MARY CHAMBERLAIN was b
and spent her childhood there. A
Politics from the University of Edinburgh and an M.Sc.
in International Relations from the London School of
Economics, she worked at the Foreign and Common-
wealth Office and at the Richardson Institute for Conflict
and Peace Research. In 1972 she left London to live in the
Fens, where she taught Liberal Studies at the Norfolk
College of Arts and Technology. While there, she wrote
her first book, the highly acclaimed *Fenwomen: A Portrait of
Women in an English Village*, published by Virago in association with Quartet Books in 1975. In 1977 she returned
to London, where she teaches Communications at the
London College of Printing. She lives in South London
with her husband and two daughters.

The woman healer is as old as history. Today, superseded
by the institutions of modern medicine, her wisdom
remains in the guise of 'old wives' tales' handed down from
mother to daughter, through the generations. Recently
there has been a revival of interest in the old ways, and this
study of the history and practice of 'the old wife' re-
establishes the importance of her traditions as a valuable
source of medical knowledge. Using extensive research
into archives and original texts, and numerous conver-
sations with women in city and countryside, Mary
Chamberlain presents a stimulating challenge to orthodox medical practice and an illuminating history and
compendium of female wisdom which goes back to the
earliest times.

OLD WIVES' TALES

Their history, remedies and spells

MARY CHAMBERLAIN

Virago

Published by VIRAGO PRESS Limited
Ely House, 37 Dover Street, London W1X 4HS

Copyright © Mary Chamberlain 1981

Typeset by Jubal Multiwrite Limited
and printed in Great Britain by litho
at The Anchor Press, Tiptree, Essex

British Library Cataloguing in Publication Data

Chamberlain, Mary
  Old wives' tales
  1. Folk-lore
  I. Title
  398   GR72

  ISBN 0-86068-015-0
  ISBN 0-86068-016-9   PBK

Contents

For Rosie and Kate

Acknowledgements

I would like to thank first and foremost my husband, Peter Lane, who not only gave me invaluable practical and moral support throughout the writing of this book, but also advised and criticised my ideas and drafts with judgement and infinite patience. I would also like to thank Carol Fisher for her helpful comments on all the drafts, Anna Coote and Ann Oakley for their criticisms of the final draft and Ursula Owen at Virago for all her help in the compiling and writing of the book.

I am indebted to Belinda Ackerman of the Association of Radical Midwives, Philip Corrigan, Auriel Hill of the Association for the Improvement in Maternity Services, Jane Mace, Nancy MacKeith, Angela Phillips and Kathy Savage for their comments and contributions to individual chapters. In addition, James Cornford, Kevin Crossley-Holland, Jean Donnison, Roger Fieldsend, Mike Fisher, Alastair Kerr, Arthur Lane, Alan Maryon-Davis, John Pickstone, Enid Porter, Bill Williams, Bob Williamson, the staff of the Department of Egyptian Antiquities of the British Museum, and the staff of the Library of the Wellcome Institute for the History of Medicine, all helped direct me to sources or answered questions and to them I am grateful.

I also owe a debt to the East Suffolk Federation of Women's Institutes, whose members contributed enormously to the collection of remedies, to Radio Orwell for inviting me to do a 'phone-in' programme on Old Wives' Tales, to Lambeth Social Services for allowing me to interview residents in their Homes for the Elderly and to the residents themselves, to the Matron and residents of Glebe House, Woodbridge, Suffolk (Suffolk Social Services) for the same, to Mrs Coker, Mrs Copping, Mrs Heiser, Mrs Murray, Mr Stronger and Mrs Wallace for their interviews, and to the Earl of Albemarle, Mr Richard Allnutt, Lt Col. R.B. Longe, the Earl of Stradbroke and the Suffolk Record Office for permission to use their material on remedies. There are many other people to whom I have spoken throughout the research for this book and who, wittingly or unwittingly, have given me material and thanks are due to them.

Finally, I must thank my aunt, Lilian Hewson, who told me a great deal about my great-grandmother, and my parents who told me many old wives' tales as well as looking after my children at various stages in writing the book. To them I am especially grateful.

Mary Chamberlain, London 1981

PART ONE

 OLD WIVES

CHAPTER ONE

Introduction

They called my great-grandmother the 'Angel of Alsace Street'.[1] If anyone was in labour, she would be there with her basins and rags delivering the babies and attending the mothers. If anyone was sick, the first person they would fly to was old grandma. When neighbours died, she laid them out. She took care of her local community in birth and death, and for much of the period in between. And she did this for little or no remuneration. She was an 'old wife', a handywoman.

My great-grandmother, and others like her, were familiar figures in most working-class communities until well into this century. They were the usual resort for the sick and poor. Doctors existed, but they were often too expensive for the family budget, or simply unpopular. In preference, the first treatment for the sick was usually at home, with the advice of a wise and trusted neighbour.

Some old wives, like Mrs Mapp, the eighteenth-century bone-setter from Epsom, or Margaret Kennox, the Elizabethan herbalist, acquired legendary fame; but for the most part they were local figures, often indistinguishable from other members of the community. What skills or knowledge they possessed they held *inter-alia*. For they were also mothers and workers. In 1894 in Whitechapel, for instance, a poor woman

aged nineteen was dying of blood poisoning a month after

delivering herself of a still born child. A doctor was summoned, but when he found he was not to be paid 'refused to do anything' and left. The Poor Law medical officer's locum was then called but he refused to help without a fee or a Relief Order. During this month and for twenty days afterwards, the woman's only attention came from a 'handywoman' at a nearby newsvendor's shop.[2]

On the whole, the old wife did not earn her living exclusively from her practice, and she held no formal qualifications. Entry into the ranks of the old wives was achieved through experience or a form of apprenticeship. My great-grandmother had sixteen children, and this was deemed sufficient qualification. Another woman, Mrs Coker, though she ultimately entered service, began a midwifery apprenticeship under her mother, an 'old wife', in the 1890s. This is how she described it:

> Of course there was no help in those days, it was all home nursing, no hospital. It's all so different now. They just used to send for her. Sometimes I think that's how she got her asthma, getting out of a hot bed and going out in the streets in the middle of the night to these people. . .
>
> I used to watch her bringing the baby into the world and cut the cord. I know I wasn't very old but I was quite capable. I could now, if necessary. Nobody about and anyone was in trouble I could help. . . She was a marvellous midwife. They told her she got the nerve of a thousand people because she had her photo taken with two dead babies in her arms. Well, I take after her for nerves. Nothing has ever feared me. . .
>
> What you need most is nerve. I'd go with her, and rub their backs and keep them walking. It was important to keep them walking, helped speed up the labour. . .[3]

Not all old wives were midwives. Some were general healers and others held quite specific skills, like wart-charming. Those specific skills which required little basic knowledge were often surrounded in mystery and secrecy, and would be passed down through families. A Suffolk wart-charmer explained:

> I learnt the cure from my aunt, before she died she told me. She didn't like to feel that it was lost. So she told me how to do it up. It seems to work, it seems to have cured everybody that I've given it

to. My aunt always said you mustn't tell anybody what you put in it, but she thought it was a shame to lose it, that's why she passed it on to me. . .[4]

'Charming' burns was often likewise shrouded in secrecy and, particularly in rural areas in the nineteenth century and earlier, certain individuals were believed to hold special properties of healing and prophecy. The seventh daughter of a seventh daughter was often sought out for these skills.

But with these examples we begin to approach the fanciful and what is now a popular perception of the 'old wife'. The Shorter *Oxford English Dictionary* defines an old wife as 'an old woman, now usu. disparagingly'. 'Old wives' tales' it registers as 'trivial stories, such as are told by garrulous old women'. Indeed, the ultimate dismissal for a piece of advice is to term it 'an old wives' tale'.

Throughout recent history old wives have been for the most part middle-aged or elderly women. But their age and sex were virtues, and they were consulted for their wisdom and experience, for their acquired skills or knowledge. They achieved what local reputation they had from their successes in the area of health care. They were the custodians of communal and community medical knowledge. But this knowledge was free and freely given. With little or no money at stake there was no need to preserve a 'closed' profession in terms of entry, training and dissemination of knowledge. Old wives' tales – the body of popular medical lore – have now almost died, killed off by the monopoly achieved by the medical profession and its intellectual hegemony over scientific ideas. They are now regarded largely as superstition – as ritual devoid of content. This view ignores the context in which old wives and old wives' tales found currency. It ignores also an approach to health care which sought as much comfort in explanation and participation (albeit often in a ritualistic way) as in a solution. Old wives' tales and the old wife represented communal health care – they were a neighbourhood resource with no barriers of class, education or money to separate them from the community.

Yet the rôle of these women as unofficial healers is one that has been largely ignored by medical histories. We are now accustomed to think of doctors and healers as men. We are led to believe that this was always so. The history of medicine is on the whole seen to be the history of great men and discoveries in science. It is also a history of medical institutions and professions. But the story of women in health care is vitally important. The old wives' tale should be heard, not only to redress a historical imbalance, but also for the insights it may now throw on modern medical practices.

The purpose of this book is, therefore, to restore the memory of the old wife and her place in the community and to collect some old wives' tales before they are lost. It tells the story of women as 'unofficial' healers and looks at some of the advice and remedies they offered. It attempts to place old wives and old wives' tales in a social and historical context and to offer an explanation of how our perception of the old wife has developed. 'The healer's role', as the medical anthropologist David Landy points out, '. . . is a key role since the healer is dealing with matters of life and death and what happens to the curer may be an important barometer of what is going on in the total process of socio-cultural change.'[5]

The book is divided into two parts: the first traces the old wife in history and the second catalogues some old wives' tales. But first, some words of warning: in tracing the rôle of women as *unofficial* healers we must, by definition, also trace the development of *official* healers. The one cannot exist without the other. But decisions as to who was deemed 'unofficial' or 'official' and, therefore, whose form of medical practice became legitimate and orthodox depended not on the nature of medical practice but on the relationship of the practitioners to what constituted political power in any one period.

Our current perceptions of medical orthodoxy and

legitimacy have been determined by this relationship as it has existed through different periods of history. Its origins go back to the classical periods of Greece and Rome, and earlier. Chapter 2 looks at the old wife in this formative period of Western medicine. Chapter 3 traces the attitudes of the Roman Catholic Church towards medicine and assesses its rôle in the formation of the medical profession and in the development of an association between healing and witchcraft. This chapter starts in Europe in the Dark Ages but ends by assessing the nature of witchcraft and the state of the medical profession in England in the Middle Ages. Chapter 4 looks at England in the eighteenth century, principally, and at the beginnings of the professional organisation of doctors and its implications for the old wife. Chapter 5 traces the erosion of domestic medicine in the nineteenth and twentieth centuries after the economic, social and political changes of that period. In particular, it looks at how the old wife survived in certain, limited, areas where the state and doctors chose not to enter. Old wives began as goddesses but ended as back-street abortionists.

Tracing a small thread through such a large historical and geographical area has necessarily resulted in some simplifications both of arguments and, more crucially, historical processes. I am fully aware of this. But I hope that distortions which might arise from this do not detract from the overall theme of the book.

Where possible, I have tried to use primary sources. This was easier for the second half of the book than for the first; for the historical narrative I have had to rely largely on secondary sources, particularly for the early and medieval periods. These sources have been written from a particular perspective where references to old wives are few and, when they do occur, are placed either in a small footnote or in a negative context. This in itself is indicative of the place women as healers have been granted in history, but it makes it difficult to build up an independent portrait of the old wife and her place in society at any particular time.

But the problem of obtaining sources on old wives is wider than this. For the old wife was more than a healer. She was a woman and, latterly, predominantly working-class. Until relatively recently, little historical effort has been expended on working-class, social or women's histories. The evidence relating to these areas is, therefore, often thin. For the commonplaces of the common people are rarely documented, even by themselves. There are few oral and even fewer written sources with which to document the old wives' tale. We can only discover a limited amount. The rest has been constructed from the gaps and silences in testimony. The silences are often overwhelming. For many of my deductions, there is no conclusive evidence. In time, more evidence may be unearthed. Till then we can best reiterate Adrienne Rich's sentiments when she wrote:

> . . . with a painful consciousness of my own Western cultural perspective and that of most of the sources available to me; painful because it says so much about how female culture is fragmented by the male cultures, boundaries, groupings in which women live. However, at this point any broad study of female culture can at best be partial, and what any writer hopes – and knows – is that others like her, with different training, background and tools, are putting together other parts of this immense half-buried mosaic in the shape of a woman's face.[6]

Old wives played a central rôle in what Rich describes as 'female culture'. The disparity between the official record and actual experience is often enormous. I hope this book begins to close this gap a little.

Old Wives' Tales is a history of the old wife and her rôle in domestic medicine. It is a history of women as unofficial healers, for women were the main practitioners of this art. It is not a history of alternatives to the doctor. There is, therefore, no discussion of men who practised 'domestic' medicine or offered alternatives to orthodox practice, even though in some instances what they offered was indistinguishable from that offered by women. Occasionally they are mentioned in the text but without comment. Similarly, there is no discussion of what we now call 'alternative' medicine, for example homeopathy or acupuncture. Herbalism does feature, particularly in Chapter 5 and in the second half of the book which lists cures and remedies. This is because herbalism, and remedies using herbal ingredients, were an aspect of domestic medicine. But the book is not a history of herbalism, nor a handbook for herbalists. It is the old wife's tale.

CHAPTER TWO

From Goddess to Sorceress: women healers in Assyria, Egypt, Greece and Rome

Men generally have a view of the nature of their society. They also have views concerning what validates the society's arrangements. The two things, image and validation, never are and cannot be wholly distinct. . . A society can possess a world creation story, in which the creation of the world and the foundations of society itself are tied up: the cosmic and social foundation stones may be identical or both may be invoked to validate the social order. . .[1]

Let us begin with a tale. There was a garden of paradise in Sumar, which had four rivers, including the Euphrates and Tigris. The great mother goddess Ninchursag allowed eight beautiful plants to grow in this garden, though she forbade the inhabitants to eat from them. Enki, the water god, defied Ninchursag and ate from them and she, angry about it, condemned him to death though she did not expel him from the garden. Enki fell ill, eight of his organs were affected and his strength began to fail him. But a fox was able to persuade Ninchursag to save Enki from death. She then enquired about his suffering and created one healing deity for each of his sick organs.[2]

Ancient cultures believed that medicine was the prerogative of women, a prerogative ordained by the goddess and reflected in practice. Yet the history of medicine usually begins with the 'father' of medicine, the Greek physician Hippocrates. This beginning reflects the need of doctors to show the antique but scientific basis of their profession. It also reflects assumptions regarding the rightful practitioners of medicine. For within the Hippocratic tradition of medicine, which dominated European medical thought until the seventeenth century at least, women had few rights and little rôle or scope. Moreover, as inheritors of this tradition we now have particular notions of what is medically orthodox and what is not. 'Old wives' tales' have been placed firmly in the camp of the medically unorthodox and the inferior. Within such a perspective there is little room for assessing either the value of the methods or the social importance of 'unorthodox' practice.

The gap between our current perceptions of medicine and the prime rôle enjoyed by women in healing in those early pre-classical cultures is enormous. We cannot know for certain how this gap developed, but certain themes current in modern attitudes towards medicine can be traced backwards through time. The themes concern the development of scientific orthodoxy through its association with political and religious elites. The tradition we have now inherited has its origins variously in Egypt, Greece, Rome and Palestine. This chapter attempts to outline some of the more important elements relating to the practices of medicine in these ancient cultures.

THE RELIGIOUS EXPLANATION
OF DISEASE AND HEALTH

The earliest explanations of disease were religious. Among many ancient cultures and many 'primitive' cultures studied by anthropologists, the same phenomenon has been recorded. Medicine and religion were so closely inter-related that it was impossible to disentangle the two. The deities who created life or commanded death were also responsible for health and sickness. The Sumerians held Ninchursag, the goddess of life, accountable for health and childbirth. The Assyrian goddess Ishtar was both mother goddess and goddess of health. Isis, the great goddess of the Egyptians, was also their physician. The Minoans, Myceneans, Cretans and early Greeks also worshipped female deities of healing and life. The goddess of death was also the goddess of resurrection. Gula, the Assyrian goddess of death, was labelled 'the great physician'. Isis carried about her symbols of death. In the cycle of existence, life and death were inextricable.

But if the benign deities were attributed with knowledge of health and were held responsible for it, malign demons were charged with sickness and ill health. It is believed that the Sumerians were the first to personify the demons of disease. Such personification also developed among the peoples of Mesopotamia, Egypt, Greece and Rome and among the northern Teutonic tribes. The Israelites believed that it was the Destroying Angel who stood by the threshing floor of Ornan the Jebusite, and that Satan afflicted Job. The Anglo-Saxons believed that the spirits of sickness were called elves or dwarves and fired arrows or darts – known as 'elf-shot' – at their victims. The belief in the power of demons to bring on sickness is an element in Christian exorcism rites.

Cures were thought to be effected, in the first place, by prayer or command to the deity or demons. But oral rites were always accompanied by practical measures. These practical measures were given authority by their creation and use by the goddess. An Egyptian remedy for a headache, for instance, states that it was:

> made by the goddess Isis for the god Ea himself, in order to drive away the pains in his head:
>
> | | |
> |---|---|
> | Coriander berries | 1 |
> | Berries of the Xaset plant | 1 |
> | Wormwood | 1 |
> | Berries of the Sames plant | 1 |
> | Juniper berries | 1 |
> | Honey | 1 |
>
> To be mixed and smeared on the head.[3]

Prayer and practice were important factors in the treatment of the sick. For the fear generated by the unknown and arbitrary nature of sickness could be assuaged by appeals to the supernatural, while practical treatment secured an immediate sensation of relief and control. The remedy was believed to work partly because of its method, partly because of the intrinsic worth of its ingredients, but largely because of the power of its practitioners. The pharmacological base may not have been well founded, yet it represented a process of experimentation which was essentially scientific. For though failure and success could be explained in terms of the wrath or good will of the deities, the approach remained fundamentally empirical. The priestessess were required not only to know the properties and attributes of the healing deities and the appropriate prayers and incantations but also to have an extensive knowledge of botany, minerals, and animal derivatives used in medical prescriptions. Indeed, the Sumerians, Egyptians and Assyrians, for instance, had an impressive list of drugs used in the treatment of specific diseases in the form of pills, suppositories, lotions or ointments.

PRIESTESSES, HEALERS AND MIDWIVES

The religious explanation of illness and its treatment helped support and perpetuate the position of its earthly functionaries. The practitioners of healing in the pre-classical cultures of the Near and Middle East were also the religious guardians.

> In nearly all areas of the world, goddessess were extolled as healers, dispensers of curative herbs, roots, plants and other medical aids, casting the priestesses who attended the shrines into the role of physicians of those who worshipped there.[4]

In Sumer, Assyria, Egypt and Greece until about the third millennium the practice of healing was almost exclusively in the hands of priestesses. And within those societies, the rôle of priestess was paramount. In Sumer, for instance, there were many kinds of priestesses whose importance in the economic, political, cultural and social life of the country was enormous. Business was conducted in the temple and there is evidence that writing was developed there by women: 'It was the goddess Nidaba in Sumer who was paid honour as the one who initially invented clay tablets and the art of writing. . . The official scribe of the Sumerian heaven was a woman. . .'[5] Archeological evidence indicates that the earliest examples of writing were discovered at the temple of the Queen of Heaven in Erech, in Sumer, over 5000 years ago.[6]

Links between spiritual leaders and political rulers were also strong. Nearly all the high priestesses of the god Nanner in Ur were members of the royal family. In Assyria and Egypt, similarly, priestesses were called from high-born and royal families. A picture on the wall of the tomb of King Ramses III in Egypt shows Isis in the rôle of healer and the priestess/physician as intermediary. So close were the links between high priestesses and ruler that many of the queens of those ancient cultures were also temple physicians. In the grave of Queen Shubad of Ur, 3000 BC, there was buried not only food for her journey but also her prescriptions for stopping pain and medical instruments of bronze and flint.

Many of the Egyptian queens were also notable physicians, for example Queen Mentuhetep (2300 BC), Hatshepsut (1500 BC) and Cleopatra (100 BC). Pictures on the walls of temples and tombs of Egypt often illustrate women in their rôle of priestess/physician, and the writings of Diodorus, Euripides, Pliny and Herodotus testify to their eminence.

Yet among the women healers in Egypt and elsewhere there was some separation of rôles. Midwifery was exclusively a woman's concern, but was not necessarily conducted by a priestess. Priestesses were limited in number and high in rank. It was sufficient that they attended the sick who presented themselves for treatment at the temple. There were not enough of them to attend every confinement. And there were other reasons to explain why midwifery was separate from the temple ritual. Religion depends on mystery – on explaining or comprehending the unknown, but childbirth is a common, mechanical event. The midwife might have had skills, but they were craft skills perfected by practice, though recognised for their importance. In Sumer, midwives were educated and trained; in Egypt, midwifery was an area delineated for women and midwives were also educated and trained. The Ebers Papyrus,[7] which contains guidance on midwifery, indicates that knowledge of gynaecology and obstetrics was quite advanced, including not only childbirth and abortion but a range of other problems from breast cancer to prolapse of the womb.

Nevertheless, midwives could not ignore religion. Consequently, the goddesses kindly disposed towards pregnant women and those in labour were invoked, and the demons of birth, who were believed to devour babies and kill their mothers, were warded off. The relief of labour pains was sought through prayer and practical measures. A spell to relieve the pains of labour and facilitate birth, set down in the Leiden Papyrus (approximately second century AD) ends with the rubric: 'Say the words four times over a dwarf of clay to be placed on the forehead of the woman who is giving birth'; while the Sumerians invoked the sympathy of Ereshkigal or the wife of the god Etana.

Midwifery was 'subcontracted' from the priestess who, for practical reasons, needed to delegate this area of activity, and could do so to women who could be safely trusted to proceed according to the correct cultural and religious practices. The mystery relating to creation lies not in the act of childbirth, but in conception and in protecting the health of the newborn child and its mother; in these areas the priestesses would again have been invoked. But it was likely, too, that the midwife, the one 'who knows the inside',[8] would also have been approached. The division of rôle between midwife and priestess/physician was thin but nevertheless functional. It implied no inferiority on the part of the midwife, nor rivalry with the priestess. Yet it was a division with important implication for the future.

There is evidence that other functions were delegated too. The earliest known chemists were two Mesopotamian women of the thirteenth century BC. Like the midwives, specific functions – in this case the dispensing of medicines and experimentation with new formulae – would only have been delegated to people who could be trusted. And in this early period the priestesses would also have made up their own prescriptions.

THE ENTRY OF THE GODS:
RELIGION VERSUS MEDICINE

The near monopoly of the priestesses over medicine was ultimately eroded. The process was slow and by no means uniform. Among the different cultures of the Middle and Near East the process of erosion took different forms. But the cultural exchange between Egyptians, Greeks, Romans and Hebrews meant that, by the end of the Roman Empire in approximately the fourth century AD, the rôle of women in medicine had been radically altered. Women were no longer the official arbiters and practitioners of medicine but, within medicine, social and scientific deviants.

The first step 'in the limitation of the status of women' was, as Briffault suggests, 'to take over from them the monopoly of the religious functions'.[9] And, we might add, the medical function. We do not know for certain why and how this monopoly was eroded and it is not within the scope of this book to document or discuss the research and large number of theories which relate to this period of change. What does seem clear, however, is that changes in the religion and culture of those early societies appear to have coincided with the Indo-European invasions of the Near and Middle East which occurred between the second and third millennium BC.[10] Their introduction into the cultures of the East was invariably marked by the emergence of a powerful male god transplanted from the religions of the Indo-European invaders. Among the Assyrians and Egyptians, the myths of creation were rewritten and the male deities began to acquire an equal, if not superior, position to the female deities. If the myths, as allegory, are to be believed, the battle was a bloody one, 'I cannot help but recall', wrote Merlin Stone, 'the Greek legend of the Goddess known as Hera, whose worship appears to survive from Mycenaean times, and Her thwarted rebellion against Her newly assigned husband Zeus, surely an allegorical reminder of those who struggled for the primacy of the Goddess – and lost.'[11]

Whether the invasions themselves were directly responsible for changes in society, or whether they coincided with and gave impetus to changes already occurring, cannot be known.

Whether the invasions themselves were directly responsible for changes in society, or whether they coincided with and gave impetus to changes already occurring, cannot be known. But the result was that the primacy given to women in the process of creation, and in the 'world view' of those cultures, began to be displaced. By the eighteenth dynasty in Egypt (1570–1300 BC) women had been relegated to the rôle of temple musicians, no longer enjoying the status even of 'clergy'. Previously the goddess Hat-hor, for instance, had been served by eighty-one priestesses and eighteen priests and Neith had been attended solely by priestesses. With this displacement from the temple went, necessarily, a displacement from medicine. Male healing deities began to emerge – Ea among the Assyrians and Ptah in Egypt. And as early as 3133 BC an Egyptian queen named Nitocris appointed a man – Imhotep – court physician (though other sources have placed him later, at the court of King Hoser, 2980–2900 BC). He appears to have been the first male physician to be appointed court physician. He soon became 'patron' of doctors because of his association with 'science and learning', and was elevated to the rank of god, joining Ptah. The Greeks later identified him with their own 'god' of healing, Aesculapius.

EGYPT: THE DECLINE OF THE HEALER AND THE RISE OF THE SURGEON

The introduction of men into medicine signalled fundamental changes in the nature of medical practice in Egypt. Medicine began to develop independently from religion; it began to be anti-mystical. More important, the soothing incantations and balms of the priestesses began to be replaced by the surgeon's knife. For male medicine in Egypt emerged alongside the practice of embalming which, by 2300 BC, had been perfected as a technique. The Egyptian embalmers were always men[12] and their practice led them to a detailed knowledge of anatomy and surgery. Their findings were written down and used by embalmers and surgeons alike. The Smith Papyrus, which dates from approximately 3000 BC, contains medical prescriptions which deal primarily with techniques for dealing with injuries, and clear advice for avoiding inoperable cases. Religion plays little part here in the diagnosis or treatment of injury. The ultimate authority for surgery was vested not in divine inspiration but in human knowledge. Sickness was rooted in the body and its causes were explicable; this knowledge became the prerogative of men. Male medicine began to stand for knowledge and discovery and women's medicine for superstition.

In line with the growing separation of medicine and religion, medical schools were established at Heliopolis and Sais, Memphis and (later) Alexandria, where both surgeons and embalmers were trained. Moses is said to have studied at Heliopolis, and Sais and Alexandria were the centres of exchange between Greek and Egyptian physicians and surgeons. The entry of women into these schools was restricted. Significantly, the school at Sais specialised in gynaecology and obstetrics, and although there is evidence that women studied there,[13] the Kahum

Papyrus (dated approximately 2500 BC and thought to have originated at Sais) deals with gynaecology as well as veterinary diseases and primarily contains guidance for surgical practices. It is likely, therefore, that surgeons – and therefore men – would have been called in to perform Caesarian sections and other obstetric or gynaecological surgery. It is possible that some midwives were trained in these techniques, but the evidence seems to suggest that on the whole the more complicated aspects of midwifery involving surgery began to be removed from their jurisdiction. Certainly, by 1560 BC, podalic version (the turning of the foetus into a birth presentation) was no longer practised by midwives but by priests.

Nevertheless, religion still had a rôle to play in the diagnosis and prognosis of the patient and even conferred its authority on to the new techniques of surgery and embalming. Isis, after all, gathered the slain body of Osiris and mummified him to preserve his pieces intact. Moreover, anatomy and surgery were inadequate for coping with every physical ailment. Traditional medicine therefore continued to operate alongside the new. What was known and could be repaired became the subject of the more secular practice of surgery, while what was unknown remained within the scope of a religious medical approach. But within the temple, this approach was now in the charge of priests.

Whatever claims to success the surgeons may have made, surgery throughout the Egyptian period was highly dangerous and extremely painful to the patient,[14] undertaken in an emergency when all else had failed. And the costs of embalming and surgery were high and therefore accessible only to the wealthy. The Egyptian poor dealt with their dead and dying by the traditional and only means available to them. They buried their dead in the desert and tried to cure or soothe their dying by traditional and non-surgical methods. Nevertheless, the removal of women from the temples necessarily reduced women's status even in traditional medicine, while that of the male priest/physician who replaced them increased proportionately.

The status of priest/physician was enhanced too by the association of the male sex with surgery, science and courtly circles. Women continued to practise but without the authority of either science or religion. Indeed, the prime area in which they continued – largely because the separation from the temple had occurred earlier – was midwifery. But even here there were important differences. First, in relation to the temple midwives were now seen as inferior. Paradoxically, because of (or, perhaps, despite) this, their practice became broader.

Women's and children's complaints, as well as questions relating to sterility or conception, were now perceived to be midwives' responsibility. Whereas before the priestess/physician and midwife would have shared this area of medicine, these were now seen as essentially women's questions of which temple priests could be expected to know little. Also, even if the priest was consulted over a sickness or injury, nursing the patient back to health remained the task of women at home. This had always been so. But whereas formerly there was no gender separation between physician and nurse, there now was, and the gender separation also signified the split between the public and private rôle of women in medicine. Healing began to emerge as separate from the public, male, world of medicine, and became submerged in the domestic world.

THE HEBREWS: ONE RELIGION, ONE MEDICINE

By the second millennium BC the primacy of the woman in healing in Egypt had been challenged. But, though it was now diminished and less public, her rôle within medicine was still tolerated. In ancient Egypt – as in Greece – there remained a link between polytheism and a multiplicity of permitted methods of medicine and healing. Although the status of the methods shifted, essentially they were allowed to co-exist.

The peaceful co-existence of a variety of medical methods is a theme lacking in modern Western medicine. For the origins of this we must turn first to the Hebrews and then to the classical cultures of Greece and Rome, where the associations between men, science and orthodoxy were more rigorously developed. Ancient Hebrew society was patriarchal, hierarchical and authoritarian. It permitted one male God, and Him alone. It is not surprising, therefore, that the Lord God, Yahveh, was also the supreme healer of the sick. It is clear that the Hebrews knew that deities elsewhere claimed this healing function and that the practice of healing was often in the hands of women, especially in Egypt. Given the Hebrew belief in the low status of women, it is clear too that they did not wish this practice to become established within their own society.

> If you will lend your ear to the laws and observe all the statutes, you will never contract any of the diseases of Egypt, *for the Lord is your Physician* . . . . (Ex.15:26)

> . . . and will take away sickness, *machalo,* from your midst . . . . (Ex.23:25)

The Hebrews tried to identify the practice of healing firmly with their god. They also anticipated early Christian attitudes – that sickness was the result of sin and that God alone had sole authority to heal. The elder in each generation was endowed with divine powers, under the direct guidance of Yahveh, to lead, instruct, judge and heal – an endowment first given to Adam 'to subdue the earth and to have dominion over every living thing'. (Gen.1:28) Indeed, the story of creation which dramatised the downfall of woman and of the serpent who had symbolised the power and knowledge of woman, necessarily also symbolised the end of the preponderance of women in healing and the end of the relationship between women and healing. For the snake was a symbol not only of the water goddess but also of healing. The two were closely connected.

> In contrast to the Indo-Europeans, to whom Earth was the Great Mother, the Old Europeans created maternal images out of water and air divinities, the Snake and the Bird Goddess. A divinity who nurtures the world with moisture, giving rain, the divine food which metaphorically was also understood as mother's milk, naturally became a nurse or mother. Indeed the terracotta figurines of an anthropomorphic snake or bird holding a baby are encountered at various periods and in many regions of old Europe and in Minoan, Cypriote and Mycenaean cultures as well.[15]

The Egyptian goddess, Au Zet, the great serpent, was also a goddess of healing. For Hebrew society the symbolism of crushing the serpent meant the crushing not only of woman's social position but also of her rôle in healing.

Although it was the Hebrew religion which provided the ultimate authority for the practice of medicine, it stood in marked contrast to Egyptian practice. The Hebrews' knowledge of anatomy was minimal and consequently their surgery crude and limited. The emphasis was rather on sanitation, hygiene and the prevention of disease. The treatment of sickness relied principally on the use of herbs and spices, such as mandrake, saffron, camphor, myrrh, cinnamon, senna, balm of Gilead, oil and wine for wounds and aconite and curare for poisons. But the execution of medicine was believed to be the prerogative of men, bestowed by a male God. Any resort to methods beyond permitted Hebrew practice was denounced. Moses – himself a student at Heliopolis – was well versed in Egyptian medicine, and continually denounced its practices:

> Regard not them that have familiar spirits; neither seek after wizards to be defiled by them: I *am* the Lord your God. (Lev.19:31)

> A man also or woman that hath a familiar spirit or that is a wizard, shall surely be put to death; they shall stone them with stones; their blood shall be upon them. (Lev.20:27)

> There shall not be found among you anyone that maketh his son or daughters to pass through fire, or that useth divination, or an

observer of times, or an enchanter, or a witch, or a charmer, or a
consulter with familiar spirits, or a wizard or a necromancer.
(Deut. 18:10–11)

It is clear from these promulgations that practices
antithetical to the Jews were continuing and that women,
particularly Egyptian women, were to some extent responsible. Indeed, the extent to which they were defying
the promulgations is made clear by references to midwives in the Old Testament. For women who found
favour were those who restricted their rôle to midwifery,
defied Egypt and found Yahveh's favour – in other
words, those who submitted to male control.

> . . . and the King of Egypt spake to the Hebrew midwives (of which
> the name of one was Shiprah and the name of the other Puah).
> And he said, When ye do the office of a midwife to the Hebrew
> women, and see them upon the stools; if it be a son, then ye shall
> kill him; but if it be a daughter, then she shall live.
> But the midwives feared God, and did not as the King of Egypt
> commanded them but saved the men children alive.
> And the King of Egypt called for the midwives and said unto them,
> Why have ye done this thing, and have saved the men children
> alive?
> And the midwives said unto Pharaoh, Because the Hebrew women
> are not as the Egyptian women: for they are lively, and are
> delivered ere the midwives come in unto them.
> Therefore God dealt with the midwives: and the people multiplied
> and waxed very mighty.
> And it came to pass, because the midwives feared God, that he
> made them houses. (Ex. 1:15–21).

The emphasis on God as sole healer, and a male, is one
which is repeated throughout the New Testament in
accounts of miracles and feats of healing performed by
the Son of God.

THE GREEKS: SCIENCE AND MEDICINE

The Greek contribution to the development of medical
ideas and attitudes was the establishment of the criteria
for scientific and medical ideas and discoveries. Although the Greeks were not as dogmatic as the Hebrews

on the form medicine should take, the criteria laid down by the Hippocratic 'school' of medicine came to dominate, through its adoption by the Romans, all subsequent Western medical thought.

The Dorian invasions of the second millennium BC introduced into classical Greek culture the Indo-European God Dyaus Pitar, who became known in Greece as Zeus and in Rome as Jupiter. And – as in Egypt – male healing deities began to arise. However,

> ... while the feminine Gods were generally gentle, sympathetic and careful not to injure mortals, the most powerful gods were masculine and far more often angry, resentful, harmful and cruel than their consorts.[16]

Indeed, the most famous of the healing gods was Aesculapius, the son of Apollo. According to legend, he had several children, all of whom became doctors. Homer mentions only his sons as healing the battle wounds of Troy, while Pindar (520–440 BC) says of one of his sons:

> Each of his several bane he cured;
> This felt the charm's enchanting sound;
> That drank th'elixir's soothing cup;
> Some with soft hands in sheltering bands be bound
> Or plied the searching steel and bade the lame leap up.[17]

Aesculapius also had two daughters, Hygeia and Panacea (now, interestingly, household words for the maintenance of health), and it is significant that their rôle in medicine is largely ignored or forgotten. From about the seventh century BC, Hygeia is rarely seen alone in her representations. Usually she is depicted introducing patients to Aesculapius, or administering treatment on his advice. Occasionally she is seen with a snake, and often with a basket of herbs, but she is always modest and beautiful. This is a symbolic representation of the ideal, if not the actual, position of women within Greek medicine at that time. For among the early Greeks the social position of women and their place in medical care was actually more central. As Jacquetta Hawkes points out, the lowly position of women in classical Greece was greatly exaggerated by the 'bias of nineteenth-century scholarship'; she suggests that in classical Greece

> just as in Crete, women shared the power of the Goddess both psychologically and socially; priestesses were of high standing and priestly associations of women were formed round temples and holy places. There was an influential one, for example, associated with the famous temple of Artemis (Diana) at Ephesus.[18]

Even Homer, who praised Aesculapius' sons, mentions that Helen as 'healer outweighs many others in value', and that Agamede 'understood as many drugs as the wide earth flourishes', for she was the daughter of Augeas of Elis

> Agamede, with the golden hair,
> A leech was she, and well she knew
> All herbs that on ground that grew.
> (Iliad XI 739–745)

Virgil, in the *Aeneid*, (I,83) tells that Medea, the wife of Jason who won the golden fleece, knew magic and could cure insanity. In Homer's time, however, the tradition of Aesculapius and male medicine was strong and the connections between Greek and Egyptian medicine, particularly in the fields of anatomy and surgery, well established.

> From Paeon sprung their patron god imparts
> To all Pharian race his healing arts . . . .

By the time of Hippocrates (460–377 BC) traditional medicine (incorporating both herb lore and religious ritual and practised in the temples primarily by religious functionaries, often women) was coming into serious disrepute, and the more secular practices, as epitomised by the Aesculapian tradition which incorporated surgery and science, were coming into favour. Aristophanes (450–380 BC) , Herondas a century later, Euripedes and Socrates all scorned traditional medico-religious

practices. The schools of medicine established by Hippocrates in Cos and Larissa were essentially philosophical
and speculative, based on reason and logic. The workings
of the body were allowed no mystery: they all conformed
to logical principles. The main emphasis of the schools
was on anatomy and surgery; health was governed by
four 'humours', or fluids in the body (blood, phlegm,
choler and black choler), the relative proportions of
which determined physical or mental well-being. Sickness was the result of imbalance within the body.

Although it was the Hippocratic 'school' of medicine
which came to dominate European medical practice
until the eighteenth century, in classical Greece it was one
'school' among many. The schools at Cnidos, Rhodes
and Cyrene (which all date from about the sixth and fifth
centuries BC) were, in their day, as popular. But women
were excluded from them, and only the wealthy could
afford the treatment which they offered. Temple practices necessarily still continued, not only for those who
could not afford the trained physician, but also for those
who still believed in religion as a curative agent.
Herodotus, for instance, mentions the Aesculapia or
health resorts, where many patients went to be cured.
Significantly, however, the diagnosis of disease was, even
here, in the hands of laymen and priests, even though
often based on 'mystical' criteria, such as the interpretation of dreams.

Although women were excluded from the medical
schools and from temple practice, they continued to play
a significant rôle in healing at home, among the poor and
among women. Their skills necessarily relied primarily
on herbal knowledge (Aristotle's wife, Pythias, was a great
botanist and Queen Artemesia of the fourth century BC
was said to know every herb used in medicine) in
conjunction with prayers and incantations. But docu-
mentation refers to women mainly in their rôle as
midwives. Greek physicians, such as Hippocrates, and
post-Hippocratic writers who taught obstetrics and

gynaecology, occasionally credit their knowledge to midwives. Midwifery itself, because it dealt with women and was conducted by women, had low status. Nevertheless, the knowledge that midwives possessed was impressive. Pythagoras' wife won a debate with Eurphon, a well-known contemporary physician, arguing that a foetus was viable before the seventh month. Pliny records (though without dates) Lais and Sotira, who wrote books on abortions and sterility and Philista, the sister of Pyrrhus (318–272), who was an *obstetrix* and Victoria the 'gynecia'. It was the obstetrix who attended births. These women also performed abortions, but qualifications for midwifery were generally skill born of long experience and, as Hurd-Mead records, 'she cared for the patient for fifteen days after the birth of the baby, which she turned over to a wet-nurse of her own selection, and received her fee on a piece of dry bread'.[19]

But in Greek society women healers were placed, by reason of their sex and their methods, outside the intellectual traditions of medicine. For the male medical schools, and above all the Hippocratic school, had begun to formulate not only a procedure for medical investigation but the establishment of hypotheses about the workings of the body based on their experiments and findings. Ironically, these hypotheses became translated into immutable 'laws' of nature, and it was not until the seventeenth and eighteenth centuries that they began to be challenged in any rigorous way by official medical practitioners. Yet, because the initial procedure for investigation conformed to certain principles, because it was divorced from religion, and because it was men who had charge of this learning, medicine was believed to have come of age – to have become a science. Those who challenged the new precepts were condemned to obscurity. Pliny, for instance, thought that women healers should be as quiet and inconspicuous as possible so that 'after they are dead no one would know that they had lived'. Or they were condemned to public trial, like

Agnodice, the 'midwife of Athens'.

Agnodice practised medicine in Athens around the fourth century BC. She wore men's clothing in her practice and when this was discovered she was accused of practising under false pretences. Her trial, however, became something of a *cause célèbre*, during which the women of Athens demanded that the judges release her, arguing 'You are not our husbands, but our enemies if you condemn Agnodice, who saves our lives.'[20] The judges appear to have bowed to this pressure and released her. Interestingly, among the crimes that Agnodice was purported to have committed was that of abortion. It appears too that she performed successful Caesarian operations. It is likely that her accusers were motivated by professional rivalry, for evidence elsewhere indicates that Agnodice was not the only woman doing such medical work.

THE ROMANS: MEDICINE AND
THE RETURN OF RELIGION
Before the fall of Greece, Roman medicine displayed characteristics reminiscent of other ancient cultures. That is, it combined religious ritual with practical measures and the execution of this function was vested in women, either in the temple or at home. Pliny records that 'Roman people for more than 600 years were not, indeed, without medicine, but they were without physicians', and Cato indicates that the average family had a good supply of home remedies. Significantly, however, by the third century BC these women were beginning to be ridiculed and condemned by the intellectuals of the day. Plautus (254–184 BC), Terence (195–159 BC) and Ovid (43 BC–18 AD) all ridiculed their practice, particularly in midwifery, and characterised the midwife, in perhaps the first of the stereotypes, as a superstitious drunk. After the fall of Greece, the Romans began to institute their own medical schools, based primarily on the teachings of the Hippocratic school. In line with

Greek practice, women were excluded from these schools.

The Roman emperor was seen as the father of the people and was, in many cases, deified. The Roman gods and the Roman religion were guardians of the empire. The position of the man within the family reflected that of the emperor. He was the unqualified head of the household, his position upheld by both the legal and religious system. Indeed, throughout Roman society, it was the men who held positions of authority and leadership. Learning and science, religion and law, were all the preserves of men. Yet, as in other cultures, women continued to practise healing, primarily among the poorer parts of Roman society, for the cost of being treated by trained doctors was high.

Lanciani, writing in the second century AD, described the city of Rome with its 800,000 inhabitants, its contaminated drinking water, its clogged sewers and its public refuse pits in which the poor were buried along with the rubbish. The rich were cremated and lived in the more salubrious areas of the city. Many of the wealthy had their own private hospitals for the treatment of their family and household. For the poor, medical treatment remained traditional – home remedies and the local midwife. Indeed, according to Soranus, the public demanded a midwife. She was known, variously, as a *medicae*, an *obstetricae*, or a *sagae* – a wise woman.

Popular attitudes seem to have accepted these women as performing valuable functions. Second-century tombstone inscriptions praise the woman who was a *medica* or a *saga*. And Pliny also mentions by name *sagae* like Elephantis and Salpe and Sotira, who were experts not only in midwifery but also in the use of traditional remedies for curing a wide range of diseases. Photius mentions an *honesta matrona* who could cure epilepsy and sterility in the first century AD, a description similar to that given by Scribonius Largus to another healer called Africana. Octavia, sister of Augustus and wife of Mark

Anthony, and Messalina, were also both reputed to be skilled in domestic medicine. And the second-century midwife, Aspasia, was well known and regarded for her skills and knowledge.

But however popular or famous women healers may have been, they nevertheless operated within a cultural framework which denigrated their work. Cato classed them all as abortionists. Tertullian (150–230 AD) hurled sarcasm at their methods. Galen (129–201 AD) refers to traditional medicine as 'old wives' tales' and 'Egyptian quackeries'. Praise for their work is rare. Even twentieth-century medical historians such as the German, Harless, mention that they were empiricists and midwives. Baas suggests that the *medicae* and *sagae* were the worst sinners against Hippocratic law (which directs a doctor's duty to, broadly speaking, work for the relief of suffering and the prevention of death), and adds that they were all prostitutes and abortionists. But these attitudes are hardly surprising. For their practice was at variance with the medical theory and practice of the day and potentially a challenge to a patriarchal ideology. And yet, in their rôle as midwives, the life and death of the heir might be very closely controlled by women.

Women as empiricists, with their use of herbs and drugs, were often seen as poisoners. In addition, their use of charms and incantations implicitly challenged the techniques of the male temple priests and male religion. The greatest sanction which the Romans used against dissidents was to brand them as magicians and sorcerers, for which the penalty was death. Women healers often met this fate. Caligula's insanity was attributed to drugs and magic used against him by his wife, and she was executed. The early Christians were similarly branded as magicians and executed, and it is no coincidence that some of the early Christian martyrs, like Theodosia, Nicerata and Thekla, were principally *sagae* or midwives.

Nevertheless, the Romans drew a distinction between

belief in sorcery and its actual practice. The former, as Helen Trimp explains, was tolerated:

> In the polytheistic world of classical times, where the deities of the underworld and death were part of the pantheon and most deities had both good and evil aspects, the belief was generally included as one among many.[21]

The latter was only condemned when used for 'evil' purposes – an attitude reflected in the civil law of pre-Christian Roman emperors. Sorcery used for evil purposes – especially if it carried political undertones – was a capital offence.

The belief in sorcery as such implied a belief in the power of demons to cause sickness, death, pestilence and plague. Sorcerers, it was believed, knew how to conjure up demons and use them for their own purposes. Demons were thought to be the cause of anti-social occurrences, and they could also be appealed to, or commanded, to provide the cure. That this was an ancient belief has already been testified: that its practitioners were believed to be able to render evil as well as good was inevitable, for the same process was implied in either act.

The conversion of the Roman empire to Christianity crystallised attitudes towards women and women healers. The Roman gods were replaced by one all-powerful God whose duties included healing, and who delegated the rôle of healing to His chosen successors. Thus men were confirmed in their role as official healer and Galenic medicine – the most prominent Roman medical 'school' – was confirmed as Christian medicine.

But the midwives and *sagae* represented an open challenge to the Church's views on sickness and disease as well as on the rôle and position of women. Women's healing practices were interpreted as paganism. Moreover, the early Christian Church of Rome drew no distinction between the beneficial acts of 'sorcery' and *maleficarium* – the power to work harm. Its main preoccupation, then and throughout the 'Dark Ages' which followed the fall of the Roman Empire, was in eradicating paganism. Belief in demons was pagan and therefore the belief, and any practice based on this belief, whether criminal or not, had to be eliminated. As Christianity spread throughout Europe, old laws were revised to deal with this new consideration.

CHAPTER THREE

From Sorceress to Witch: the old wife in medieval Europe and seventeenth-century England

By the end of the Roman Empire (approximately the fourth century AD), notions of medical orthodoxy had begun to take firm shape. Reflecting essentially the cultural ideology of the Romans, treatment of the sick and diseased resided primarily with men, and the use of humoural and mechanical precepts was the basis of their diagnosis and practice. Although only the wealthy could afford Roman physicians, this approach to medicine had great normative influence. Under Christianity magico-religious precepts became firmly equated with paganism, and its practitioners outlawed.

Yet the gap between official ideology and actual practice, during the Roman Empire and after, was enormous. For the poor had little choice but to continue with home remedies and unorthodox practitioners. This duality of medical practice remained a feature of European medicine until the twentieth century.

Between the twelfth and seventeenth centuries the theological arguments which held that the spiritual deficiency of women laid them open to temptation by the Devil were translated into lay terms. By the seventeenth century spiritual deficiency had become intellectual deficiency: women were not merely open to the temptations of sensuality but were motivated by illogicality and irrationality. In both arguments, women's bodies were seen to be the cause of their fundamental weakness; under the first, those women who attempted to heal committed a sinful act, and under the second they were guilty of an act of stupidity. Since women know their own limitations, the argument continued, it could only be malice which motivated their actions. The prosecution of many thousands of women for witchcraft was one manifestation of this change in attitudes.[1] Yet even the terrible persecution of women did not eliminate their rôle as healers and midwives, for the social needs of the poor ensured their continuing work. Nevertheless, the prosecutions are an important turning-point in that they enshrined in legislation official attitudes towards women and healing. This chapter looks principally at the development of this legislation.

It must, however, be pointed out that the prime motivation of witchcraft prosecutions was not to eliminate women in healing. The period of witchcraft prosecutions – beginning in Europe in the fourteenth century and ending in England in the seventeenth – was far too long, differentiated and complex to support such a simple argument. Nevertheless, it was during this period that theological arguments against women in medicine became conflated into the more familiar intellectual and social arguments of today, and physicians began to perceive themselves as members of a profession and to demand protection to ensure that a monopoly be guaranteed and preserved.

HEALING, PAGANISM AND THE OLD WIFE

The pre-Christian Roman belief in *maleficarium* was also held by the Teutonic tribes of Northern Europe who, prior to Christianity, drew a distinction – similar to that of the Romans – between belief in sorcery and its actual practice. The belief was tolerated but the practice, when used for anti-social purposes, condemned. Moreover, any unforeseen or unwanted tragedy could be blamed on *maleficarium*. There was, in a sense, no defence against the accusation. For instance, the sixth-century Merovingian Queen, Fredegond, became convinced that the death of her two sons in an epidemic was the result of sorcery. She accused the mother of her stepson's mistress of the crime and had her executed. A little later, another son died of dysentery and a number of women, who had originally been employed to cure him, were accused of sorcery and executed.

The execution of alleged sorcerers for lethal acts of sorcery was written into the law of the Lombards in Northern Italy, the Alamanni of the Rhine and the Saxons before their conquest by Charlemagne in the eighth century. When Christianity began to spread through Europe, from about the fifth century, the Church's blanket condemnation of sorcery could therefore draw on elements in the existing cultures compatible with this belief. But the Church's condemnation was motivated to a large extent by the attitudes it held towards healing itself. Blame for the sins of the world was allocated firmly to Satan. Sickness, disease, pestilence and death, however, were interpreted as evidence of God seeking divine vengeance on the sinful individual or community. Prior to Christianity, sickness was considered to be the result of the evil machinations of demons activated either independently or through the intervention of an intermediary, and the cure was effected through propitiating or punishing the demons or their agents. Under Christianity, sickness now became evidence of the power and justice of a beneficent God. Indeed, it almost became an honour to be sick, for it meant that God had singled out the sufferer for His special attentions. Sickness, therefore, was the result of sin and healing a matter of forgiveness. Anyone who declared otherwise and sought relief from pain in means other than prayer was to be condemned.

The Synod of Ancyra in 314 forbade the curing of sickness by 'occult' means – a decree repeated in 375 at the Synod of Laodicaea, in 506 at the Synod of Agde and at later synods in 511, 533, 573 and 603. 'It is enough', declared Bishop William Blois as late as 1229, 'that the sick should receive the Body of the Lord once a week and Unction once a year.'[2]

Any attempt to cure was evidence either of paganism or devilish inspiration, or both. Healing therefore became associated with sorcery. But, as in Roman society, it was also inevitably associated with women – among the Celtic and Teutonic tribes the traditional healers and midwives were women, and in Teutonic writings and those of Tacitus which deal with these Northern tribes, only women are mentioned as healers. To what extent these women were also priestesses of the old religion is not known. What mattered to the Church Fathers was that their rôle as healers smacked of magic and therefore paganism, and was to be condemned. The virulence of the early Church's attack on paganism was married with its condemnation of women – an attitude inherited from Hebrew and Roman culture. Indeed, it is likely that the misogynism of the early Church was further fuelled by contact with the Teutonic tribes and the pre-eminence of women in healing in those tribes.[3] In addition, the Teutonic concept of *maleficarium* was, in itself, inherently suspicious of women. For women were considered capable of causing not merely sickness and death but also, significantly, impotence. Both sorcery and healing were women's 'magic'. The new association of magic with the devil was therefore acceptable in a culture which already believed that women were capable of *maleficarium*.

The association between healing, sorcery and the Devil became enshrined in canon and civil law. The seventh-century bishop St Eligius commanded that

> Before all things I declare and testify to you that you shall observe none of the impious customs of the pagans, neither sorcerers nor diviners, nor soothsayers, nor must you presume for any cause nor for any sickness to consult or inquire of them . . . .
> Let none presume to hang amulets on the neck of man or beast even though they be made by the clergy and called holy things

and contain the words of the Scripture for they are fraught not with the remedy of Christ, but the poison of the Devil . . . .
But let he who is sick trust only in the mercy of God and receive the sacrament of the Body and Blood of Christ and according to the apostles the prayer of faith shall save the sick and the Lord shall raise him up.[4]

The secular laws of Cnut forbade the performance of 'wiccecraeft' (witchcraft) and the chanting of runes was likewise prohibited. (A rune was a whispered charm and the Anglo-Saxon word *leod rune* or *hel rune* meant a witch.) In Europe, Theodore's penitentials specifically attack the worship of demons. Indeed, the faintest glimmer of deference or respect paid to women, whether acknowledging their rôle as healers or as mere remnants of pagan worship, was stamped upon. Theodore directed: 'If anyone on the Kalends of January walks as a stag or as a little old woman . . . . shall do penance for three years, for this is devilish . . . . '[5] (Kalends, or Calends, were the first day in any month in the Roman calendar.) St Eligius commanded:

Let none on the Calends of January join in the wicked and ridiculous things, like dressing like old women or like stags or folleries, nor make feasts lasting all night, nor keep up the custom of gifts and intemperate drinking.[6]

Medicine was a sinful act and the practice of healing, especially if it succeeded, 'could only be by the help of devils and whoever sought to do anything, even good, by such means must be God's enemy.'[7]

The healer was no longer in control of the demons (as she had been considered to be under the old 'pagan' beliefs), but was their servant. One of the recommendations made to the Emperor Louis the Pious in 829 after the Synod of Paris, to reduce paganism (which, it was argued, still survived in the cult of sorcery), was that those guilty should 'be subjected to discipline and punished by the Prince; all the more severely because their wicked and overweening audacity does not shrink from serving the devil.'[8] Aelfric, in England, declared: 'It is not allowed to any Christian man to fetch his health from any stone, nor from any tree, unless it be the holy sign of the rood.'[9] Both are clear references to traditional healing. (The temptation to turn to it, however, must have been strong. Bede remarks that in the great plague of Cadwallader's time, in the seventh century, many of the East Saxons lately converted to Christianity, reverted to 'paganism').

The directives were aimed necessarily, not just at the practice but also at the practitioners. Charlemagne's son was advised by the Frankish bishops not 'to suffer a witch to live'. In England King Alfred declared: 'the women who are wont to receive enchanters and workers of phantasm, and witches, suffer thou not to live . . . .'[10] The laws of Edward and Guthrum were marginally more humane: 'If witches or diviners or poisoners be found anywhere within the land, let them be driven from the country and the people cleansed.'[11]

MEDICINE AND PRIESTS:
THE CHURCH'S CONTRADICTIONS

Yet for all this the policy of the Church was ambiguous, if not contradictory. Officially it condemned all healing practices; unofficially, it was prepared to condone those practices if they could be seen to be firmly within the control of the Church. Thus, for instance, the Church had commanded that in every community there be appointed 'at least one widow to assist women who are striken with illness.'[12] This widow, however, had to restrict herself to midwifery and related areas and was accountable to the priest. In many ways she was similar to the Hebrew midwives who were permitted and tolerated if they conceded their authority to God. It was also clearly an attempt to accommodate and control the main practitioners of healing.

The Church's contradictory attitude is seen more clearly in its position on priests and healing. Officially the Church condemned priests who practised medicine. The

Synod of Laodicea in 366 forbade the priesthood the study and practice of medicine and this was repeated in a series of directives culminating in the Synod of Ratisbon in 877. The Lateran Treaty of 1125 forbade the attendance of monks and priests on the sick in any capacity other than as ministers of religion. This decree was swiftly followed in 1131 by further restrictions prohibiting the study of medicine by monks and priests and directing, interestingly, that they confine their rôle as physicians strictly to their own monasteries. Eight years later, in 1139, yet another Lateran Council threatened all who neglected its order with the severest penalties and suspension of their position as priests – obviously to little avail. Pope Alexander III, at the Council of Tours in 1163, maintained the Devil was at work in those priests who pursued medicine. And in 1215 Innocent III issued yet another decree threatening anathema to any priest who practised surgery or performed any operations in which instruments of either steel or fire were utilised and directing that priests should refuse benediction to all those who professed or pursued surgery.

The Church's policy was to effect the transition from paganism to Christianity as smoothly as possible. Christian churches were built on pagan religious sites, and Church festivals coincided with pagan rites. But since the Church's pronouncements on healing were diametrically opposed to pagan practice, such practices could not be so readily assimilated. Traditional healers were women and their practices diabolical. Only the priest, by making intercessions to God for forgiveness, was in a position to comfort the sick. Prayer and piety could cure all. Any priest who dared to resort to more secular methods was to be condemned.

But the Church needed converts. And it recognised that its doctrines were most vulnerable at the point where its teaching was most fundamental: on matters of life and death. Faced with the reality of sickness, faith alone is often painfully inadequate. The temptation to turn to a

promise of earthly help in the present rather than
spiritual help in the future must have been enormous.
Although the penalties for the practice of medicine were
severe, there were, for the priests, ways round the
prohibition. Although invocations to the demons of
disease were diabolical, intercession to the saints, God's
chosen emissaries, was permissible. Any cure effected by
the former was evidence of the operation of supernatural
forces which could only come from the demons as a
result of a pact with the Devil, but any cure effected by the
latter was evidence of a miracle and of God's ultimate
generosity. Relics, saints and holy wells (all with impec-
cable theological pedigrees) were superimposed on
ancient beliefs in the power of amulets, deities and
magical springs. The division of labour among the saintly
brotherhood and sisterhood replaced that of the ancient
deities and astrological symbols.

> The saints of the Romanists have usurped the place of the zodiacal
> constellations in their governance of the parts of man's body, and
> that 'for every limbe they have a saint.' Thus St Otilia keepes the
> head instead of Aries: St Blasius is appointed to governe the necke
> instead of Taurus: St Lawrence keepes the backe and shoulders
> instead of Gemini, Cancer and Leo: St Erasmus rules the belly with
> the entrayles, in the place of Libra and Scorpius: in the stead of
> Sagittarius, Capricornus, Aquarius and Pisces, the holy Church of
> Rome hath elected St Burgarde, St Rochus, St Qurinus, St John
> and many others, which governe the thighes, feets, shinnes and
> knees.[13]

Aelfric, after condemning a sick man who sought to
improve his health 'with unallowed practices or at
accursed enchantements or at any witchcraft', recommended instead that he 'seek his health at holy relics'.[14]
    The matter did not rest with the saints and their relics.
The old incantations were cynically converted into
prayers. A ninth-century German manuscript contains a
charm originally addressed to Herba Cucumeris. The
dedication is crossed out and in its place are the words:
'*quod hic sequitur non valet, sed pro hoc dicatur, paternoster et
credo . . . .* ' ('that which follows has no value unless the

Lord's Prayer or the Creed are said.') The Teutonic methods of medicine, with their emphasis on wort cunning (herbal cures), were likewise transformed. God in His mercy had provided natural antidotes to sickness in the form of herbs and plants, and the Biblical statement that God had power over 'words, herb and stone' gave further sanction and appeal to those remedies which contained them.

These Christianised spells filtered through into popular usage. Indeed, traffic in medical remedies was undoubtedly two-way, for they became as much a part of the midwives' and healers' repertoire as they did that of the priests and monks. (See Chapter 7 for further examples.)

Throughout the Dark Ages European peasants incorporated existing religious traditions into their own. As the French historian E. LeRoy Ladurie points out:

> In the case of peasant societies in western Europe, rural religion essentially means a form of Christianity, interpreted according to the ways of local folklore. In theory, by the heyday of rural civilisation (thirteenth to eighteenth centuries), the most flagrant elements of paganism had long since been eradicated from peasant religious practices: the animistic worship of trees, stones, plants and creatures had disappeared. Set in wooden statues, the moonstones had become black Madonnas. Christian missionaries were until quite late on (the seventh century) burning idols representing mythical monsters and chopping down tree-gods. Legions of Christian saints peremptorily occupied the sites of sacred springs and woods, giving personal and human form to the old paganism of folklore. They could not root it out entirely: St Medard or St Swithun controls the rain; Saint Barbara protects from storms. And hundreds of miracle-working saints conveniently posted at every curative spring keep watch over the respective organs, from head to foot, of the invalids coming to be cured. The Church did indeed – especially after the Council of Trent (1545 and after) – rather half-heartedly remind villagers that the saints and even the Virgin were able merely to intercede with the Trinity. But to the peasants who prayed to St Joseph or St Anthony such casuistry meant nothing: from their point of view, the saint quite definitely had personal power, and he did not have to go through the Almighty in order to grant small favours on earth. In this sense, the saint remained a minor rural deity.[15]

Within this context, wise women were able to maintain the legitimacy of their rôle. They could use Christianity to sanction their position as effectively and as clearly as the priests might use traditional remedies to acquire their position. Ultimately, however, their position was vulnerable for, unlike the priests, in the final resort they could not claim protection under the Church's umbrella.

HEALING AND HERESY:
THE CHURCH'S RESOLUTION

From the eleventh century a discernible shift in the Church's thinking on both healing and paganism occurred. In the eleventh century a school of medicine was founded at Salerno, a rival to the Arab school of medicine at Cordova. It appears to have been the first such school established since the fall of the Roman Empire, and its method and teaching was derived from 'classical' sources – Hippocrates and Galen – newly rediscovered in the hands of Arab and Jewish scholars. The school was highly influential and, despite the Church's strictures on the study and practice of medicine, attracted scholars from throughout Europe including, initially, women. (One of the most famous of Salerno's teachers was Trotula, who wrote a definitive work on the diseases of women. Subsequent medical historians have either denied her existence or claimed she was a man. She is now largely remembered as Dame Trot, of nursery-rhyme fame).

It was a school which only the wealthy could afford to attend and its influence was such that the Church was forced to relax some of its prohibitions against the study and practice of medicine, to the extent, for instance, that it permitted physicians to marry, whereas initially they had been bound by the priestly code of celibacy. Nevertheless, the Church retained a firm hold over the curriculum and practice of medicine not only in Salerno but in other medical schools based on the model of Salerno which were set up in the emerging universities of Europe.

The study of medicine was concerned, primarily, with the study of theology, and the new university-trained physicians were not allowed to practise without first calling a priest to aid and advise them. Nor were they allowed to treat a patient who refused confession. The doctors' practice consisted largely of bleedings and cuppings (drawing blood by cutting the skin and applying a 'cupping glass'), 'christianised incantations' (prayer) and astrology. Indeed, because practical experience was absent in their training, what practical knowledge they had was derived largely from wise women. In the thirteenth century, for instance, one professor at Oxford rode forty miles to get a prescription from an old woman who cured jaundice with the cooked juice of plantain, whilst Paracelsus in 1527 burned his medical texts, confessing that he 'had learned from the sorceress all he knew'.

Galen and Hippocrates were permitted subjects of study, for their texts contained little that was overtly pagan. As Ehrenreich and English point out, medical students,

> like other scholarly young gentlemen, spent years studying Plato Aristotle and Christian theology. Their medical theory was largely restricted to the works of Galen, the ancient Roman physician who stressed the theory of 'complexions' or 'temperaments' of men, 'wherefore the choleric are wrathful, the sanguine are kindly, the melancholy are envious' and so on. While a student, a doctor rarely saw any patients at all, and no experiments of any kind were taught.[16]

In 1400 the library at New College, Oxford, contained only the following medical books: two copies of Galen, one copy each of Rhazes, Averroes, Hippocrates, Gilbert, Avicenna, Bernard Gordon and Dioscorides, the *Rosa Anglica* of John of Gaddesdon, and the *Esculapii de Morborum Origine Liber* bound up with *Trotula Curandarum Aegritudinum Mulierum Liber*.

But however limited the physician's knowledge, the Church was now prepared, officially, to sanction medicine so long as it remained within its theological and practical jurisdiction. Coinciding with this shift in thinking came a corresponding change within theology as regards healing. On the one hand the Church accepted some medical practice as beneficial; on the other, those who practised healing without Church sanction were now even more heavily condemned.

Whereas before sorcery and healing were evidence of paganism – albeit inspired by Satan – they now became heresy, a far more serious crime in the eyes of the Church and one which commanded the death penalty. The theocratic union between the Austrian Frederick II and Pope Innocent III in the thirteenth century had resulted in the notion that a crime against the emperor was also a crime against the Pope, and *vice versa*. Thus heresy became treason, and treason heresy. And the penalty for treason was capital punishment.

There were numerous signs of the control exercised by the Church over medical practitioners. Thus Pope John XXII urged Etienne, the Bishop of Paris, to prohibit those unlearned in the art of medicine (*ignari*) and old wives (*mulieres vetulae*) from practising in Paris and its suburbs. He maintained that most of them were fortune-tellers. Antonion Guaineri asked for lenience if his work the *De Egritudinibus Capitis* appeared to contain 'old wives' tales'. And while the Popes resided in Avignon between 1305 and 1377, they strictly enforced laws against 'irregular' practitioners:

> Women and old ladies and lay brothers and rustics and some apothecaries and many herbalists, in addition to scholars not yet learned in the faculty of medicine, are to be ignored by the science of medicine and are ignorant of the make-up (humours) of men.[17]

The trial of Jacobie Felicie in 1322, accused of curing her 'patient of internal illness and wounds or of external abscesses' and 'of visiting the sick assiduoysly' and continuing 'to examine the urine in the manner of physicians, feel the pulse, and touch the body and limbs', culminated in her being prohibited from practising medicine in or near Paris under pain of excommunication and a fine of sixy Paris pounds. Jacobie Felicie maintained that she was not one of the *ydiotas et fatuos usurpantes* ('idiotic and foolish usurpers'). Her prosecution arose from her success. She succeeded where university-educated physicians had failed and, though she had been trained, it was a training achieved through practice rather than a study of logic and philosophy.

A further Church edict of 1421 forbade women to practise medicine or surgery under pain of imprisonment, and a later edict of Sixtus IV prohibited the practice of medicine or surgery by 'Jews or Gentiles, men or women, who were not graduates of a university'.

Those, therefore, who practised medicine without a university training, did so in open defiance of the Church and the civil authorities. Success in those areas could only be achieved through the Devil's intervention.

> The Biblical statement 'we have entered into a league with death; we have made a covenant with hell' (Is.28:5) which had since the days of St Augustine implied the possibility of a pact with Satan, was taken to be the explanation of the witch's power over men's bodies and over natural forces – a power which was never doubted in popular belief.[18]

Significantly, the vast majority of those who continued to practise medicine as midwives and healers were women. 'For St Augustine says in Book 83', wrote the authors of the *Malleus Mallificarium*, the 'textbook' of the witchcraft Inquisition:

> This evil, which is of the devil, creeps in by all the sensual approaches: he places himself in figures, he adapts himself to colours, he attaches himself to sounds, he lurks in angry and wrongful conversation, he abides in smells, he impregnates with flavours and fills with certain exhalations all the channels of understanding.

The Devil was always conceptualised in masculine terms. It was insufficient that women alone should epitomise total evil: they could only do it after they had been subjected to a male – albeit evil – authority. The new Christian patriarchy could not, it appears, allow women autonomy even in this area, for by doing so they would also permit the notion that women were capable of the opposite: total good. The subjection of women, concept-ually, to the power of Satan enabled the Church to argue that women, by their nature, were susceptible to his influence, and that any suspicion or practice of sorcery, healing or magic, was done not through the initiative of women, but under the direct authority of Satan. The Church's attitude necessarily raised the status and power of Satan and, by the same token, increased the status of the 'witch'. As late as the seventeenth century an Essex clergyman declared: 'The ministers of Satan, under the name of Wisemen and Wisewomen are at hand, by his appointment, to resolve, direct and helpe ignorant and unsettled persons, in cases of distraction, losse or other outward calamities.'[19]

HEALING AND HERESY:
THE PHYSICIAN'S RESPONSE
The exclusion of women from the universities, and therefore from access to learning, was justified on the grounds that their intellects were deficient, largely be-cause they were governed by the senses rather than reason. Those women who practised medicine without a formal education were sinning not only against Christ, but against their own sex, for their 'natural' incomp-etence as healers necessarily meant that they did themselves a disservice whenever they practised. The physicians were not slow to develop this theme.

In the fourteenth century John of Ardenne described in scathing terms the treatment to which some women practitioners had 'subjected' his patients. One patient, with an injured finger, was treated for six months by a woman who used only 'drynk of Antioch and other pillules', while another, who had been 'hauntyng or usyng the medycines of ladies' for a swollen and aching arm, 'evermore had hymself worse'. Though John of Ardenne did describe his methods of treatment, he omitted to mention that they were virtually identical with those of the 'ladies'. And perhaps a further inkling of his motives for discrediting women's remedies can be gleaned from the fact that he described them as 'ladies bountiful', since they charged no fee. He, on the other hand, believed in charging a great deal. For one operation for fistula, for instance, in 1370, he charged £40 in cash, a new suit of clothes and a pension of 100 shillings a year.

John of Mirfield, a physician of St Bartholomew's and a close contemporary, wrote about the

> worthless and presumptuous women (who) usurp this professsion to themselves and abuse it; who, possessing neither natural ability nor professional knowledge, make the greatest possible mistakes (thanks to their stupidity) and very often kill their patients; for they work without wisdom and from no certain foundations, but in a casual fashion, nor are they thoroughly acquainted with the causes or even the names of the maladies which they claim they are competent to cure.[20]

In 1544 Thomas Gale, surgeon to Queen Elizabeth, complained that:

> I did see in the two hospitals of London, called St Thomas's and St Bartholomew's to the number of 300 and odd poore people were diseased of sore arms and legs, feet and hands, with other parts of the body so grievously affected that 120 of them could never be recovered without the loss of limb. All these were brought to that mischief *by witches, by women*.[21] (*my italics*)

One of the most coherent arguments against women healers was put forward in the seventeenth century by John Cotta in his *Short Discoveries of the Unobserved Dangers of Severall sorts of ignorant and unconsiderate practisers of Physicken in England (1612).*

> . . . *Here therefore are men warned of advising with women counsellors*. We cannot but acknowledge and with honor mention the graces of womanhood, wherein by their destined propierty, they are right

and true soveraignes of affection; but yet, seeing their authority in learned knowledge cannot be authentical, neither hath God and nature made them commissioners in the sessions of learned reason and understanding (without which in cases of life and death, there ought to be no daring or attempt at all). *It is rash cruelty in them even there to do well*, where, unto the not judiciously foreseeing, that well might have proved ill, and that ill is oft no lesse than death, or else at least the way to death, which is the hazard of health. Their counsels for this cause in matters of so great and dangerous consequent, modestie, nature, law and their own sexe hath ever exempted. We may justly here *taxe their dangerous whisperings* about the sicke, wherein their prevalence oft being too great, they cause the weak sense of the diseased, while they are not themselves; and make just and wise proceedings suspected and with danger suspended . . . . if women then profess no arts, nor as maisters of sciences can prove their rules, let them with sobrietie governe the great rule of themselves and so shall they be most harmlessly happy and being freed from the unhappiness of having their hands so commonly in others misshaps, unto the dishonour of womanhood.[22] (*my italics*)

Even if one spurned the theological explanation for women's inferiority, within the medical knowledge of the day there could be found sufficient explanations for women's 'natural' inferiority. The Hippocratic tradition held that women were governed by the womb and were therefore 'naturally' hysterical and incapable of logic and reason. Moreover, as John Cotta declared, women took advantage of the sick:

Oft and much babbling inculcation in the weake braines of the sicke may easily prevaile with them, to forget that which their owne good hath taught them, and also by a borrowed opinion from others indiscreete words, to corrupt their owne sense. . . . . Such persons are the curse of God and the sinne of man (for they that) persuade the sicke that they have no needs of the Physition, call God a lyar, who expressly saith otherwise; and make themselves wiser than their creator, who hath ordained the Physition for the good of man.[23]

Women were not only theologically suspect and intellectually deficient but they also posed another, professional, threat. The rôle and position of the old wives could be seen, as Pennethorne Hughes points out, as analogous to that of the Jews who

> were branded as usurers because no one but a Jew was permitted to lend money under the medieval system, and they were allowed few other professions. In the same way, witches had largely a monopoly of the powers of healing – the dual powers of healing and harming – because of the medieval injunctions against medicine.[24]

The Church's restrictions on the study and practice of medicine limited the physician's own scientific autonomy. Traditional healers, free from these restrictions, were able to experiment. Indeed their methods were primarily empirical and intensely practical. Their education may have been lacking in formal logic, but it was one achieved through experience, a position which the physicians could not hope to match.

> The study of anatomy, long prohibited by the Church began with her (old wife): this is why she is accused of robbing graves and selling children to the devil. The study of poisons, of chemistry and pharmacology, began with her as well . . . . [25]

The attitudes of the physicians, therefore, were coloured by rivalry over clients and their recognition that traditional healers could experiment with new healing methods, while they could not. 'Women, the sicke and the ignorant', lamented John Cotta,

> preferring their owne private ointments, plaisters ceareclothes, drinkes, potions, glysters and diets, because by time and custome they are become familarly knowne ynto them, and now are of their owne domesticall preparation, and therefore are by their knowledge, acquaintance and avouching of them, growne into some credite and reputation with them . . . . With this insinuation and officious promise of their knowne, gentle and pleasant medicines, and of undoubted food from this their owne protested proofs and experience, many allure the sicke miserably to beguile themselves.[26]

Moreover, just as the Church wished to divest itself of any association with magic, the physicians too wished to disassociate themselves from the connection between medicine and magic. For while healing remained associated in popular thinking with magic, it necessarily distracted from the appeal of more mechanistic forms of medicine. And while healing remained associated with women, male physicians would have little opportunity of establishing their rights within health care.

The number of university-trained physicians was limited. In 1500, for instance, although there are no records in England which specify the number of qualified physicians, in Paris at that time (a city of comparable size) there were 21. In 1566, when the city had grown, the university faculty arrived at the official figure of 81. In England in 1535 only 108 students graduated from Oxford from all disciplines and in 1566 only 54 graduated. Those that practised had, as John of Salisbury commented, only two maxims: 'Never mind the poor; never refuse money from the rich.'

> Emperors and kings and popes and the richest barons had sundry doctors of Salerno, or Moorish or Jewish physicians; but the main body of every state, the whole world we may say, consulted no one but the Saga, the Wise woman.[27]

The situation remained the same from the twelfth to the sixteenth century and beyond. Physicians were few and far between, and expensive. But in addition their methods had little to recommend them in popular thinking. Disease appeared frightening and irrational. 'We saw two prestys standing togeder', wrote a fifteenth-century physician, Dr Forrester, 'and speaking togeder and we saw both of them dye sodenly. Also in die proximi we se the wyf of a taylour taken and sodenly dyed. Another yonge man walking by the street fell down sodenly....'[28] (The disease was most likely to have been the 'English Sweat' – a fatal fever.)

The causes of sickness were little understood: magico-religious diagnosis and treatment of disease offered a seemingly sensible explanation and solution. It was, moreover, a system that was no better or worse than the practice of contemporary physicians. In some cases the treatment was identical. 'Charming is in as great request as physic', wrote William Perkins in *A Discourse of the Damned Art of Witchcraft*, published in 1608, 'and Charmers more sought unto than physicians in time of need.'

As late as 1735, a doctor wrote:

> The common people when incapable of penetrating the reasons of their bodily sufferings are exceeding prone to charge them on the influence and operation of superior powers; believing, as their phrase is, that they are under an evil tongue or afflicted by some mischievous eye, (they) impute their maladies to necromancy and witchcraft, (and) are inclined to use spells, charms and anti-magical remedies for their cure.[29]

Indeed, as Defoe wrote in his novel *Journal of the Plague Year 1665*, the common people:

> ran to Conjurers and Witches and all Sorts of Deceivers to know what should become of them; who fed their Fears and kept them always alarm'd and awake, on purpose to delude them and pick their Pockets. So they were as mad upon running after Quacks and Mountebanks and every practising Old Woman for Medicines and Remedies .... [30]

Though undoubtedly many were as unscrupulous as Defoe portrays them, nevertheless the reluctance of villagers and others to forgo their traditional healers resembles, as Keith Thomas suggests:

> the unwillingness of some primitive peoples today to rely exclusively upon the newly introduced Western medicine. They notice that men die, even in hospitals, and that the Europeans have virtually no remedy fo such complaints as sterility and impotence. They therefore stick to their traditional remedies, some of which afford a degree of psychological release and reassurance not to be found in Western medicine. They cherish the dramatic side of magical healing, the ritual acting out of sickness, and the symbolic treatment of disease in its social context. Primitive psychotherapy, in particular, can compare favourably with its modern rivals. If this is true today, when medical techniques have made such striking advances, we can hardly wonder at· the attitude of 17th century

villagers, when medical therapy still proceeded along its traditional paths of purging and bloodletting. There is little more reason for asking why the wizards were able to retain their prestige than for enquiring how it was that the pretensions of Galenic physicians remained so long unchallenged.[31]

THE OLD WIVES IN PRACTICE

Healing was seen as part of a woman's normal duty. Until the seventeenth century, the population of Britain was essentially rural and the pattern of social organisation based on the family and, by extension, the village community. The economy was similarly organised around domestic production. Therefore the contribution towards the family's survival made by its members, of either sex, was considered to be of equal importance. Though there was a division of labour in terms of work appropriate to sex, the value of occupations was not clearly defined by sex. Cooking or weaving were as essential to the family's survival as hoeing or fishing.

As well as contributing to domestic production, women also contributed other, less quantifiable, skills. Two of the most important functions performed by women of the family were teacher and doctor. They were, moreover, regarded as natural rôles. As Alice Clark described it: 'many of the services which are now ranked as professional were thought to be specially suited to the genius of women and were accordingly allotted to them in the natural division of labour within the family.'[32]

Women were still expected to be versed in the treatment of ailments and in the preparation of drugs and remedies. *The Compleat Serving Maid* of 1704 declared that the housekeeper should:

> have a competent knowledge of Physick and Chyrurgery, that they be able to help their maimed, sick and indigent Neighbours; for Commonly, all good and Charitable Ladies make this a part of their Housekeeper's business.[33]

Notions of charity meant that women of all classes were expected to provide services not only within their family but also in the community. The rôle of women in healing was merely an extension of their domestic rôle – a rôle which was as much incumbent on wealthier women as on poorer ones. One of the hallmarks of a 'lady of Quality' was that she treat the sick and needy. 'The Character of a Good Woman', as Timothy Rogers described, was one who: 'distributes among the Indigent, Money and Books, and Cloaths and Physick, as the severall Circumstances may require', to relieve

> her poorer Neighbours in sudden Distress, when a Doctor is not at Hand, or when they have no Money to buy what may be necessary for them; and the charitableness of her Physick is often attended by some cure or other that is remarkable. God gives a peculiar blessing to this practice of those Women who have no other design in this Matter but the doing Good . . . . [34]

'Ladies of Quality' played a crucial role in healing, operating in parallel with the (few) physicians, apothecaries and surgeons. 'Ladies were the ordinary practitioners of domestic medicine and the skilled chatelaine could reduce fractures, probe and dress wounds, or burns and prepare herbal remedies . . . . '[35]

During the Civil War, for instance, a number of noble women like Lady Anne Halkett, 'who had studied medicine and surgery in order to help the poor', received the thanks of Charles II for care of the wounded on the battlefield of Dunbar.

Others too gained renown. Lady Falkland had a wide reputation with her 'antidotes against infection and of Cordials, and other several sorts of Physick for such of her Neighbours as should need them (which) amounted yearly to very considerable summes . . . . '[36]

Similarly, a Mrs Elizabeth Bedell 'was very famous and expert in Chirurgery, which she continually practices upon the multitudes that flocked to her and, still gratis, without respect of persons, poor or rich.' The Rev. R. Josselin enters in his diary of 1673: 'My L. Honeywood send her coach for me: yr I stay'd to March 10 in wch time my Lady was my nurse and Phisitian and I hope for much good .... they considered ye scurvy, I took purge and other things for it.'[37]

Among the poorer classes the woman healer was an equally familiar figure. Moreover, although the social pattern and distribution of disease in the medieval and early modern period was fairly uniform, some diseases were more prevalent among the urban poor. Plague, for instance, although endemic in Britain from the fourteenth century, was largely an affliction of the poor: 'they have some little plague in England well nigh every year', wrote the Venetian ambassador to London in 1554, 'for which they are not accostomed to make sanitary provisions, as it does usually make great progress; the cases for the most part occur amongst the lower classes, as if their dissolute mode of life impaired their constitutions.'[38]

Similarly, typhus was largely confined to the poor in overcrowded conditions, and at this time whooping cough was also an affliction of the poorer classes. 'Chincofe', as it was originally called, first makes its appearance in medical writings in the sixteenth century. It undoubtedly existed before, but was not mentioned by physicians because it was not a complaint among the classes from which they drew their support. Till then, as Willis remarks, in the *Pharmaceutice Rationalis* of 1674, 'chincofe' was left to the management of 'old women'.

When syphilis first made its appearance at the end of the fifteenth century, cures for the wealthy were entrusted to surgeons. The poor resorted to 'wise women', of whom William Cloves wrote disparagingly in 1579:

> . . . yet I do not mean to speak of the old woman at Newington, beyond St George's Fields, unto whom the people do resort as unto an oracle; neither will I speak of the woman on the Bankside who is as cunning as the horse at Cross Keys; nor yet of the cunning woman in Seacole Lane who have more skill in her cole basket than judgement in urine, or knowledge in physic or surgery nor of many others who are compared to 'moths in Clothes' to 'canker' and to 'rust in iron'.[39]

Nevertheless, not all diseases were confined to a particular class, and throughout the medieval period until approximately the seventeenth century, both 'Ladies of Quality' and wise women treated both the wealthy and the poor for a wide variety of diseases. 'Old women in the country give burnt purple in the drink, for it has an occult property of curing smallpox', wrote Gilbert, adding a recommendation. Sir Ralph Verney counselled his wife:

> give the child no physick but such as midwives and old women, with the doctor's approbation, doe prescribe; for assure yourself that they by experience know better than any phisitian how to treat such infants.[40]

Elsewhere in the Verney memoirs, Sir Ralph talks of an eruption on his leg which would not heal. The advice he received ranged from bathing in asses' milk to a home-prepared lotion 'so violent a drop would fech of the skin wher it touched', to being recommended an old woman who was alleged to have an infallible 'oyntment for yumurs'.[41]

Adam Martindale described his illness as 'a vehement fermentation in my body .... ugly dry scurfe, eating deep and spreading broad', and the subsequent cure when

> some skilful men, or so esteemed, being consulted and differing much in their opinions, we were left to these three bad choices .... in this greate straite God sent us in much mercie a poore Woman who by a salve made of nothing but Celandine and a little of the Mosse of ashe root, shred and boyled in May butter tooke it cleare away in a short time, and though after a space there was some new breakings out, yet these being annointed with the same salve .... were absolutely cleared away.[42]

In medieval communities the wise woman was a central figure not only because of the vital nature of her rôle as healer, but also because that rôle itself reflected a position of trust.[43] As Christina Hole points out: 'their value to the community lay in the fact that they were women and trusted and were called upon in cases of illness and trouble, when no stranger, however learned, would have been consulted.'[44]

ATTEMPTS TO CONTROL:
(1) THE CASE OF THE MIDWIVES

The first attempts at control were aimed at midwives. The *Malleus Maleficarium* stated that midwives 'surpass all other witches in their crimes'. Midwives were an identifiable group; they also dealt exclusively with women at a moment when women were, in medieval eyes, at their most female – in childbirth. In England, some of the earliest legislation was directed specifically at midwives. Legislation of 1512 declared that all midwives had to obtain a licence from the Bishop's Court before they could practise. The 1584 oath taken by midwives (at the direction of the Bishop of Chester) clearly specifies the reasons. It commanded that midwives should not use 'any witchcraft, charms, relics or invocation to any saint in the time of travail'.[45] And if required to christen the child they would use only plain water in the 'apt and accostomed form' and 'none other profane words'. Midwives, moreover, were required only to attend childbirths, and not to extend their skills to more general practice. In 1661 and 1677 two midwives were barred from practice on suspicion of witchcraft and in 1664 a Mrs Peppar, midwife, was charged for using charms before Sir Francis Liddle, Mayor, in Newcastle-upon-Tyne. The evidence reads that: 'Margaret, wife of Robert Pyle, pittman, sayther, that about half a yeare agoe, her husband, being not well, sent his water to Mrs Pepper, midwife, and one that uses to cast water.'[46]

When infant mortality was high, the midwife – as the one who first handled the newborn child – was likely to be a prime target for blame. It made little difference whether the child died at birth or subsequently – if witchcraft was sought as an explanation for its death, then the woman present at its birth was the one with obvious access to witchcraft.

Though the life and soul of the child were the main source of concern, midwives' techniques also came under suspicion. If they tried to lessen the pain of labour or speed the delivery that, too, was often evidence of witchcraft. The rationale here was different from that associated with healing. Birth, and the pains of birth, far from being inexplicable, were the subject of rival explanations. For the Church the pain of labour was God's punishment for the sin of Eve. For the midwives it was a 'natural', almost mechanical process and they therefore sought methods to relieve the pains and aid the delivery.

By our standards their knowledge was limited but it was nevertheless based on a knowledge of the body, and not in a belief of the soul. Thus ergot or a draught of darnel, poppy, henbane, bryony root or pearlwort were used by medieval midwives to hasten labour, incantations were employed to 'soothe' the mother, the lode stone was widely believed to be efficacious in 'drawing' out the baby and girdles, similarly, were thought to be useful in speeding labour and easing pains. Labour girdles – used by Ancient Assyrian midwives also – were condemned by both Catholic and Reformation Churches, along with 'purses, Mesures of our Lady or such other Superstitious Things, to be occupied about the Woman while she laboureth, to make her believe to have the better spede by it'.[47] Indeed, the extent to which the midwives' techniques had been given *ad hoc* 'Christian' authority is shown by an inventory of the sacred relics at the convent of St Austin in Bristow in 1536, which stated:

> I send you also our Lady's girdle of Bruton, red silk, sent to women travailing, which shall not miscarry in partu. I send you also Mary Magdalen's girdle: and that is wrapped and covered with White: sent also with great reverence to women travailing.[48]

One can imagine the fury of the pre-Reformation Church fathers in finding that the midwives not only defied the Church's explanation of the pains of childbirth but also invoked the Mother of Christ – who, sinless, enjoyed a painless childbirth – for help during labour.

Midwives were popular and their popularity increased with the degree of help they could offer. A medieval saying had it 'the better the witch, the better the midwife'. Midwives who possessed 'virgins' nuts' – kidney-shaped stones marked with a cross – were in great demand, and the stone would be clutched by the labouring woman. Urine too, would be scattered on women in labour and many midwives carried their own 'groaning malt' (containing pain-relieving drugs), which they gave to women in labour to help alleviate the pains.

By the seventeenth century the ranks of the physicians (and, in particular, the surgeon and apothecaries) were growing. Anxious to increase the scope of their practices they began to regard midwifery, especially among the middle classes, as a potentially lucrative area of work. Attempts to incorporate it into male medical practice were made, accompanied by a great deal of propaganda against the alleged ignorance, clumsiness and incompetence of midwives.

Generally, the average physician lost no opportunity to abuse women healers and midwives. Thomas Sydenham (1624–89) called them ignorant old women. Thomas Fuller (1654–1734) declared that they infested the sacred precincts of medicine. Daniel Whistler (1620–1684) waxed lyrical on the native female empirics who undertook to cure rickets by bleeding from the ears, along with a warm bath at full moon, applying the blood to the bleedings on the ribs and other medicaments to spine and joint.[49] John Jones warned nurses in 1579 to take counsel only of learned and expert physicians and not to rely on the apothecary or every presuming practitioner, vain Paracelsian or 'tattling dame'. Robert Burton (1577–1640) bemoaned the 'common practice of some to first go to a witch and then to a physician'. He also railed against the use of 'kitchen physic' by country people.[50]

ATTEMPTS TO CONTROL:
(2) THE RÔLE OF THE PHYSICIANS

Although midwives were an identifiable target for both the Church and physicians, it was the general healer who especially attracted the opprobrium of the physicians. The traditional healer was more of a professional threat and a serious rival. The physicians needed status and recognition and while this was in theory provided by Church patronage, in practice they had little social recognition. Garrison, for instance, described the average seventeenth century physician as:

> a sterile pedant and coxcomb, red heeled, long robed, big wigged, square bonnetted, pompous and disdainful in manner, making a vain parade of his Latin and instead of studying and caring for his patient, trying to overawe them by long tirades of technical drivel, which only concealed his ignorance of what he supposed to be their diseases.[51]

Much of the argument and effort which went into consolidating their professional position was directed not at improving their knowledge and practice but in attacking the rivals – the wise women. The case of the English physicians provides a useful study of this. By the fifteenth century, the physicians had sufficient political leverage to demand stronger legal protection and control, initially from the Church and, after the Reformation, from the State.

From their start in the thirteenth century, the universities of Oxford and Cambridge excluded women as students. Women had continued to practise medicine, not only as healers but also as surgeons. They became barbers and members of the barbers' guilds. The Lincoln Guild ordinances of 1369 refer to the 'brothers and sisters' of the Guild and the Guild of Surgeons founded in 1389 admitted women. But in 1421 the universities petitioned Parliament to give authority to the Privy Council to make and enforce regulations which would restrict medical practice to trained and competent physicians. In other words, to allow no man to practise 'fisyk' without having studied in 'scholes of Fisyk . . . . undure peyne of long emprisonement and payng xl li (£40) to the Kyng'. They also asked that no woman be permitted to use the 'practyse of Fisyk undre the same payne'.

In 1423 an unsuccessful attempt was made to found a college for physicians in London. It was not until 100 years later that physicians secured the legal status they demanded. An act of 1512 laid down that none could practise physic or surgery unless they were graduates of Oxford or Cambridge or licensed by the Bishop of the Diocese, not only on the grounds that non-graduates and non-licentiates were 'ignorant persons' but, more particularly, that these 'common artificers, as smiths, weavers and women boldly and customably, take upon them great cures and things of great difficulty, in the which they partly use sorcery and witchcraft . . . . to the . . . . grevious hurt, damage and destruction of the King's liege people.'[52]

Since women were excluded from the universities they were not, legally, entitled to practise medicine. The Church sponsored the 1512 Act partly because it had the experience and organisational skills to administer it at a time when the State machinery was underdeveloped, and partly because the offences committed – sorcery and witchcraft – were then indictable offences under Canon Law. This Act was not repealed until 1948.

In 1518 a Charter was granted to the College of Physicians. The Act of Incorporation embodied much of the spirit, if not the actual language, of the 1512 Act, denouncing unqualified physicians as

> ignorant persons of whom the great part have no manner of insight nor any kind of learning, soke also no lettres in the boke so far forth that common artificers as smyths, wevers and women boldly and continually take upon them great cures and things of great difficulty in which they partly use sorcery and witchcraft, partly apply such medicines unto the disease as be very noyous and nothing merely therefore to the high displeasure of God . . . . [53]

This was followed by a series of Acts generally strengthening the position of the physicians. However, in 1542 a further Act was passed which exempted from the penalties laid down by the 1512 Act

> divers honest persons, as well men as women, whom God hath endowed with the knowledge and the nature, kind and operation of certain herbs, roots and waters, and the using and ministering of them to such as be pained with customable disease.

Only those who practised without charging a fee, however, were exempt. This Act was a tacit admission that the Act of 1512 had failed to eliminate the 'great multitude of ignorant persons' who presumed to practise medicine. It was also indicative of pressure for the Act to be amended, not so much from the 'common artificers' (they were hardly in a position to organise sufficiently to demand repeal) but from the physicians themselves. In 1540 Henry VIII had united the Corporation of Barbers with that of the Surgeons, who had immediately abused their privileged monopoly position by 'minding their own lucres and nothing to the profit or ease of the diseased'. Competition from another fee-charging body was not what the physicians had in mind as a way of securing their own professional monopoly status. It appears that they would rather retain 'divers honest persons' who would act as a convenient foil to their profession – providing that they were male. Between 1572 and 1603 nineteen women were tried under the 1518 legislation, prosecutions that were initiated by the College, and between 1624 and 1640 thirty women were prosecuted.

ATTEMPTS TO CONTROL:
(3) THE OLD WIFE AND THE WITCHCRAFT LAWS
The legislation described was a precursor of more sinister legislation. The association, already present in the eleventh and twelfth centuries, between non-orthodox medical practitioners and heresy, had already been

translated in Europe into a full-scale witch-hunt. The mood of persecution now began to filter across the Channel.

The 1563 Act 'agaynst Conjuracions, Inchantments and Witchecraftes' laid down the death penalty, on a first conviction, for using 'witchecraft Enchantment, Charme or Sorcerie, wherby any p(er)son shall happen to be killed or destroyed'. For *intending* to provoke 'any p(er)son to unlawful love, or to hurte or destroye any p(er)son in his or her Body, Member or Goodes' the death penalty was applied on a second conviction. This Act was strengthened in 1604. Any attempt to cure by 'unauthorised' persons could be used as evidence of witchcraft; any untoward injury or illness could likewise be attributed to witchcraft. Thus any attempt to cure which failed and resulted in a worsening of the patient's condition, or his or her death, could be, and was, interpreted as a deliberate act of witchcraft.

One of the depositions of the Archdeaconry Court in Essex, against Elizabeth Lowys, for instance, reads:

Item, that about M(ar)ch last, gooinge to Comes House, she (the depositer of this evidence) wente to the said Lowys wiffes hous, and then they talked about a sore arme of hers. And then she (ie Elizabeth Lowys) counselled her to goo to a woman under Munchewoode. And goynge thith(e)r, the folkes tolld her husbande and her that she was a wychte.

It(em). the saide Lewys wif did then and there aske how Johnson drink did worke. And she this deponent aunswerid that yt was as yt did. Then the said Lewys wif said, 'lett hym com and speke with me.'

Item. That this depo(nen)t goynge to her for monnye, viz, vi^s viii which she collde not spare, and aft(e)r that she had two piges and one of them sodenlie died, and the other ev(er) pyned tyll she was fayne to sell yt. And she judgeth that yt is the doinge of the said Lowys wiff. And then she this depo(nen)t fell sicke, w(i)th her husband and child w(i)th all, in pain and grief.

Item. that on(e) maye even, being at Canell(es) hous, John Cannell his child being sicke, (it) laye w(i)th the neck clene awrye, the face und(er) the lift (sic) shollder, and the right arme drawen with the hands clene backwarde and upwarde, the shullder pynt before the brest pight (sic), the bodie lyinge from yt an other waie, not right but wrythinge, and the right legge clene backwarde behinde the boddie –contrarie to all nature; as they suppose the verye doinge of the said Lowys wif.[54]

Most of the accusations were plainly ridiculous. An entry in the parish register of Wells-next-the-Sea in Norfolk records the drowning of fourteen sailors 'brought to pass by the detestable working of an inexorable witche of King's Lynn whose name was Mother Gabley, by the boiling or rather labouring of certyn Eggs in a payle full of colde water'. Other charges accused witches of causing their victims to vomit pins or nails, have fits or drop dead. Witches were accused of performing super-human feats which could not possibly have been true and which were, therefore, impossible to deny.

Moreover, witchcraft, like murder by poison, was treated as a crime apart, in which the normal legal requirements for evidence were attenuated. 'Common fame', or mere interest in the sick, was considered sufficient evidence to establish intent if not actual practice. Thus, once common or legal interest was directed towards someone it would be very difficult to establish innocence. Guilt was established at accusation and accusation was proof enough.

By European standards, English legislation was mild. In Europe, as in England, the doctor's evidence at a trial was significant, for it was they alone who could determine whether 'sickness' or 'death' was attributable to natural causes or to witchcraft. The *Malleus Maleficarium* stated this explicitly: 'and if it is asked how it is possible to distinguish whether an illness is caused by witchcraft or by some natural physical defect, we answer that the first (way) is by means of the judgement of doctors.'[55]

In England, the 'cunning man' (who acted as a kind of intermediary between the accusers and the judiciary and determined whether or not witchcraft had been employed and, if so, whether there was a case for prosecution) was often a doctor. Indeed, a doctor had, by law, to be consulted before a prosecution could take place. As Alan MacFarlane points out:

> Perhaps the best evidence that medical practitioners were unlikely to provide a bulwark against witchcraft prosecutions is the fact that nearly a third of the twenty-three cunning men whose professions are known were either surgeons or physicians.[56]

Moreover, the practice of witchcraft as a system of explanation and blame was used as efficiently by the physicians to explain their own failure to diagnose or cure. In 1624, for example, at Wivenhoe in Essex, a two-year-old child

> 'shrieked and cried out that it was lame.' Master Dauber, a surgeon, declared that there was 'no natural cause for its lameness'. Supernatural causes were therefore investigated and Mary Johnson, a seaman's wife, was charged with witchcraft.[57]

Thomas Ady wrote:

> Seldom goeth any man or woman to a physician for cure of any disease but one question they ask the physician is 'Sir, do you not think this party is in an ill handling, or under an ill tongue?' or, more plainly, 'Sir, do you not think the party is bewitched?' And to this many an ignorant physician will answer 'Yes, verily'. The reason is *ignorantiae pallium maleficium et incantatio* – a cloak for the physician's ignorance. When he cannot find the nature of the disease, he saith the party is bewitched.[58]

More significantly, as Ehrenreich and English point out:

> the distinction between 'female' superstition and 'male' medicine was made final by the very roles of the doctor and witch at the trial. The trial in one stroke established the male physician on a moral and intellectual plane vastly above the female healer he was called to judge. It placed him on the side of God and Law, a professional on par with lawyers, theologians while it placed her on the side of darkness, evil and magic.[59]

WHEN WAS A WITCH A WITCH?

But what of the common people? In England, particularly, they were not slow in turning over to the law those
suspected of witchcraft. Although legislation may have
reflected official thinking, the law could only be sustained
by those who were prepared to use the powers it granted.
In England, unlike Europe, with one exception no witch-
hunts were deliberately directed from a 'higher' authority
like the Church.

The kinds of sickness and deaths for which explanations in witchcraft would be sought were those cases not
instantly attributable to an obvious cause, such as a slow,
lingering or sudden death – perhaps a heart attack.
Plague or smallpox, though lethal, had symptoms which
could be diagnosed, and ran a specific social and medical
course. Explanations for these were not needed or
sought in the supernatural, though the patient might well
resort to a wise woman for cure or comfort. Failure to
cure common and discernible ailments rarely resulted in
accusations of witchcraft. Rather, it was those areas least
open to diagnosis and therefore least amenable to
explanation and treatment where possible witchcraft
would be suspected, and it is precisely in those areas that
accusations of witchcraft were most common.

If a witch was presumed to be present in a village, ills
and death were often readily attributed to her on the
rather doubtful logic that if she had not existed the
incidents would not have occurred. Moreover, in the
popular mind, there was little doubt that a wise woman
had negative powers of harming as well as positive ones
of healing. In periods of witch-hunting these attributes
were given legal and articulate expression by both
Church and State, and provided the mechanism by
which accusations could legitimately be made.

Although not every wise woman was accused of
witchcraft and not everyone accused of witchcraft was a
wise woman, the activities of the wise woman and the
connections, in the public imagination, of women with

sorcery, healing and *maleficarium*, meant that these activities were under public scrunity, and they could be
readily employed as weapons against any woman who
went against the accepted mores or offended the public
or an individual in some way. Wise women already stood
out and evidence suggests that the women most likely to
be accused of witchcraft were the most outspoken of
them – the scolds. Constantly recurring phrases in the
accusations of witchcraft are 'a busy woman of her
tongue', 'devilishe of her tonge', 'for scolding and railing
of most men, or rather every man when they do anything
in the town's business or affairs contrary to her own mind
or not pleasing to her', 'for a common scold and
disturber of the whole Parish', for 'terming the parish-
ioners to be a company of jackdaws'.

Being outspoken was clearly outside male definitions
of acceptable and reasonable female behaviour. But
more than that, women were forced to be outspoken in
the absence of customary legal practice in order to
uphold their (albeit tenuous) rights. As Alice Clark
explains, by the seventeenth century there were changes
which

> abrogated custom in favour of law, in effect eliminated women
> from what was equivalent to a share in the custody and interpret-
> ations of the law which henceforward remained in men's hands.
> We can see this in the succession of laws passed by men which
> deprived women of their property rights . . . [60]

Moreover, as Keith Thomas points out, the period was
also one which saw a change in attitudes to charity and
beggary. Indeed, the State now defined poverty and
provided welfare strictly within those definitions. This
meant that the poor were no longer cared for on an *ad hoc*
community basis, neither was there adequate provision
for them under the new Poor Law statutes. They were
caught in a situation which left them with neither legal
nor moral protection for their rights. It meant that
begging for alms was often the only way to survive,
especially for old women and widows. Many of the

accusations were made against women who begged for alms by people who had denied them alms and who could assuage their guilt and justify their meanness by accusing the beggar of witchcraft.

Finally, one crucial area in which women were subject to accusations of witchcraft was sexuality. The elevation by the Church and society at large of the 'male' virtues of rationality and intellect took place partly to isolate the rational man from the power of the flesh – a power which was greatly feared. By projecting this fear on to women, the object of that fear could be isolated and so dealt with. It was a fear of the unknown and the uncontrollable and this could easily be translated into witchcraft.

The notion of witchcraft and the persecution of witches was, therefore, more than the mere condemnation of magic and the devil. It was a visible way of demonstrating male power. LeRoy Ladurie sums up the social and psychological aspects of witchcraft when he suggests that: 'the witch thus represents the revenge of the beggarwoman against the rich, and of women against the "phallocracy" of male-dominated society'.[61]

Some 85 per cent of those persecuted for witchcraft were women,[62] and many of those were accused of attempting to heal – but by magic, not medicine. Since the distinction between the physician's and the wise woman's practice was thin (doctors relied more than wise women on humoural pathology in their diagnosis, but both used similar if not identical drugs, herbs and charms in their treatment), the only reliable yardstick which could be used to differentiate the two was one of authority. Physicians, trained and sanctioned by both Church and State, used medicine – the rest used magic. The connection between healing and witchcraft was only one dimension of witchcraft persecutions, but for the old wife it was crucial. In this period the rôle of women as healers began to be placed under public scrutiny and doctors were established as legitimate medical practitioners. The period also reflected social changes in the status of women. Ultimately these changes (which continued throughout the eighteenth century) had a far more deleterious effect on the rôle of the old wife in English society than any association of healing with sorcery, or the damning of the woman healer by the physicians.

CHAPTER FOUR

From Expert to Charlatan: the old wife and the medical profession in eighteenth-century England

Although the numbers persecuted for witchcraft in England must have run into thousands, the old wife and the system of medicine she represented survived throughout the Middle Ages and up till the mid-eighteenth century. Three crucial constraints were present in society which ensured her survival. First, the intellectual climate and ideology was essentially that of a pre-industrial age, and was based on a rural economy and pattern of life. Second, that economy itself meant a pattern of social organisation in which women had a definite and accepted rôle, especially in areas of health care. And third, the nature and rôle of the medical profession itself did not represent an effective challenge, either in terms of political power or in the superiority of its practice, until at least the end of the eighteenth century.

Traditional medicine will survive as long as the culture from which it originates is not challenged or displaced. As the medical anthropologist David Landy points out, 'It is from the culture of his [the traditional curer's] membership group that he [sic] draws his sanctions as healer and from the maintenance of its values and practices that he retains the legitimation of his rôle.'[1]

Once the social supports are withdrawn and the legitimising base removed, the rôle of the traditional curer and the status of traditional medicine is placed in question. This is further challenged if a new system of medicine is introduced. And if that system is based on a different ideological and socio-political support from that of traditional medicine, the traditional curer must adapt to survive, or perish.

In Europe generally and in Britain in particular, the social changes which occurred in the eighteenth and nineteenth centuries constituted a challenge to the old wife far more serious than that of the witchcraft pro-secutions. The nature of these changes fundamentally transformed the communities which had previously sanctioned the old wife, and helped refine the male medical elite who became increasingly powerful in terms of their political base and social acceptance. The rôle of the old wife became attenuated and in many areas the practice of traditional medicine gradually atrophied. At the beginning of the eighteenth century the old wife was an acceptable and viable alternative to the physician. Within the space of a century she, and traditional medicine, had begun to stand for what they now represent in common mythology: a symbol of superstitious and outdated women's advice.

FROM OLD WIFE TO DOCTOR'S ASSISTANT: THE CASE OF THE RICH

Despite the threat of witchcraft throughout the medieval period and beyond, the services of women were often used by choice by the wealthier classes (and of necessity by the poorer classes) in preference to those of male physicians. 'For Goddys sake be war what medesyns ye take of any fysissyans of London', wrote Margaret Paston to her husband John in 1464. 'I schal never trust to hem because of your fadir and myn onkyl, whose sowlys God assoyle.'[2]

For the most part women practised 'physic' without, as Adam Smith observed, 'exciting a murmur or com-plaint'. Indeed, in some cases they even had royal patronage. Margaret Kennox, who practised in London

without a licence, not only included Sir Francis Walsing-
ham among her clientèle, but was saved from prosecution
and punishment by the Royal College of Physicians
through the personal intervention of Elizabeth I.

By the seventeenth century some of the conditions
which ultimately led to the general demise of the rôle of
the old wife were discernible. It was the position of the
old wife among the wealthy classes which was the most
vulnerable. The employment of a physician for curing
disorders was, from an early time, a choice open to
members of the wealthy classes. Although it was not until
the eighteenth century that physicians gained something
like a monopoly on the practice of medicine among this
class, it seems that as early as the fifteenth century the
physicians represented a sufficient threat for the 'Lady of
Quality' to adapt her rôle and sometimes to accommodate the physicians' practice. This took two forms.
First, an *ad hoc* division of labour began to be established
whereby the more mundane sicknesses and those thought
to have a supernatural origin would be treated at home
by women. New illnesses like syphilis or illnesses new to
members of that class (like whooping cough or, in some
cases, typhus) would be referred to the physician. Second,
the treatment offered by the old wife would now incorporate remedies from the practice of the physician.
For instance, in 1765 Mrs Cappe described her friend
Mrs Lindsey as:

> visiting the sick, studying the case if any difficulty occurred (for she
> had a good medical library, and great acuteness in the dis-
> crimination of diseases) and in prescribing and making up
> medicines. She was careful, always, to obtain the best drugs from
> the Apothecary's Hall and generally administered them in person;
> and such was her knowledge, her care and her assiduity, that if the
> disease was not absolutely incurable, she generally succeeded.[3]

From the seventeenth century new drugs obtained
from, and sometimes prepared by, the apothecaries
began to replace the more traditional herbal medicines
used by physicians. Only wealthy old wives would have

had access to these as well as to the medical treatises of the day, and they undoubtedly incorporated new ideas and ingredients recommended by the physicians. Certainly the ingredients were more expensive than those available to women of the poorer classes,[4] who retained their use of herbs. The divide between physicians and old wives began to open up. It was a divide which quickly became characterised in class terms.

In addition, some women learned their skills from actual partnerships with male practitioners in their family. The widow of Sir William Read, occulist to William and Anne in 1719, advertised herself as:

> The Lady Read, in Durham Yard, in the Strand, having obtain'd (by several Years Experience) a peculiar manner of Couching of Cateracts, and Curing most Diseases of the Eyes by the late Sir William Read's Method and Medicines. She hath had great Success in curing Multitudes that were Blind and defective in their sight, particularly, several who were born Blind. She is to be advis'd with as above; where may be had . . . all the other Medicines Sir William used in his practice.[5]

The result of all this was that the wealthy wise woman's experience became more limited as more 'cases' were referred to the physician. Moreover, the accommodation of 'orthodox' practices did little to enhance, and probably restricted, the development of her own empirical tradition and approach to medical practice. These changes undoubtedly eased the way for the transition which occurred in the eighteenth century, when medical care among the middle and upper classes moved progressively from women practitioners of medicine to male physicians – especially as more areas of medical care (such as midwifery) became legitimate areas of male activity.

THE SURVIVAL OF THE OLD WIFE: THE CASE OF THE POOR

The poor were forced to use more empirical methods not only in their treatment of known diseases but also in their treatment of hitherto unknown diseases. They used cheaper, more traditional ingredients (such as herbs), which were more accessible and the knowledge of which could be transmitted more readily. Pertelot, in Chaucer's *Canterbury Tales* (the 'Nonnes Priest Tale'), says:

> I shal myself to herbes techen you
> Then shal be for youre helpe and for youre prow.
> And in oure yeerd the herbes shal I fynde . . .
> . . . of Lawriol, centaure and fumetere,
> Or elles of ellebore that groweth there
> Of Kataphee, or of gaitrys beryis
> Of herne yve growing in our yeerd, ther mery is
> Pekke hem up right as they grow, and ete them up.

'I was told', wrote William Boghurst in his account of the Plague of London of 1665, 'by an ancient woman that in Somersetshire the spotted fever (typhus) was very epidemical so that whole families died; but being told that plantan (plaintain) was very good, all of them almost took it, whereas before they died very fast.'[6]

It is impossible to determine the extent to which women practised medicine either 'professionally' (ie for a fee) or charitably. Some certainly were prosecuted for practising medicine without a licence. Yet, significantly, the State itself, and some of the medical authorities, conferred a legitimacy on certain categories of old wife. In this respect the State clearly saw them as 'professionals'.

St Bartholomew's Hospital employed women for the treatment of skin diseases, the last one being appointed as late as 1708. The Plague Orders of 1581, which attempted to control plague by isolating and quarantining its victims, mention the appointment of:

> two honest and discreete matrons within euery parish who shall bee sworn truely to search the body of euery person as shall happen to dye within the same parish, to the ende that they make true reporte to the clarke of the parish church of all such as shall dye of the plague, that the same clerke may make the like reporte and certificate to the wardens of the parish clerkes thereof according to the oder in that behalfe heretofore provided . . .
> . . . If the viewers through favour or corruption shall giue wrong certificate, or shall refuse to serue being thereto appointed, then to

punish them by imprisonment in such sorte as may serue for the terror of others . . . [7]

These searchers became a familiar feature of the plague, and though they were carried out initially to confirm the cause of death, by the seventeenth century they had become more diagnostic, and the rôle of the women more akin to that of physician and nurse than coroner. In 1637, for instance, it was agreed

with old Frewyn and his wief, that she shall presentlye goe into the house of Henry Merrifield and aidinge and helpinge to the said Merrifield and his wief, during the time of their visitacion (plague) . . . She shall have dyett with them, and six weeks after their visitacion ended. And old Frewyn to have 2s a week duringe all that tyme paid him and 2s in hand. And she shall have 2s a weeke kept for her and paid her in the end of the sixe weekes after . . .

And later:

It was thought fitt the Woman keeper and Merrifielde's wenche in the Pest-house, it beinge above vj weekes past since any one dyed there, should be at libertie and goe hence to her husbande's house, she havinge done her best endevour to ayre and cleanse all the beddes and beddinge and other things in both the houses . . . for her mayntenance vj weekes after the ceassinge of the sicknes, she keepinge the wenche with her, they shal be paid 3s weeke for and towards their mayntenance during the vj weekes.

In 1639 it was agreed:

Agree to geve Widowe Lovejoye in full satisfaction for all her paynes taken in and about the visited people in this Towne in this last visitacion xls. in money, and cloth to make her a kirtle and a wascote, and their favour towards her two sonnes-in-lawe (beinge forreynours) about their fredome. [8]

Similarly, the 1536 Act against vagabonds provided that the local authority should receive its poor 'most charitably'. Medical and nursing care was eventually included within notions of charity. In many cases, however, it was not the doctor who was called in under the provisions of the Poor Law, but the wise woman.

Records from Norwich, for instance, show that in 1571 a Deacon paid 'iiid to Glavin's wife to heal Tom Parker's leg', while Mr Thomas Meaumont paid '6/8 to Mother Colls for healing a broken legge of Margurette Pairs, a poor widow in the Normans'. In Barnstable in 1585, 'wydow Yard' received 5/- for healing a poor maid's leg. In 1578 Johanna Salisbury received 3/4 for healing Mary Notte and a similar payment was made to Margaret Cruste. In Hastings in 1601 payment was made to 'Mother Middleton for twoe nights watchinge with Widow Coxe's child being sick'. In 1651 in Dorchester 'Unto the Widdow Foote xs for curing of the Widow Huchins' lame legg at present; and xs more when the cure is finished'.

At Cowden, the overseers paid '10/- to Goodwife Welles for curing Eliz. Skinner's hand'; to 'Goody Halliday, for nursing him and his family five weeks £1.5s'; to 'Goody Nye for assisting in nursing 2s 6d'; to 'Goody Peckham for nursing a beggar, 5s. For nursing Wickham's boy with the small pocks 12s.' In Hertfordshire a woman was paid 15/- for attendance over three weeks on a woman and her illegitimate child and 15/- was given to Widow Thurston 'for healing of Stannard's son' in 1640.

The attempt to license midwives in the seventeenth century was as much an attempt to control them as a *de facto* recognition of their services. The State policy of persecuting some women practitioners as witches while incorporating others into the system as paid healers is not as contradictory as might at first appear. Notions of professionalism and a clear demarcation of occupational boundaries were not as yet an integral and defined part of the consciousness of society and the State. The period of the Civil war and the Restoration was one of economic, social and ideological transition, during which apparent anomalies occur. However, although some wise women were persecuted as witches, those who suffered most, as was made clear earlier, were the most outspoken, the 'scolds', often the women most critical of social change.

The women most likely to be paid or appointed by State institutions were those least critical of the State and social changes and resultant shifts in responsibilities.

There was, too, another argument for the State employing wise women. In line with Elizabethan attitudes to the poor, it was considered undesirable that vagrants and vagabonds, the 'undeserving' poor on relief, should receive better treatment than the more deserving members of their class who could afford to pay. Money was therefore not lightly given for doctors' fees, and substitute medical treatment had to be provided which was compatible with class; by employing the local 'wise woman', the skills and services of the 'respectable' poor would be acknowledged and utilised.

Finally, sheer expediency demanded the use of the services of these old wives. While some doctors were prepared to treat plague victims and the recipients of Parish Relief, practice in both those areas was unprofitable and unpopular with physicians. The ordnance of 1675, for instance, which commanded the newly-formed Royal College of Physicians to provide its services free to victims of the plague, was bitterly opposed by the College and, consequently, inoperable. Similarly, few physicians were prepared to offer their services in exchange for the renumeration provided by the Poor Law. There was little choice but to turn to the services of the old wives.

THE STATUS AND ORGANISATION OF THE PHYSICIANS

In fact, as was stated earlier, physicians in the seventeenth and eighteenth centuries had little to offer. Bleedings and purgings were a common form of treatment and there was considerable popular cynicism of their skills. 'An experienced old woman', wrote Thomas Hobbes 'is far preferable to the most learned and inexperienced physician.' Science had nothing to offer, Bacon sardonically observed, 'with its much iteration but little addition . . .

Old women', he continued 'are more happy many times in their cures than learned physicians'.

Moreover, as a profession, the doctors were split. Formal recognition of the physician's exclusive status had been demanded and granted in the sixteenth century by Henry VIII. This recognition, however, extended only to Fellows of the Royal College of Physicians. During the period of the persecution of the witches the Royal College had made selective prosecutions but was ultimately unsuccessful in eliminating competition. The prosecutions were principally a demonstration of power by a new organisation.

However, the Royal College was unrepresentative of the range of medical practitioners. Its authority and membership was that of an elite minority, and the exercise of this authority, ironically, merely highlighted the gap between Fellows of the Royal College of Physicians and the rest, Licentiates and non-Licentiates alike. Prosecutions by the Royal College, rather than increasing its status, merely antagonised those not privy to the same protective privileges as members. Indeed, as late as the 1800s, the Royal College of Physicians represented only five per cent of medical practitioners in England and Wales, and that included Licentiates, extra-Licentiates and Fellows (179 in all).

In addition to the physicians there were the surgeons who, in 1545, established themselves as a city company separate from the Barbers. In 1617 the Apothecaries similarly separated themselves from the Grocers and established by Royal Charter their own Society of Apothecaries. Few surgeons could exist by surgery alone and many were therefore also members of the Society of Apothecaries. In theory, apothecaries were not entitled to prescribe or diagnose, only to dispense or sell drugs, but in 1703 a judgement was passed which effectively gave them the legal right to diagnose and prescribe providing they did not charge for those services. This judgement severely challenged the authority of the physicians, who considered themselves the only body capable of diagnosis, and the battle for medical jurisdiction between the physicians and the surgeon/apothecaries was one which proceeded to occupy them throughout the eighteenth century and for a good part of the nineteenth.

The splits within the medical profession meant that physicians were not in a position to develop a medical monopoly. As long as this continued, and as long as the support for physician's skills remained minimal, their development as an autonomous profession remained limited. They were merely one system of healing in a broad spectrum which began to emerge in the eighteenth century and which included old wives, surgeons, apothecaries and pedlars of patent remedies.

PURITANISM, CAPITALISM, THE MEDICAL PROFESSION AND OLD WIVES

While the employment of some old wives – and the prosecution of others – throughout the seventeenth century marked the contradictions of the period, it also marked the beginnings of more fundamental changes. The development of capitalism and the growth of Puritanism meant that social class began to stand not merely as an indicator of relative wealth or poverty, but also as a metaphor for social and moral value. The employment of wise women under the Poor Law in the seventeenth century did not merely confirm their rôle – it also conferred on that rôle a lower social status and consequently social worth. Indeed, it set the context and terms for all subsequent arguments over health care, many of which still prevail today.

The Poor Law reflected some of the crucial changes occurring within society, defined the poor as a separate class and differentiated within it. The poor were defined not only in terms of access to wealth but also in terms of access to fundamental, and increasingly professional, services. Hitherto the treatment of the sick had varied between classes in two ways: in treatment available and in patterns of disease. Distinctions in treatment were based on practice, with no moral overtones as to the value of treatment. This distinction was now enshrined by statute, and by the custom and practice of the Poor Law Commissioners. The poor, simply because they were poor, could not expect and did not 'deserve' to receive the range of treatment available to the wealthier members of the community. Second-class status deserved second-class treatment. In specific terms women's practice was identified with inferior provision (a status still dogging the nursing profession). In general terms, the situation cleared the ground for general practitioners to expand their services and seek professional recognition from the class which not only could pay but, precisely because it could pay, deserved better treatment (an argument which echoed throughout the nineteenth century and is still heard today in the debate over private versus public medical provision). But, more immediately, it meant that the old wife was now associated with the poor and this association the poor themselves were increasingly reluctant to accept.

There was also change in the intellectual climate – change which, ultimately, could not sanction traditional medicine. This change was part of broader social and economic changes which had fundamental implications for the status of women, rural society and the new professional institutions.

By the latter half of the eighteenth century the pattern of social organisation which had hitherto sanctioned and protected women's domestic and productive rôles had begun to break down. The expansion in trade and industry not only disrupted the traditional rural social organisation by attracting ever-increasing numbers into the cities and the factories, but also declared redundant the family as a unit of production. Labour was beginning to become more specialised and centralised; on the whole, family industry could not compete with the scale of production in the new factories. Men (and women too) were forced to abandon the domestic unit as a source of livelihood and sell their labour on the open market. But labour became valued according to the economic reward accruing to it. The valuable skills were now the saleable skills. And saleable skills were, almost by definition, those capable of being used beyond the family unit and introduced into the market.

But the new urban immigrants who sought work in the towns and cities brought with them redundant rural skills. For the purposes of the new economy, they were unskilled. All they could sell was their physical strength and labour. Women and children were also forced to sell their labour, for the new economy, on the whole, paid wages too low for any one man to support a wife and family. If the unskilled labourer could sell no more than his physical strength, his wife and children could sell even less. The woman and her children were 'lesser' versions of the man. In theory, lacking the physical strength of the man, the woman could only do less work. And being of lesser economic value, she became of lesser social value.

Although wealthier women were not forced to sell their labour, their rôle and status also began to be devalued in those areas which had hitherto been their prerogative, namely healing and teaching. Being skills which required intellectual rather than manual dexterity, these began to be concentrated in that section of the population which defined itself in terms not of selling labour, but of providing services. Doctors, along with teachers and lawyers, began to see themselves in terms of 'professions'. And together with some of the older trade and occupational groups, they began to define themselves not in terms of locality (as the old Guilds and the old licensing system for physicians had done) and occupation, but in terms of status and expertise. The professions became increasingly closed to outsiders, especially women: entry became more restrictive and their policies more protective.

THE GROWTH OF THE MEDICAL PROFESSION AND THE RISE OF THE MIDDLE CLASSES

The intellectual mood of the eighteenth century meant a move away from the 'arts' of the Middle Ages and towards the cognitive sciences and ideas of progress and enlightenment. With this came the desire to protect these areas of knowledge from those unable to comprehend its complexities. Knowledge itself began to be institutionalised, and became expertise. Knowledge without expertise became skilful deceit. 'Cunning' changed its meaning from 'knowledge' to 'craftiness', and the cunning woman, once an expert, was now a charlatan.

> Expertise is not mere knowledge. It is the practice of knowledge, organised socially, and serving as a focus for the practitioner's commitment . . . he develops around it an ideology with the best of intentions, an imperialism that stresses the technical superiority of his work and capacity to perform it. This imperialistic ideology is built into the perspective that his training and practice create. It cannot be overcome by ethical dedication to the public interest because it is sincerely believed in as the only proper way to serve the public interest. And it hardens when an occupation develops the autonomy of a profession and a place of dominance in a division of labour and when expertise becomes an institutional status rather than a capacity.[9]

By the eighteenth century the authority of the Royal College had begun to be challenged by a growing body of general practitioners, the surgeons and the apothecaries. The former, especially, demanded equal entry into the small and closed professional world of the Royal College. Fellowship was still limited to a few: the Licentiates increasingly took on duties of a general nature and began to demand equal status and recognition with the Fellows. (Fellows were full members of the Royal College; Licentiates merely had a licence to practise).

The system of licensing and registration of medical practitioners were chaotic. At the turn of the nineteenth century there were nineteen different licensing bodies, the majority of which were concerned with the licensing of surgeon/apothecaries. The multiplicity of licensing authorities permitted the easy expansion in numbers of legitimate medical practitioners – an expansion which was beyond the control of the Royal College and necessarily represented another challenge to its authority and jurisdiction. In addition, the surgeon/apothecaries were claiming – as were the Licentiates – the same status and rights as the Physicians.

The increase in numbers of legitimate medical practitioners, especially surgeon/apothecaries, was closely linked to the expansion of the middle classes. This group, as Parry and Parry point out in *The Rise of the Medical Profession*, 'produced a massive increase in the market for medical care'. Indeed, this market was necessary to the development as a profession of the general practitioner. It was not, however, a sufficient condition. The size of the market created the demand and the nature of the market determined the type of medical attention that would meet this demand.

The nature and growth of the new 'division of labour' in medical care was not uniform. It affected different skills and different classes at different periods. In terms of healing, the first women to lose their rôle as healers were those who had treated the upper classes. The physicians had support among this class already and the establishment of the Royal College aided in the consolidation of this practice. It was in this social group that healing skills were first removed from the home and trusted to the male expert 'beyond'. The rôle of healer and the necessary skills had already become diluted here by the willingness to employ the physician for many categories of sickness at the expense of traditional medicine.

As the middle class grew and began to create a consciousness modelled on the behaviour and standards of their 'superiors', one way to differentiate themselves from the 'lower orders' and to confirm their new status

was to employ, increasingly, 'professional' help in traditional domestic areas. Healing, like education, was
provided by those whose value was recognised in economic terms: the professional physician. Indeed, the
hallmark of the middle classes was their ability to pay for
services hitherto provided free in the home, and the
hallmark of a 'lady of quality' became idleness. A
necessary corollary was the middle-class willingness to
defer to the experts. It was among this group, for
instance, that the 'man-midwife' became popular, and
midwifery was one of the major areas into which general
practitioners could expand their practices. Even home
nursing was a skill to be bought and, if not bought, was
undertaken only with the supervision of the physician.
Dr William Buchan introduces his *Domestic Remedies* of
1789 with the following:

> We have indeed ventured to recommend some simple medicines
> in almost every disease; but even these should only be administered
> by people of better understanding. We would have the ignorant
> omit them altogether and attend solely to the diet and other parts
> of the regimen.

Diagnostic or prescriptive initiatives increasingly became the prerogative of the physician, not of women, for
as Dr John Connolly explained in *The Physician* of 1832
'. . . this publication is not meant to supercede an
application of the sick to persons competent to cure
them, but to show that it is only such persons that they
can safely trust'.

As the incentive to practise healing by middle-class
old wives became reduced, the skills available and the
sources of acquiring knowledge became, proportionately,
more limited.

> When no professional services were available, it was to the women
> of the family rather than to the man, that the sick and wounded
> turned for medicine and healing [but gradually] women were
> excluded from the sources of learning which were slowly being
> organised outside the family circle, and were thus unable to
> remain in professions for which they were so eminently suited.[10]

Middle-class women were excluded circumstantially from acquiring an empirical training and formally from acquiring a university medical training. Furthermore, throughout the eighteenth century, the number of new hospitals increased. In London, for instance, five general hospitals specifically for the care of the sick poor were founded in addition to the two (St Bartholomew's and St Thomas's) already in existence. Although it was not until the nineteenth century that hospitals began to play a major rôle in medical education, already by the eighteenth century many physicians, surgeons and apothecaries would voluntarily supplement their formal training with a spell of observation in these hospitals. One result was that medical practitioners' training became more rooted in practice and less reliant on theory.

Ultimately this led to improvements in medical science, but it also had immediate implications for the practices of women in healing. It increased the authority of the medical practitioner by providing many of them with experience that women could not claim to have had and, indeed, were denied the opportunity of acquiring. And the experience substantiated the practitioners' claims to carry out a proper diagnosis based on physical examination rather than mere theory. Their practice appeared therefore more empirical and, in a sense, more like that of the old wife – but with an important difference as J. Peterson points out:

> Less reliance was placed on the patient's description of his own symptoms and more importance placed on the medical man's evaluation of the physical signs of disease which he observed in the patient. In a subtle way, authority about the patient's physical condition shifted from patient to doctor as the doctor became less dependent on the patient for knowledge of the patient's condition.[11]

This shift in authority increased their standing with patients. This, together with the attempts by an increasing range and number of general practitioners to achieve comparable status with the Fellows of the Royal College, led them to develop more protective and restrictive conditions of entry to the profession, and to become more expansionist in their policy. Midwifery, for instance, the woman's area *par excellence*, became included in the practice of the general practitioner for, it was argued, only they had the intellectual skills, practical experience, physical strength and moral integrity to perform in that area. In addition to being squeezed out professionally, middle-class wise women were also caught in the crossfire of the class aspirations of male practitioners. On the one hand

> The Royal College of Physicians had established a thriving oligarchy in which royal patients, appointments at the great new voluntary hospitals of the century university chairs and knight-hoods rotated among the Fellows, to the fury of the surgeons and even of their own Licentiates. There was still less room for women within that circle of privilege. At the same time, social and economic changes were forcing them out of family practice.[12]

The physicians had, typically, been recruited from the 'second sons of gentry, or the sons of clergy'. The surgeon/apothecaries, however, came from a lower class and wished not only to consolidate their practice among the middle classes but to achieve entry into those ranks themselves. Indeed, many of the surgeon/apothecaries

> had served a rough-and-ready apprenticeship training as surgeon/apothecaries in the armed forces of the Crown. It has been said that by the end of the century (18th) more than half the medical men in practice in Britain had service qualifications. They entered the profession with no preliminary education, apart from a chance meeting with the recruiting officer or the press gang and many of them were remarkably tough customers. Competition with them was cut throat competition, and the women could not survive it.[13]

Middle-class women in the eighteenth century reflected the class of their husbands. They could not themselves define their own class status. The requirements of symbolic status meant that not only did they defer to the male, especially in terms of expertise but they did nothing to challenge male status – either in terms of claiming rank with the physicians or pulling rank with the surgeons/apothecaries. Both courses would have demeaned their position and that of their husbands. They would also have demeaned the status of the professional group upon whom they relied, paradoxically, to define their own status.

Thus the growing limitation in the performance, scope and social rôle of the middle-class women healers created a vacuum which the increasing number of medical practitioners in the eighteenth century could fill. Although there remained some 'sceptics' who felt that there was not much to choose between the physician and the 'wise woman', for the most part the latter became increasingly inoperative among the middle classes, and those classes had little choice but to opt for the professional male practitioner in times of sickness and, increasingly, of childbirth.

SICKNESS AND POVERTY: OLD WIVES FOR THE POOR AND THE CHALLENGE OF PATENT REMEDIES

Doctors did not, until the mid-nineteenth century, see expansion of their practice among the working classes as a means of achieving professional recognition or status. Throughout the eighteenth century they were essentially concerned with demarcation disputes for control of lucrative middle-class practice. For the working classes, however, the services of a medical practitioner were financially beyond their reach. Medical provision for the poor working class remained largely in the hands of women – the group which had, traditionally, provided this service. Nevertheless, although the circumstances which surrounded the working-class old wife were historically and socially different from those of the middle classes, the erosion in the rôle of the old wife followed broadly similar stages: first, she adapted her practice to accommodate the pressures of a new and alternative medicine; second, her rôle as a result of this became diminished; and third, her social standing within the community in which she practised was reduced.

The move to the cities which continued throughout the eighteenth and nineteenth centuries necessarily changed the rôle, scope and social perceptions of the old wife. The nature of work and domestic life were substantially different in cities and rural areas. For the first time, a divide opened up between urban and rural communities – a divide marked not merely by social organisation but, significantly, by quality of life and cultural expectations.

Rural poverty had always existed. Enclosures (the appropriation of the common land) begun in the fifteenth century intensified an already high level of agrarian poverty. For those rural poor displaced from their livelihood there was little choice but theft or death. Even for those able to work on the land, survival was hard. But with the expansion of manufacture and industry came the hope of employment. Throughout the eighteenth and nineteenth centuries increasing numbers of agrarian poor emigrated to the cities. And although the cities expanded enormously the rate of expansion was too slow to provide adequate employment and, especially, accommodation for all rural refugees.

In terms of health, immigration caused more problems than it solved. Between 1801 and 1851 London grew from a population of under one million to two and a quarter million. Manchester in 1800 had a population of 70,000, but by 1841 its population had reached 243,000. Living conditions were appalling, overcrowding the norm. The *House of Commons Committee on Mendicity and Vagrancy* of 1814–5 gave the example of George Yard, Whitechapel, where there were forty houses in which 2000 people were living. And in 1835 the newly formed Manchester Statistical Society counted 3,500 cellar dwellings housing 15,000 people or 12 per cent of the working-class population of the city.

Conditions in the crowded dwellings were exacerbated

by the window tax, which left many dwellings dark and airless, and by a lack of sanitary and waste disposal provision: such conditions greatly aggravated the prevalence and incidence of disease. Plague had died out in the seventeenth century, but 'fever' remained a major killer. 'In London now', wrote Sir John Coke to Lord Brooke in 1625, 'the tenth person dieth not of those that are sick, and generally the plague seems changed into an ague.'[14]

Although there was no differentiation between 'fevers' in official records until the mid-nineteenth century, influenza, malarial fevers and particularly typhus (spotted fever) and typhoid (relapsing fever) were the major diseases. The typhus epidemic of 1817–9 'visited almost every town and village in the United Kingdom'. In 1847 (when records had become more specific), out of a total of 57,925 recorded deaths in England and Wales, typhus alone accounted for 30,320. Although typhus and typhoid were by no means new diseases, the scale increased in proportion to the degree of overcrowding. 'Fevers' were largely adult diseases; children were prone, usually fatally, to smallpox, measles, whooping cough, scarlatina, croup and diarrhoea and, from the mid-nineteenth century, diphtheria. Dysentery – 'griping in the guts' – was a major problem for all age groups, and when cholera came to Britain in 1831 it, too, was most prevalent in the poorest and dirtiest quarters.

Overcrowding and inadequate diet meant, simply, poor health. Some diseases, like plague and typhus (nicknamed 'gaol' or 'workhouse' fever because of the high incidence of the disease in those institutions), were related to class but on the whole the distribution of disease up to the eighteenth century affected all classes more or less equally. By the eighteenth century, however, the distribution of disease had begun to change. The declining living conditions of the urban poor stood in contrast to the improving conditions of the middle- and upper-class city dweller. Many diseases like typhus and cholera became synonymous with poverty; other diseases too were far more prevalent among the working classes. Practices such as the pawning of clothes and bed linen spread infection far more rapidly among the poor, and working-class living conditions generated disease which spread much faster and further than in the wide, paved streets and spacious squares of the wealthy. The middle classes had available to them the services of the 'professional', even though their success rate for curing diseases was limited; but then the wealthier classes did not have to contend with the major 'killer' diseases of the working classes, nor with poverty and malnutrition – a major variable in the recovery of the patient. Indeed some diseases were virtually unknown to physicians. The urban poor also had to contend with far higher rates of disease than their rural counterparts. Whooping cough, for instance, had a far lower rate of occurrence in the country. And, as has been made clear in earlier chapters, even if the working classes could have afforded the services of the physicians,[15] the number of the latter prepared to practise in the 'slums' was limited.

Although some fever and general hospitals had been set up towards the end of the eighteenth century, they were seen more as Houses of Death than as Houses of Recovery and were rarely voluntarily visited. Notions of public health care in the seventeenth and eighteenth centuries were minimal, and the few institutions that existed had, as their primary function, a responsibility to maintain public order, not a responsibility to health. Not surprisingly, as Dr John Hunter, an ex-army doctor, observed in 1780:

though the fever (typhus) in the confined habitations of the poor does not rise to the same degree of violence as in the jails and hospitals, yet the destruction of the human species occasioned by it must be much greater, from its being so widely spread among a class of people whose number bears a large proportion to that of the whole inhabitants. There are but a few of the sick, so far as I have been able to learn, that find their way into the great hospitals of London.[16]

Slums were 'but little known to the physicians'; and even then the physicians' success would have been limited partly because of the limitations of medical science itself and partly because many of the diseases of the poor were essentially social in origin.

The move to the cities therefore increased the prevalence of disease within a context in which there was even less provision for medical help. For the move also displaced the old wife from her traditional social base and, more crucially, from her source of ingredients. In 1848 it was still possible for Mrs Gaskell to remember the activities of such as Alice Wilson (in her novel *Mary Barton*), as she gathered herbs and continued her rôle from an urban (Manchester) rather than a rural base:

> She had been out all day in the fields, gathering wild herbs for drinks and medicine, for in addition to her invaluable qualities as a sick nurse and her worldly occupation as a washer woman, she added a considerable knowledge of hedge and field simples; and on fine days, when no more profitable occupation offered itself, she used to ramble off into the lanes and meadows as far as her legs could carry her. This evening she had returned loaded with nettles and her first object was to light a candle and see to hang them up in bunches in every available place in her cellar room . . . the cellar window . . . was oddly festooned with all manner of hedgerow, ditch and field plants, which we are accustomed to call valueless, but which have a powerful effect either for good or for evil, and consequently much used among the poor. The room was strewed, hung and darkened with these bundles, which emitted no very fragrant odour in their process of drying.

Remember, though, that Mrs Gaskell was recalling a period before urban expansion had begun in earnest. As cities increased in size and immigrants extended into second and third generations, it became increasingly difficult for a city-dweller to gather natural ingredients. And with this came an inevitable decrease in herbal lore, until now almost always transmitted orally, and the use of traditional herbal remedies. What remained to the old wife was, broadly, the form – the charms and ceremonies – but not the content of herbal treatments. 'The domestic treatment of disease among our poor', commented a writer in *Notes and Queries*, 1859, 'consists chiefly of charms and ceremonies and even when material remedies are employed as much importance is attached to the rites as to the agents used.'

Though charms and ceremonies were an integral part of traditional healing, they were relevant to a pre-industrial, rural age. In an urban environment, epitomised by the technology of new forms of manufacture and based on a belief in science and technology, they appeared anachronistic and became redundant. Indeed, things 'rural' began to assume an aura of 'backwardness', and much traditional medical lore either atrophied or became extinct.

Moreover, the old wife, particularly in the cities, had to compete with new forms of medical care. With the poor health conditions generated by urban overcrowding new medical practitioners emerged, foremost among them the peddlers of patent medicines and the quacks. In the early 1830s, Dr Andrew Ure remarked:

> Nothing strikes the eyes of a stranger more in Manchester than the swarms of empirical practitioners of medicine. Nearly a dozen of them may be found clustered together in the main streets; all prepared with drastic pills and alternative potions to prey upon credulous spinners.[17]

Patent or market medicines only became viable after the mid-seventeenth century with the introduction of new drugs and preparations (see section on remedies). Since the ingredients in medicines did not have to be disclosed (the first tax on patent medicines, in 1783, was imposed only if the ingredients were not disclosed and most manufacturers preferred to pay the tax rather than expose their remedies), the field was wide open to fraud. The cost of these medicines was relatively high.[18]

Apart from more dubious manufacturers of drugs, there was now an increase in the number of chemist shops. In Nottingham, with a population of 10,770 in 1739, there were three surgeons and six physicians (the surgeons hardly left room for 'one physician to gain genteel bread') and three chemists. In 1874, with a population of 134,000, there were 69 physicians and 82 chemists. The chemists themselves offered what was termed 'counter practice' (treatment over the shop counter) which, although it undercut the physicians and apothecaries, was still expensive. And representing progress and science, visible and easily accessible, advertising widely and promising unimaginable cures, the chemists proved destructive to traditional methods of healing. A 'Dr Uytrecht, Oculist' advertised in the *Nottingham Journal* of 1784 that

> he has restored many afflicted with blindness of sight and many deaf to perfect hearing. His operations and cures (by the blessing of God) have been great and unexpected, that even the most versed in physic, and eminent in the (medical) profession, were astonished to see such wonderful and uncommon cures, many of which have been several times mentioned in the newspapers.[19]

By comparison, the old wife appeared even more backward and remote. Druggists were part and parcel of the new urban environment and the old wife was inextricably linked with the past. But there remained certain areas of practice which she adapted to accommodate these new urban conditions, and one particular rôle which she was capable of sustaining.

In the domestic preparation of remedies, the old herbal ingredients began to be replaced by ingredients sold by the druggists and chemists. Even if patent medicines could not be afforded, some of the basic ingredients could be purchased readily and made up at home. These were either adaptations of traditional herbal recipes or were copied from many of the 'domestic recipe' books which came on to the market from the seventeenth century onwards.

Yet the incorporation of manufactured ingredients into traditional domestic recipes mirrored, in some ways, the pattern of incorporation of new medical methods undertaken two centuries earlier among middle-class women – with parallel results. For the compromise in practice between the traditional and the new was ultimately to the detriment of the traditional. Just as the absorption of 'orthodox' methods and ingredients into old wives' lore had earlier eased the encroachment by physicians on to the old wives' practice among the middle classes, so the patented and bought ingredients destroyed the important empirical approach to domestic treatment and paved the way for the purchase of patent medicines on a large scale in the latter part of the nineteenth century. Moreover, the sale of patent remedies had behind it the force of capitalist enterprise – a force with which the old wife was not equipped to compete.

In general terms, the old wife and traditional medicine had, by the nineteenth century, become associated with medical treatment for the working class and for women. This combination meant that it was seen as inferior treatment. The absence of male professional medical attention for the working class led to two important nineteenth-century movements: the revival of herbalism, representing the nineteenth-century spirit of self-help, and the formation of the Friendly Societies and 'sick clubs' representing the spirit of benevolence and charity. Both movements represented different means of achieving the same end: medical treatment comparable with that available to the middle classes – in other words, male physicians. Between these two movements the old wife, such as she now was, was squeezed out even further.

Throughout the latter half of the seventeenth century and the eighteenth century, the interest shown by the medical profession in working-class health was negligible. The demise of the old wife was ultimately linked with changes in her social base as well as changes in the nature of the competition. She was not equipped in terms of education or skill to enter into the field and market for patent medicines, while the organisation of the medical profession meant that there was no need for her to organise herself professionally, even had it been possible to do so. The nature of her work and practice was always diffuse and the status acquired had always been derived from direct contact with her clients and the community. It had never relied, as did the status of physicians, on a professional 'guarantee'.

There remained one area of medical help in which no medicines or chemists could compete. This area was midwifery, and among the urban working classes the old wife continued to sustain her rôle in this area. Indeed, it was not until the twentieth-century that this area was taken over by the medical profession (and then not in its entirety until the 1968 Abortion Act).

Midwives were the first – and only – category of old wives to attempt to organise themselves professionally, for reasons peculiar to the nature of midwifery. Midwifery was singled out as a function separate from general healing. From the early sixteenth century the Church and State, both in Europe and in England, attempted to control its practice by prohibiting the use of 'magic'. In the seventeenth and eighteenth centuries midwives were challenged by the arrival of male accoucheurs who introduced forceps and other technical aids in their practice, denied their use to the midwives and thereby hoped to differentiate themselves from and elevate themselves above the midwives. As Jean Donnison points out midwifery could, especially among the upper and middle classes, be a lucrative profession in itself, and general practitioners saw in it a useful way of expanding the scope of their practices.

Efforts were made to educate, if not incorporate, what Percival Willoughby in the seventeenth century called the 'meanest' sort of woman who had taken up midwifery 'for the getting of a shilling or two'. The meanest sort of midwife, however, who incorporated other healing arts into her practice, saw no need to organise. Her practice was multifarious, located specifically in one class; and in those areas the medical profession did eventually pose the kind of threat they presented for middle-class midwives. The lack of organisation and of a professional status conferred by an institution also resulted in a lack of identification and formal recognition of the midwife, at a time when more pronounced divisions of labour meant that these were both valued and necessary. Indeed, by comparison with other, emerging, groups the old wife became less visible. And parallel with this came movements in society which resulted in women generally becoming less visible – and less valued. The domestic world was fast losing its prime position.

Early moves at organisation were made by middle-class midwives working in middle-class practices to prevent encroachment by doctors and man-midwives on their livelihood. Although their attempts to organise into a distinct profession were unsuccessful, they did at least help to distinguish this area of health care as a discrete one and, paradoxically, to sustain women's monopoly often on an informal basis, in healing practice among the urban poor of the nineteenth and early twentieth centuries.

CHAPTER FIVE

Alternatives for the Sick: the old wife and the sick poor in nineteenth- and twentieth-century England

Of the *wise women* (a class of practitioners, by the by, still to be found in many rural villages and in certain parts of London) in whom our ancestors had as much confidence as we of the present generation have in the members of the College of Physicians, we question if two score, including Margaret Kennox and Mrs Woodhouse of the Elizabethan era, could be rescued from oblivion. (John Cordy Jeaffreson, *A Book About Doctors*, 1861)

The social problems which sickness creates for the poor are often far more significant than the illness itself. For sickness generates poverty. It involves extra expenditure on food, medicines and doctors at a time when ability to earn ceases. For the poor to fall sick in the nineteenth century was a major disaster. Few working people earned enough in healthy days to save for sickness. Indeed, the Industrial Revolution had meant an increase in the numbers of unemployed and those forced to live on or below subsistence wages. Sickness for the poor often represented the threat of destitution.

For the sick poor, in town and country, the old wife remained a viable form of medical care. Whatever her methods or the source of her ingredients, she could be afforded by the poor and, in terms of success, there was often little to differentiate her from the licensed practitioner, the physician, surgeon or apothecary. Indeed, among working-class people the doctor inspired more fear than trust with his regime of 'starving, purging, blistering and blooding'. It was only among the middle and upper classes that the doctor enjoyed a popularity and status – often far higher than his expertise warranted. Medical science had still to make the qualitative advances which would distinguish it as the superior form of medical treatment.

For working people, access to doctors was usually through a charitable institution – one of the voluntary hospitals or dispensaries which had been set up towards the end of the eighteenth century. However, even here access was limited,[1] for many hospitals and dispensaries pursued policies of restrictive entry, reserving it only for accident cases or those with a letter of referral from subscribers to the hospital charity or one of the governors. Another form of access to doctors was through fever hospitals but in this case entry was compulsory and there was no guarantee of a cure. Conditions in these hospitals were appalling, and working-class dislike of them occasionally manifested itself in violence. In Manchester in 1832, for instance, hostility was so strong that rioting against one of the cholera hospitals broke out in the streets.

THE RESURGENCE OF HERBALISM – WITH A DIFFERENCE

Dislike and fear of the medical profession and a correspondingly increased popularity for traditional remedies account in large part for a renewed interest in 'herbalism' in the early part of the nineteenth century. Compared to the state of medical science at the time, many of the traditional remedies of the old wife were soundly based and reasonably efficacious. The new herbalism had a strong anti-doctor bias.

The earliest manifestation of the 'new' herbalism was published in the eighteenth century by the Methodist preacher, John Wesley. His *Primitive Physic or an Easy and Natural Method of Curing Most Diseases* went through countless editions from its first appearance in 1747. Most of the remedies were herbal ones gathered by himself and other lay preachers on their missions round the country. The book represented very much the spirit of dissent and of self-help – an expression of hope that 'every man of common sense (except in some rare cases) may prescribe to himself or his neighbour'. It also reflected the feeling that medical knowledge was becoming institutionalised and the people alienated from it. Wesley's intentions were made explicit in the introduction to the book:

> Physicians now began to be held in admiration, as persons who are something more than human; and profit attended their employ, as well as honour; so that they had not two eighty reasons for keeping the bulk of mankind at a distance, that they might not pry into the mysteries of the profession. To this end, they increased those difficulties by design, which began in a manner by accident. They filled their writings with an abundance of technical terms, utterly unintelligible to plain men. They affected to deliver their rules, and to reason upon them, in an abstruse and philosophical manner. They represented the critical knowledge of anatomy, natural philosophy, (and what not, some of them insisting on that of astronomy and astrology too) as necessarily previous to the understanding of the art of healing. Those who understood only how to restore the sick to health, they branded with the name empirics. They introduced into the practice abundance of compound medicines, consisting of so many ingredients that it was scarcely possible for common people to know which it was that wrought the cure; abundance of exotics, neither the nature nor names of which their own countrymen understood; of chemicals, such as they neither had skill, nor fortune, nor time to prepare; yea, and of dangerous ones, such as they could not use without hazarding life, but by the advice of a physician. And thus both their honour and gain were secured; a vast majority of mankind being utterly cut off from helping either themselves or their neighbours as once daring to attempt it.

Primitive Physic, along with other herbals remained a best-seller throughout the eighteenth and nineteenth centuries. Since the oral sources of herbal lore were disappearing in the urban context, these books represented a major source of such information. And to meet the demand for ingredients, herbal shops were established throughout the cities which both met the domestic demand and undercut the druggists.

A more organised aspect of the new herbalism was represented by movements such as that of the 'Coffinites' (so named after a 'Dr' Coffin who introduced it into the UK from America in 1841), which was widespread throughout the industrial working-class areas of Lancashire and Yorkshire. The movement was anti-doctor, stressing the need for self-help and attempting, like the temperance movement, to take some control of the social environment. Health was seen as a basic right, yet the fight for health lay with the individual. The emphasis was on natural remedies, and to this end Coffinites abhorred the use of alcohol as vehemently as they did the compounds and drugs of doctors and pharmacists. Moreover, they argued that the principles of health and good living, along with the natural remedies prescribed, should be elevated to the status of science while, at the same time, remaining fully accessible to all who wished to partake of the knowledge. A 'Dr' Skelton, in his monthly paper *Botanic Record and Family Herbal*, wrote

> It is true that the writings of Culpeper, Hill, Dr Thornton and others were held in great respect (by the working classes) . . . and that the old grandmothers and grandfathers in many of our villages mechanically prescribed various vegetable preparations, but all this was done without system of reason . . . We believe the science and practice of medicine, in order to be made truly useful, must be simplified and popularised . . . [2]

The popularity of herbalism undoubtedly helped in the overall survival of domestic medicine and the old wife. But the revival of traditional and popular medicine had subtly shifted its original centre of authority from women to men. As authors and publishers, men were perceived to be the initiators; women, the executors. And, as if to emphasise the shift, herbalism became elevated from empiricism to science. Moreover, ingredients could no longer be gleaned freely from the countryside but had to be bought from stockists in the towns and cities. The most basic and traditional health-care methods had, in keeping with the trends of nineteenth-century society, become subject to science, men and commerce.

SICKNESS, DESTITUTION AND THE POOR LAW

Despite the popularity of herbalism, the central rôle of the old wife among the working classes could not be sustained except for minor sicknesses and ailments. The traditional family and community supports which had, in a rural economy, been sufficient to support the poor at times of sickness, were now either lacking or inadequate. Under the harsh strictures of the market enonomy, once caught in the web of sickness and poverty, it was difficult to escape. Medical care, from whatever source, was no guarantee of recovery. Sickness meant a loss of wages, often destitution. However popular the old wife's form of treatment, there was no way she could solve the economic problems generated by sickness. At times of serious sickness many working people became, of necessity, destitute.

The only alternative for the destitute, short of starvation and death, was to fall back on the provisions of the Poor Law. Originally engineered to provide for the victims of poverty within a predominantly rural context, the Poor Law was now forced to accommodate increased numbers of industrial and urban poor within an ideological context which perceived poverty not as an individual's bad luck in a competitive and unequal society, but as evidence of lack of foresight. The responsibility for poverty was placed squarely on the individual's shoulders: the poor deserved condemnation rather than charity for having failed to save for rainy days. Thrift was next to godliness; anything less than thrift was ungodly and therefore immoral. The poor must by definition be immoral and, consequently, undeserving.

These notions were not new. Defoe had immortalised them in verse in the eighteenth century:

> The Lab'ring Poor, in spight of Double Pay
> Are saucy, mutinous and beggarly;
> So lavish of their money and their time,
> That want of forecast is the Nation's Crime;
> Good drunken Company is their delight,
> And what they earn by day they spend by night.

In the nineteenth century the ideas were epitomised by the New Poor Law of 1834. The average working wage in the nineteenth century was barely sufficient to sustain the worker in good times, let alone provide a surplus to save and, ignoring any correlation between sickness and poverty, the New Poor Law provided relief only for those which its officers judged to be 'incapable' of work. Incapacity, in this respect, was assessed as willingness to enter the workhouse. And the new workhouses, in line with the spirit of deterrence to unemployment, provided what were termed 'less eligible' living conditions than the poorest employed worker could provide independently. Indeed, the nineteenth-century response to the victims of the Industrial Revolution was not to provide 'most charitably' but to deter 'most harshly'.

Within these stringent attitudes and provisions there was little room for medical relief. The New Poor Law perceived its responsibility solely in terms of the 'relief of destitution', which meant, simply, preventing death from starvation or exposure. And it was usually only at this point that the Poor Law intervened with medical relief. Beatrice Webb wrote in 1909:

> The fundamental failure of the Poor Law with regard to the sick lies ... in its very nature. It is inherent in any Poor Law that it is confined to the relief of the destitute; until the man striken with disease had become so ill as to be unable to go to work he is not destitute. But when the disease has gone as far as this, it is usually too late to prevent its ravages.[3]

The Poor Law Guardians (the administrators of the

Poor Law) were vigilant in their interpretation of the 1834 Act. Medical relief was denied those who were working, even if they earned insufficient to afford medical provision. 'I think the first object', commented the Rev. E. J. Howman, a Norfolk Guardian, 'is to induce people to render themselves independent, and the narrower you can fairly draw the limit of medical relief, the sooner you will make them independent.' And Anne Digby cites the case of the Forehoe Board of Guardians, who

> approved the action of their relieving officer who in 1841 refused to authorise medical treatment to a child, who died for lack of it. The reason for refusing relief was that the Havers family, with only three children and a weekly income of 13s were thought to be able to afford to pay for their own medical treatment through a sick club.[4]

Sick clubs, like Friendly Societies, provided a relatively cheap and early form of medical insurance. Their limitations will be discussed later in this chapter.

Indeed, it was usually the Relieving Officer who diagnosed sickness in the first instance. Appointed under the Poor Law to assess individual cases of destitution and award relief as appropriate, they also judged claims for sick relief. Diagnosis was usually based primarily on an assessment of the applicant's income. To have done otherwise would, it was thought, have opened the floodgates of medical provision for all. As the Poor Law Commission itelf commented in 1841:

> This superiority of the condition of the paupers over that of the independent labourers as regards medical aid will . . . encourage a resort to the poor rates for medical relief . . . and will thus tempt the industrious labourer into pauperism.[5]

Nothing, however, could have been further from the truth. The stigma that 'pauper' status held for the working classes was not one undertaken lightly. Many would have rather died – and did – than be classified as such. Moreover, those who became paupers did so because they were destitute, for the quality of medical care offered under the Poor Law was never an incentive to apply for medical relief. Although in theory outdoor medical relief – treatment at home – was to be granted in preference to indoor relief – admission to the workhouse infirmary – in practice the principle of 'less eligibility' was applied to the sick as well as the poor. Workhouse infirmaries found themselves accommodating numbers of sick poor beyond their original capacity. And, as the workhouse proper was not to be seen as a soft option for the labourer and should not provide better conditions than he or she could provide independently, so the workhouse infirmaries were not to be seen to provide better conditions than the voluntary hospitals.

Workhouse infirmaries were no place for the sick. They were grotesquely overcrowded and filthy. No account was taken of the nutritional needs of the sick. Professional nurses were few and far between – in 1844, the twenty-two Norfolk Unions (the 'union' was a catchment area for paupers) had only four trained nurses between them. Nursing, in the workhouse infirmaries, was provided by the more 'able-bodied' inmates who often had no skills and even less incentive to care properly. Doctors were provided on the cheap, were overworked and, until 1858, often appointed with little regard to their qualifications. Drugs and dressings were not provided out of the Poor Rate. Not surprisingly, application for workhouse relief was the last, not the first, resort of the sick poor.

Nearly three-quarters of the cases of pauperism in mid-nineteenth century England and Wales involved sickness, yet the Guardians were reluctant either to improve the standard of health care provided or to make more adequate social allowances. They were constrained, not only within their narrow ideological perspective, but also by the need to reduce the Poor Rate as much as possible.

Even after 1867, when the Poor Law Board, after consistent pressure from both Poor Law Medical Officers and public opinion, began to reverse its policy *vis-à-vis* the sick poor and to encourage the separation of infirmaries from workhouses and to provide better and more humane care within the new 'state hospitals', it met with considerable and formidable opposition from the provincial Guardians. Beatrice and Sidney Webb wrote:

> In Circular after Circular to the scarcely concealed dismay of some of the officials who failed to understand this departure from 'Poor Law Principles' and of many of the Boards of Guardians, who saw no need for additional expenditure – the Poor Law Board, and afterwards the Local Government Board, strove persistently to make the six hundred Boards of Guardians understand that the policy of the preceding thirty years was to be abandoned; and that one third of all the inmates of the Poor Law institutions who were found to be sick were to be treated, without regard to 'Less Eligibility', in whatever way was best calculated to restore them to health.[6]

By the time the Royal Commission on the Poor Law reported its findings in 1909, it was found that

> Only in London, Glasgow, and a score of large towns have separate Poor Law institutions for the sick been provided. These, which have sometimes become virtually general hospitals, are a vast improvement on the workhouses, but they still suffer from 1) insufficiency of medical staff, 2) having far too few nurses, and 3) the 'deterrent' influence of the Poor Law. *Every where else the sick are still in the General Mixed Workhouse* – the maternity cases, the senile, the cancerous, the venereal, the chronically infirm, and even the infectious all together in one building, often in the same ward – where they cannot be properly treated.[7]

WORKING-CLASS RESPONSE TO DESTITUTION: FRIENDLY SOCIETIES

The old wife, like the physician, could not cure everything. Many of the illnesses of the nineteenth-century poor were related to their social conditions. The old wife may have been able to help some of the sick before their illness made them destitute, but she could never alleviate social conditions nor provide for loss of employment and wages, and was not expected to. Working-class fear of pauperisation was enormous. Their response to the prospect of destitution was to form Sick Clubs and Friendly Societies. These were essentially self-help systems, run on democratic lines, with the object of avoiding pauperisation and providing social relief for their members in times of unemployment and sickness, and funeral benefits. Incidental to this provision was scope for some benefit to cover the cost of medical expenses or to provide the services of a doctor directly.

The earliest Friendly Societies have been traced to the sixteenth century in Scotland and, in England, to the seventeenth century, where they were formed by immigrant groups (notably the Huguenots) entering Britain. But in England it was in the mid-eighteenth century that they began to be established on any scale, when a number of Acts were passed conferring legal status on these societies. The motive behind this granting of legal status was, as the preamble to an Act of 1792 stated, the 'reduction of the Poor Rate'. Throughout the nineteenth century the formation of these societies was encouraged by the State as an alternative to Poor Law Relief, for not only did it benefit the State financially by relieving it of its rôle in providing medical benefits, but it also conformed to the nineteenth-century belief in thrift and self-sufficiency. Indeed, Poor Law medical relief was denied to those people actually subscribing *or thought capable of subscribing* to a Sick Club.

The State obviously had a political and financial interest in encouraging the formation of such societies and clubs (despite the fact that a number used 'Friendly Society' status as a cover for the foundation of the then illegal Trade Unions). Nevertheless, their practical importance in the early nineteenth century should not be over-emphasised. It was only the better-off skilled worker who could afford to pay the weekly subscriptions. This excluded most women workers. In 1801 a contemporary chronicler of the Friendly Society system, Sir Frederick Eden, estimated that there were approximately 7,200

Friendly Societies with a total membership of 648,000. The Poor Law returns provide more accurate figures for later years. In 1803 there were approximately 704,350 members, which by 1815 had risen to 925,429. Areas where industry was most highly concentrated had a correspondingly high membership rate and, on the whole, the societies drew their membership from all trades rather than single trades. Yet the 1815 figure represents only 8½ per cent of the population. An investigation in 1837 of 950 men from the Nottingham hosiery and lace industry showed that only a quarter of them were members of any Friendly Society. In Liverpool, Wolverhampton and Gloucester in the 1840s club members stood at one in twelve of the population; in Bath, Cheltenham, Shrewsbury and Worcester, at one in thirty. The subscriptions to the Friendly Societies were high relative to the average wage. Not surprisingly, as late as the 1875 Royal Commission on Friendly Societies, the estimated membership stood only at 4,000,000 and represented, as the Commission stated, a 'fraction' of the population.

Their efficacy was further limited by their financial insecurity, and the local nature of their practice. Until the mid-nineteenth century when they were placed on a firmer financial footing and when larger national and commercially run units replaced the smaller local clubs, subscribers often did not receive benefits they were entitled to, for the sick club often went bankrupt or, if the subscriber had moved, payments made in one local club or society could not be carried over into another club. Indeed, Friendly Societies were renowned for their mismanagement and unreliability. Gladstone, for instance, remarked before Parliament in 1864 'of the whole error, deception, fraud and swindling, which are perpetrated upon the most helpless portion of the community, who find themselves without defence'. Nevertheless, the State considered the advantages of the Friendly Societies to be greater than their disadvantages. In 1871 a Royal

Commission[8] was appointed which investigated the area and made recommendations, and in 1875 the first of a series of Acts was passed, designed to secure and strengthen the legal and actuarial position of the Friendly Societies.

At the same time the Poor Law Inspectorates were discouraging even more vigorously the provision of outdoor medical relief, preferring instead to have all sick paupers kept within Poor Law infirmaries, principally on the grounds of finance but also as a means of retaining the principle of 'Less Eligibility' against the wishes of some of the more enlightened Commissioners. Undoubtedly, this policy of the Poor Law and the strengthened position of the Friendly Societies increased the membership of the latter, but not substantially. For any increases in spending power went, interestingly enough, on prepared medical products, on patent and patented remedies. Their sales increased enormously, often superceding the sales of herbal and other ingredients which would be bought and made up in the home.

The fact was that Friendly Societies were not necessarily a 'good buy' as far as illness was concerned. The motivating principle behind the sick clubs and Friendly Societies was to provide sickness benefit for their subscribers, rather than medical treatment for the poor—that is, to provide compensation for loss of wages rather than doctors' costs. Since they started as societies for working men, by definition the unemployed or those too sick or disabled for employment were excluded from membership. Similarly, there was often no provision for the wives or children of subscribers unless they were subscribers in their own right. Certain categories of benefit were often excluded: midwifery was rarely provided for and some serious diseases could not be treated within the terms of the subscription. The shortcomings of the Friendly Societies were indicated in evidence given to the Royal Commission on the Poor Law in 1905, when it was indicated that:

> the 'self-supporting' character of a medical club is largely an
> illusion. There are many diseases which a club doctor does not
> attempt to treat. The vast majority of notifiable cases of infectious
> diseases, lunacy, and an increasing number of cases of tuberculosis
> are treated in rate-supported institutions. Abdominal surgery,
> opthalmic surgery, any surgical operation, except the most trivial,
> and many other conditions are treated in hospitals that are
> supported by private charity. If these institutions were not
> available, clubs and provident dispensaries could not be conducted
> on their present conditions and, therefore, it is true to say that, in a
> sense, these so-called 'self-supporting' medical agencies are partly
> supported by the rates and partly by private charity.[9]

Moreover, many of the insurance provisions of these
societies were being taken over by commercial insurance
companies on the one hand and by the trade unions on
the other. Although the unions were, as the Webbs
noted, 'a bad form of Friendly Society', they were good at
protecting the rights of their members on a range of other
matters which had a more direct bearing on their
members' social and economic situation.

PREGNANCY AND POVERTY IN
NINETEENTH-CENTURY ENGLAND:
THE GAPS IN ORGANISED PROVISION

Between them, neither the Friendly Societies nor the
Poor Law provided anything like sufficient help and
protection for the sick poor. The number who went
without any official medical help was high. John Leigh,
Manchester's first Medical Officer of Health, stated in
1854 – and this was not untypical – that:

> of the whole of the children born in Manchester nearly one half die
> before they attain the age of five years, and that of those a very great
> number are attended by druggists and other unlicensed practition-
> ers. In fact . . . out of a total of 2,179 deaths, 726 had no medical
> attendance whatever.[10] [The figures apply to all deaths, not just
> children].

By far the largest category excluded from any form of

'official' provision were women. Yet women's health, generally, was of a lower standard than that of men. As Pat Thane points out:

> Poor women consistently had more deficient diets than their husbands, because they allowed their men and children more and better food.[11] Men's low or irregular earnings anyway made it impossible for many of them to support their families as official ideology dictated, even though they might wish to. Consequently, many married women went without sufficient food and suffered worse health than married men. Continual child-bearing exacerbated many wives' bad health, as ill-health and inadequate nutrition, in turn, increased the hazards associated with pregnancy and child-bearing. This is medically consistent with the longer life-expectancy of women: it is possible to survive for long periods in poor health with such debilitating chronic ailments as anaemia, due to poor diet, or repeated pregnancy, whereas men were more likely to die at younger ages from acute illnesses, and were more prone to serious occupational hazards.[12]

Interest in women's health and childbirth in particular was minimal throughout the nineteenth century. Medical practice among working-class women, particularly in midwifery, was not lucrative. Doctors, who had entered working-class practice reluctantly were even more loath to take on midwifery cases. Ironically, midwifery had been one of the major ways, as was pointed out earlier, by which the expanding medical profession had conquered the middle-class medical market. Doctors were not prepared to use the same techniques to gain the confidence of the working-class, preferring to delegate this matter to local midwives. All attempts at professionalising midwifery in the nineteenth century were bitterly opposed by the medical establishment, for they perceived that educated and organised midwives might well abandon working-class women and encroach on their lucrative middle-class preserve. The interest shown by the medical profession as a whole in the areas of obstetrics and gynaecology was slight. Obstetricians were considered very much inferior members of the profession. Maternal mortality remained almost as high in 1903 as it had in 1847, with totals of 3,800 and 3,200 respectively. Measured against 1,000 live births, the figures represent rates of 6 per 1,000 in 1847 and 4.03 per 1,000 in 1903. The rate did not fall below 1 per 1,000 until 1944–5.

The reluctance of the Friendly Societies to include maternity benefit or medical care for wives and children in their benefits was based principally on financial and actuarial principles – the same principles which excluded maternity benefits from the provisions of the National Insurance Act of 1911. These principles were based on

> the sound principle of insurance that the insured ought not to benefit financially by the occurrence of the contingency insured against; normally wives and children are not wage earners and the provision of sickness benefit for them would mean that sickness would bring money into the home.[13]

But if these principles were grounded in financial considerations, there were also ideological justifications. Women's natural functions were seen to be in child-bearing and child-rearing. Fecundity, rather than health, was the test of womanhood. Insurance could not and should not be provided for a natural function.

Much the same reasoning applied to pregnant women who requested Poor Law maternity provision. They were classified as able-bodied and as such became subject to the principle of 'Less Eligibility'. Married women who applied for a 'Relief Order', which permitted them midwifery services at home, often found it accompanied by a Removal Order (compulsory admission into the workhouse or infirmary). Consequently many married men and women were reluctant to apply for Poor Law provision. Typically, therefore, the women most likely to enter the workhouse for their confinements were single women, for whom accusations of immorality compounded their status of pauper.

Maternity provision within workhouses was dire. Inmates often acted as midwives – the mother of Dickens's Oliver Twist (who died in childbirth) was 'attended' by 'a pauper old woman who was rendered somewhat misty by an unwonted allowance of beer'. The doctor or trained midwife was only called in if the Relieving Officer deemed it necessary. Even then, they were paid the lowest of rates and were reluctant to spend much time or effort on the patient. Indeed, many midwives and doctors with private middle-class midwifery practices feared that workhouse deliveries would lose them their valuable paying patients, for the middle classes feared contagion from the doctor's contact with the poor. For this reason, as well as a reluctance to spend time with a long labour, the use of instruments in labour was far more common for pauper women than for those engaging a doctor privately. And, in addition, doctors were often paid extra for 'Instrument cases'.

The pauper wards themselves were hardly conducive to maternal or infant health. In 1842 the Sevenoaks workhouse had five women in two beds in a room which measured 10 feet 9 inches by 7 feet. In other work-houses, the maternity wards were contained within the general ward, and mothers and babies kept side by side with infectious cases and the dying (or dead). Another ward, described in 1841 by a Poor Law doctor, Dr Rogers, was a

> wretchedly damp and miserable room, nearly always over-crowded with young mothers and their infant children. That death relieved these young women of their illegitimate offspring was only to be expected, and that frequently the mothers followed in the same direction was only too true. I used to dread to go into this ward, it was so depressing. Scores and scores of distinctly preventable deaths of both mothers and children took place during my continuance in office through their being located in this horrible den.[14]

Pregnant women, as able-bodied paupers, were sub-ject to the 'deterrent gruel diet' of the workhouse. Not surprisingly the death rate in workhouses was high.

Comparing the infantile mortality statistics for the general population with those for 450 Poor Law Unions, it appears that out of every 1,000 non-pauper babies born in England and Wales amidst the unregulated conditions of the average home, twenty-five die within a week, whilst out of every 1,000 babies born in Poor Law institutions no less than *40 to 45* die within a week . . . . Lest it be supposed that this excessive mortality arises from the class of mothers dealt with, it may be added that some workhouses surmount all difficulties and lose only one or two infants by death in a whole year. Others actually in the same towns and dealing with populations of no worse class, have an infantile mortality percentage throughout the infants first year six or *even ten times as great*.[15]

Part of the explanation for these high mortality rates arose out of the lack, in many infirmaries, of quarantine facilities so that infections, once introduced, spread fatally. But part lay in the inadequacy of the nursing and hygiene arrangements. Beatrice Webb wrote:

It does not even occur to many Poor Law authorities to go to the expense of paid nurses for the actual handling of the babies, even when they leave the mother's care. We learn that 'In *all* the small Workhouses and in many of the larger ones, the infants are wholly attended to by, and are actually in charge of, aged and often *mentally defective* paupers . . .' One case is mentioned of such a pauper attendant being told to wash a baby. *She did so in boiling water*, and the child died.[16]

Yet alternative help for women in labour was limited. Few of the general hospitals built in the eighteenth century had maternity wards, and those which did required letters of recommendation before admission. Some dispensaries provided midwifery care but their small numbers and the standard of care offered made little difference. In the eighteenth century some charitable 'lying-in' hospitals had been founded. They too required letters of recommendation and usually excluded all cases of illegitimacy and often primiparous women (those in their first confinement). In addition, in all institutions which provided 'charitable' care for women in labour, the standard of hygiene meant that puerperal fever remained a constant and major killer. Many hospitals closed down, temporarily or permanently, as a result. And the standard of medical care offered was only marginally better than that provided under Poor Law auspices.

PREGNANCY AND POVERTY:
OLD WIVES AS MIDWIVES

For the majority of poor women in the nineteenth century assistance at childbirth was provided by the midwives. Occasionally druggists would be called in to help, though they were notorious for their use of instruments. They were also expensive – the average fee in the mid 1860s was a guinea. Most deliveries therefore took place in the home, with the local midwife in attendance. The more highly trained midwives for the most part practised among a middle- and upper-class clientele. Most working-class women relied on the 'local woman', whose training was essentially empirical. Yet mortality rates – 20–25 per 1,000 – were considerably lower than those of hospitals, lying-in wards and Poor Law infirmaries. The local midwife did not use instruments and required that the woman herself provide the necessary dressings and cloths. The risk of cross-infection was thereby substantially reduced.

The most obvious reason for choosing the local midwife lay in the fees she charged. The average fee in the 1840s was 2/6d, and in the 1870s 7/-. (The doctor's fee in the 1860s was a minimum of 21/- for delivery alone, with extra charges for subsequent visits and mileage travelled. It often rose to 100 guineas and more for wealthier families.) Even after the 1902 Midwives Act, the fee for a registered midwife was between 7/6d and 21/-, and that for an unregistered midwife 5/-. Most unregistered midwives also included other services – they expected to rest with the family for at least nine days after confinement, taking care not only of the mother and child but also of most if not all the other household services. Mrs C., an 'unregistered' midwife who practised in Suffolk at the turn of the century, recalls:

> You got to be there ten days. And I'd look after the father and the mother, and the baby and the other children – sometimes there'd be one and two and three and four and five and six (years). Very seldom would there be two years in between. There weren't nothing in my time to spread them . . . When I lived in I'd often sleep in a chair, to be truthful. And you took the things along with you that you wanted, that you knew the people hadn't got.[17]

This form of care was a valuable support and one which doctors and registered midwives would not undertake. Indeed, even those who might have been able to afford a trained midwife (though a midwife's fee was often equivalent to a week's wages) often preferred an untrained one for the extra help which she provided. The wife of an engine driver in Upton-upon-Severn, for instance, explained in 1892 that she

> always had the 'woman who goes about nursing' (because) she did not see the good of paying a doctor a guinea just for the time, and looking after her and the baby for a few days afterwards, when she could get a woman who would do all that was needful at the time, and wash the child when it was born, and then attend her and the child for nine or ten days, all for 5/-.[18]

In times of distress, the local woman would often waive her fee or give credit. Mrs C. recalls again:

> they give you five shillings. That was an expensive item. And how they afforded it I can't tell you. They hadn't always got the money. Where they got the money? So you'd do it free. But even then they had to give you extra, food you see. But bread was tuppence a loaf, and you could get a good loaf the next day for three ha'pence, which we often did. The ladies I went to were very nice, very kind, very grateful for what I done . . . The royalty, they had a different life. They had people to see after them. Whereas we hadn't. Who had you got? Nobody, only what you could pay for. And if you couldn't afford it, you got to do the best you could yourself.[19]

Mrs C., the daughter of a London 'woman', recalled:

> once my sister was furious because she went out to help a girl what wasn't married. Her parents had come and said she was due and my sister said 'You won't get any money there'. And my mother

said 'It doesn't matter. If she's in trouble I'm going to help.' Yes, she did and my sister was furious.[20]

Since the woman was invariably part of the local community she was much better able to recognise genuine hardship than was a system of rigid rules for determing destitution as applied by the Poor Law or the charitable institutions.

Some midwives, like Ernest Bevin's mother, did occasional work attending the childbirths of their neighbours. Others made a regular living out of the practice, often supplementing it with other medical services not available elsewhere, such as laying out the dead, advising on sick children, and treating minor ailments. The midwife was also known, and understood the conditions and customs of her own community. Moreover, compared to the doctors, her success rate in midwifery was high. Home deliveries were infinitely safer than hospital deliveries. With uncomplicated deliveries there was, in any case, little problem; with long labours, often due to poor nutrition and physical weakness (among other things), she was more patient in her attendance. She was also less likely to interfere: midwives did not use instruments and rarely inserted their hand inside a labouring woman, unlike many of the doctors and the male *accoucheurs*. The 'naturalness' of her technique often meant fewer complications and, unlike some of the doctors, she did not inspire fear. In this area, experience was a far more efficient training than the largely theoretical education of doctors.

> I learnt with Mrs Soames, a dear old lady. She's dead now. We were called out night and day . . . First of all, when we were called, we'd see that the mother was alright. We had iron bedsteads, then, so we'd make a pulley. I'd see they were ready for being delivered. We used to turn them on their right side and they'd push against the bottom of the bed. We'd manoeuvre the pulley so they could reach the bottom of the bed and push. She had to do the work – sometimes it was a long time. We didn't like a lot of straining, not on the last go. But as soon as we could see the head we knew that things were alright.

If it was a lazy baby that wouldn't work and made his mother work, Mrs Soames had a little bottle that she carried about with her, and she'd give the mother 4 or 5 drops. It had no name on it. It was only a little tiny bottle, about an inch and a half. And it would force the pains down if the pains were slow and didn't follow as they ought to. And if they hadn't started labour, Mrs Soames would give them that. But other times, some labours would only give you four lots of pain and then the baby was there. And the child worked for me. And when we knew the waters had broken – we used to call them silver water – then we knew that the baby was on its way, and we also knew, when the baby was pitched right for birth, whether it was going to be long or short.

And when we saw the baby's head, we'd ease it out, and then I got the towel ready to receive it. And we'd tie the cord with white thread, we'd leave it a length, and then tie it up. And if it fell off clean, then the baby was clean and didn't have any diseases. Same with the afterbirth. If it came out cleanly and quickly and all bloody and not clotting, then we'd love to see it because we knew all was going well. Then we'd put it in a piece of old rag and burn it – it'd crackle like anything! Or if they didn't have a fire, bury it deep so the dogs didn't scratch it out.

We'd clean the baby's eyes and nose and we'd give it a real butter ball in its mouth, to help dissolve the saliva stuff that they had in their mouth. Only just a small ball, and it had to be real butter. And we'd clean the mother, and breast them. It was all breast feeding then, and much healthier. But if they didn't have any milk, which was very seldom, it would generally flow through at the beginning, if, after the second day, if it didn't come, we'd give the baby Jersey milk, with a little cream and tepid water and a little sugar. And as it got stronger, we used to give it a thin porridge. And porridge was porridge in those days, fine oatmeal and cooked so well there were no lumps or anything.

And we never lost any children. We fed the mothers up as best we could. And always after the birth we'd give the mothers porridge and then a piece of toast, and that cleared all the little hard pieces that had formed or clotted together.[21]

Difficult births posed a problem, but the success rate of doctors at such times was little better. 'The doctors,' as Mrs C. remarked, 'needed us. They didn't use to come, only if it was a bad case.' The only baby Mrs C. ever lost was in fact due to the incompetence of the doctor after birth. (The baby bled to death after the doctor had circumcised him.) Doctors were called in emergencies, though not always paid. (Doctors who were summoned to such cases but refused to turn up for fear of not being paid were often acquitted at subsequent coroner's inquests.) 'The doctor,' recalled Flora Thompson in *Larkrise to Candleford*, 'was only seen there when . . . some difficult first confinement baffled the skill of the old woman who, as she said, saw the beginning and end of everybody.'

The Midwives Act of 1902 laid down that no person may use the title of midwife unless registered with the Central Midwives' Board and that no woman 'habitually and for gain' might attend a woman in confinement except under the supervision of a doctor, unless registered. Well after the Act, many women continued to prefer the services of the unregistered and 'untrained' midwife with her wide experience and knowledge of the social circumstances of her patients, to those of the new registered midwives. It was widely accepted that women 'knew' instinctively what was best for women in labour and for the subsequent care of mother and child. In Rotherham, for instance, 25 per cent of births in 1907 and 1908 were attended by 'old unqualified women'. One such woman, Granny Redman, dismissed the 'new fangled certified midwives' on the grounds that they 'didn't know much, how could they with only three months training.'[22]

OLD WIVES AND BIRTH CONTROL

But if need and popularity ensured her survival, there were other, politically more potent, reasons why the old wife was often preferred. Midwives were not, until 1902, recognised by the State. Working-class midwives feared little competition from doctors or others who wished to enter their field. They were, therefore, somewhat immune to charges of illegality which sometimes face the male *accoucheur*.

This immunity also placed the old wife in a favourable position within her local community. Coming from the community and therefore from the same social and economic class as the women they treated, old wives recognised well the hardships caused by large families and poverty and shared, for the most part, their patients' beliefs regarding the morality of family limitation.

Knowledge of, and access to, effective birth control methods was virtually denied the working class until the 1930s. Abortion was a major form of birth control and infanticide a close second.[23] Although it had been made a statutory offence in 1803 and successive legislation culminating in the Offences Against the Person Act of 1861 tightened up laws against it, most working women did not consider it either illegal or immoral to attempt abortion before 'quickening' (the time at which the movements of the foetus are first felt – around 16–18 weeks) – the point at which life was believed to enter the unborn child – or, indeed, to fail to revive a sickly child at birth. With infant mortality so high in the nineteenth and early twentieth century, few working-class women could afford to feel sentimental about a child who, even if born, might not survive anyway. Untrained midwives were therefore often preferred because they had 'graveyard luck' – the euphemistic term used to describe those midwives skilled at saving the mother but losing the child. In addition, what limited (traditional) birth control advice was available would also have been given by her, as would advice about how to abort early in pregnancy. The vast majority of abortionists were untrained midwives – a fact which did not escape the notice either of the authorities or of the medical profession.

Lack of State or professional interest in working-class midwifery meant that the rôle of old wives as abortionists was on the whole disguised by their other functions. Only occasionally were women prosecuted, and then usually only if they were caught red-handed, for the local community had an interest in their protection. Abortion remained one of the few methods by which women in the nineteenth and early twentieth centuries had some control over their bodies and their lives.

The reluctance of the medical profession to enter into the debate on birth control was based largely on the fear that any sympathy for the birth control cause would have laid them open to accusations of, at best, quackery and, at worst, association with the old wives. For throughout the nineteenth century the medical profession was trying to improve its image in the public eye, partly by attempts to eliminate competition from unqualified sources and partly by making sure that only 'gentlemen' were permitted to enter the profession and, once entered, were treated and paid accordingly.

The image-building attempts of doctors were aimed essentially at the bourgeoisie. The 1858 Medical Act, which established a medical register and made provision for the supervision of the education and qualifications of medical practitioners, only guaranteed the doctors a monopoly of practice in the limited area of public and commercial employment (the Poor Law and Friendly Societies). The reluctance to outlaw unqualified practitioners reflected in part middle- and upper-class doubts as to the doctor's professional competence; legislators and administrators shared these doubts. Anything, therefore, that cast a slur on the delicate position of the doctors was carefully eschewed by them. Work in all controversial areas was treated with the utmost caution: even public health and the temperance movement were initially viewed with scepticism. Indeed, the definition of what legitimately constituted medical practice was carefully controlled by the General Medical Council in order to create and retain a sharp professional distinction between themselves and all unqualified practitioners.

The definition of legitimate medical practice was based on a position of extreme conservatism. Any new movement was dismissed as being 'in our judgement, scepticism' as James Mackness noted in his *Moral Aspects of Medical Life* of 1846. Even new scientific discoveries made within the field of orthodox medical science were often greeted with as much hostility as praise, particularly within the area of childbirth (for example, the fierce debate over the use of chloroform in childbirth or the controversy over the causes of puerperal fever and the theories of Simmelweiss on this).

The position of the medical profession on birth control must be seen in this light. The main protagonists of birth control for much of the nineteenth century were regarded mostly by the middle classes as dangerous and immoral radicals in that they undermined the fundamentals of nineteenth-century bourgeois life – the family, the rôle of women and the position of the working class. Doctors' responses to birth control issues varied from silence to outright condemnation – condemnation which was couched in moral as well as medical terms, and which also singled out for particular approbation the most emotive technique of birth control, namely abortion. Abortion was associated with the working classes and their heinous practices, and the old wife was singled out among them as being responsible for perpetrating this practice. The 1861 legislation was partly the result of lobbying by the medical profession. In the debate on birth control (synonymous with abortion in the doctors' eyes), the law placed the doctors firmly on the side of the righteous.

Doctors' repugnance for dealing with birth control was also based on their limited concept of medical practice. Their conservatism in defining medical areas meant that innovations which were not firmly under their control must necessarily be regarded as quackery. Purveyors of birth-control information were therefore quacks and old wives. They were also reluctant to enter into issues which directly affected the working classes. (The doctors' support for public health measures was based as much on the fear that infection might spread to the middle classes as on humanitarian grounds.)

Midwifery, too, was a problem for doctors. They eschewed the study of midwifery itself as being 'an occupation degrading to gentlemen'. A qualification in midwifery was not considered necessary to obtain a doctor's qualification, and to have conceded that there was a valid field of study in midwifery would have conceded to the midwives that their occupation required special skills and knowledge. Association with midwifery was professionally dangerous. Where the working class was concerned, midwifery, abortion and the 'still-birth' business were one and the same in the public image. To have sanctioned the training of midwives would have exposed doctors to the implicit charge of condoning other practices.

Although many doctors had little or no knowledge of obstetrics, they were prepared to attend deliveries among the middle classes and in the charitable hospitals and Poor Law infirmaries where control and the integrity of their position were assured. The 1902 Midwives Act, which required that only midwives registered with the Central Midwives Board could use the title, was only passed after concessions had been made to the BMA and by persuading the BMA that registration was more likely to eliminate the midwife/abortionist than non-registration. Of course, it did no such thing. Legal loopholes in the Act enabled unregistered midwives to continue in practice until 1926. Thereafter they continued in their rôle as abortionist until 1968.

It is difficult to obtain sources and information on abortionists. Protected by the community, they only came to light when something went wrong and they were prosecuted. Successful cases of abortion went unrecorded. Similarly, it is difficult to gauge accurate figures on the number of women who had abortions. Studies from the twentieth century can throw some retrospective light on earlier periods. The 1936 Abortion Law Reform Association Conference reported the study of a prominent gynaecologist in Birmingham in which, of 3,000 women questioned, 35 per cent admitted to having had an abortion. A BMA report referred to in the Conference report estimated that 15 per cent of all pregnancies in

Britain were aborted criminally – figures which came to about 90,000. A survey conducted in 1966 by the National Opinion Poll for the Abortion Law Reform Association estimated, conservatively, that 85,000 women in Britain attempted to have an abortion annually.

The indications are that the majority of abortionists prosecuted were women. '. . . the people who urgently need protection', commented Mr Julius Lewin, a speaker at the 1936 conference, 'are those who suffer most by the operation of the existing law. For every doctor who appears in Court on a charge of criminal abortion, there are at least ten women.'

Studies by Moya Woodside in 1966 and Dr J. C. Weir indicated that by far the majority of abortionists were women, and of those the majority were older married women from the lower middle or working classes. Their charges were minimal – usually between £5 and £15 – and, whether money was their primary motivation or not, all regarded their rôle as one of 'helping'.

> 'The first one I ever done was a poor woman,' said one of the informants. 'She was married, had a big family, about ten children.'
>
> 'I'm not ashamed of what I've done,' said another, 'even though it's against the law. It's human nature, and women have to help each other.'[24]

Overall, as Moya Woodside observed, the sympathy of the abortionist lay with the 'pregnant married woman, often with a husband who gambled or drank, abused his children, and refused to take contraceptive precautions.'

In her novel *A Pin to See the Peepshow*, the novelist and criminologist F. Tennyson Jesse wrote:

> Mrs Humble was doing ten years for an abortion. Mrs Humble, whose husband only kept a tiny newspaper shop, and whose son was out of work, had nearly two thousand pounds laid by in the Savings Bank, and it had all been obtained by the pursuit of a profession which Mrs Humble believed to be a philanthropic one.

What, after all, had she done but help poor girls out of a trouble which civilisation would not permit to be anything else?[25]

Moreover, although the law might prosecute abortionists, the same conspiracy which had protected them in the nineteenth century operated right through into the twentieth. Among the women she served, the old wife as abortionist was often popular. 'The people down the street was ever so nice – wished me luck. Hoped I'd get off.'[26]

The rôle of abortionist was a necessary one. Until birth control became widely available, abortion remained a primary method of birth control. The majority of women who sought abortion were married and did not wish to have any more children. *The Derby Evening Telegraph* reported on 14 January 1939 the case of one woman who had died from an abortion:

The Coroner described the case as most unsavoury and most unsatisfactory. One must feel a good deal of sympathy with the woman who had died at the age of 36, and during practically the whole of her 17 years of married life had been either pregnant or recovering from pregnancy. While one could not condone it, one could well understand the desperate feeling she must have had when she found herself again pregnant . . .

The letters in *Maternity*, compiled by the Co-operative Women's Guild in 1915, provide a graphic and moving first-hand account of the desperation of many.

The mother wonders what she has to live for; if there is another baby coming she hopes it will be dead before it is born.

For fifteen years I was in a very poor state of health owing to continual pregnancy. As soon as I was over one trouble, it was all started over again . . .

I am really not a delicate woman, but having a large family, and so fast, pulled me down very much . . .

. . . when my second baby came, I had to do my own washing and baking before the weekend. Before three weeks I had to go back to working, washing and cleaning, and so I lost my milk and began with the bottle. Twice I worked to within two or three days of my

> confinement. I was a particularly strong woman when I married. There is not much strength left . . .[27]

The methods used by the women varied from instruments (typically in the twentieth century the Higginson's syringe) to herbs. Mrs C. recalled:

> They'd steep the herbs in hot water and then let them stand, for drinks. Water of rue was one of them. And they'd drink it, to see if they could disperse of it if the baby wasn't wanted. Keep on with that, every day. Rue and fennel. And they've come to me, even in my older life, and asked me what they should do, tried to get it out of me. But I would never tell them anything.[28]

And then there were drugs. By far the most dangerous of the methods used were drugs bought from the chemist. Some were prepared medicines, often marketed for 'female irregularities', as some of the more unscrupulous druggists attempted to enter the market for abortions. But others were drugs bought singly and then compounded and administered at home – such as Epsom salts, castor oil and other aperients. Many of the drugs were highly poisonous. Diachylon, for instance, was a lead compound. Women who took it often suffered lead poisoning as a result, and sometimes died. Quinine often had similarly tragic results. Others were based on mercurial compounds.

It is not clear, however, to what extent the old wife would have employed or advised the use of the more lethal drugs. Evidence seems to suggest that the reputation of certain drugs as abortifacients spread regardless of the rôle of the old wife. A Sheffield pathologist, for instance, commented that 'the news is handed from woman to woman by word of mouth, like any of the other household remedies or 'cures' which every woman knows.'[29]

Abortion was illegal until 1968 and this partly accounts for the continued approbrium in which the old wife was held by State and medical profession alike. Long after many doctors had dropped their moral objections to abortion, they continued to argue that the old wife was performing a risky medical operation, with little of the expertise and technological back-up necessary. But the fact that abortion was not made legal – and therefore safely performed by doctors – accounts for the survival of the old wife in this area of health care. Her rôle as abortionist should not, however, obscure the continuation of her other services.

Although midwives had to be registered from 1902, the use of unregistered midwives continued in country areas until the 1930s largely because, until the 1936 Midwives Act, there was no state requirement which obliged local authorities to provide midwifery services. The towns were better served, but in country areas the services of the trained midwife were not always available, and the 'woman' was therefore called in.

PUBLIC HEALTH
Until the National Health Service was established in 1946, free personal medical provision for all was not available. The latter half of the nineteenth century witnessed an increase in public health provision, with dramatic results in the overall health of the population. Fear of epidemics, particularly cholera, had led to the creation in 1847 of a General Board of Health. The Board of Health and the intervention by central authority (the Government) which it represented was politically unpopular, and subsequently went into virtual abeyance. But by the 1860s and 1870s much of this opposition to central intervention had subsided, and after a series of renewed outbreaks of disease, particularly of cholera and typhus, in the 1860s, public demand required that some effective control of both infectious diseases and their causes be implemented. Many of the recommendations of the Royal Sanitary Commission of 1868–71 were incorporated into the Public Health Act of 1872, which established medical departments within the Local Government Boards. Although these new departments had, in practice, little power *vis-à-vis* the Local Government Board they did,

nevertheless, represent the concept of an increased State rôle in public health. The Medical Officers of Health appointed under the Act themselves pressed for widening powers and did much to expand the whole concept of public health in the minds of the government and its agencies, and the public. Indeed, many of them were as much concerned with the broader issues of living and workplace conditions among the poor as with the treatment and control of infectious diseases. John Simon wrote in the *Public Health Reports* of 1867:

> Men and women, boys and girls, in scores of each using jointly one single common privy; grown persons of both sexes sleeping in common with their married parents; a woman suffering travail in the midst of the males and females of three several families, of fellow lodgers in a single room; an adult son sharing his mother's bed during her confinement – such are instances recently within my knowledge (and I might easily adduce others) of the degree and of the manner in which a people may relapse into the habits of a savage life.

It was becoming increasingly clear that the health and happiness of the majority could only be secured by putting some constraints on the individual. As early as 1840 vaccination had been introduced and it was made compulsory in 1853 and 1867, while the 1846 Nuisance Removal and Disease Prevention Act had made provision for the control of epidemics and the removal of 'nuisances', such as sewage and rubbish, likely to be injurious to the public health. Between the 1880s and 1910 a series of laws were passed covering not only the control and treatment of infectious diseases, but also sanitary measures, employment, pensions, housing, education and the health and care of the school child. Coinciding with these measures were the attempts by the Poor Law Board to expand and improve hospital facilities in an effort to encourage more people to present themselves for hospital treatment. Although many of the provincial Boards had been reluctant to comply, those Boards that had created separate hospital facilities made, as Beatrice

Webb noted,

> more striking than ever the contrast between the light, clean and
> airy newly built infirmary ward, with trained nurses, a resident
> doctor, complete equipment, and a scientifically determined
> dietary, on the one hand, and the insanitary and overcrowded
> hovel or slum tenement, on the other, in which the sick pauper had
> no other food than was provided by the pittance of Outdoor relief,
> no further nursing than his overtaxed family could supply, and no
> better medical attendance than the sparingly accorded order on
> the District Medical Officer could command.[30]

Overall, the level of public health had been improved
substantially. Yet it had only been improved in those
areas of sickness and ill health which had, traditionally,
created the greatest drain on the Poor Rate – namely
infectious disease, debilitating sickness and old age –
areas which, traditionally, the old wife would have had
little success in treating. Personal medical services had
not been improved by these provisions. Access to the
doctor was still limited by financial considerations. And
although many of the new 'State hospitals' had opened
out-patient departments for the treatment of ailments
which did not require hospitalisation, and did not
necessarily require a Relief Order, they were still not
readily available or accessible, particularly in country
areas. Moreover, the old associations with the workhouse
and the Poor Law were still strong, even in the twentieth
century.

> If you couldn't afford it (the doctor) you had the Poor Law doctor.
> He never used to charge. You paid nowt if you had the Poor Law
> doctor. They'd come round with their vaccination for nothing.
> You had to have it done, whether you wanted it or not . . . People
> thought the Poor Law doctor was . . . well, I can't say it, but
> something different to us. He used to think he was above us.[31]

The only reason the Poor Law doctor was consulted
was because people 'didn't have the money, that's why'.
The same feeling of repugnance rubbed off on to
attendance at the Poor Law hospitals and infirmaries.
Many of the hospitals in the early part of this century were

converted from old workhouses or attached to them. Despite the attempts to encourage the sick to regard them as 'infirmaries', the old associations with the workhouses were too strong: '. . . people hated the workhouse. Even when it was a hospital it was like coming out of one place into another that was practically the same.'[32]

OLD WIVES AND GENERAL HEALTH

Until the State thought it politically desirable to provide personal medical provision free of charge, the old wife remained a feature of medical care. There were some tragic consequences of this: one was reported in the *Suffolk Times and Mercury* of 16 December 1892:

> An enquiry was held on Tuesday (13 December) at the Green Man Inn, before Mr Coroner Chaston, relative to the death of Maggie Alderton Wade, aged 1 year and 9 months, the child of Henry Wade, agricultural labourer. The evidence of the mother showed that the deceased accidentally overturned upon herself, last Friday, a boiling cup of soup, sustaining scalds from which she died 40 hours later. No medical man was called in, but Mrs Brundish was sent for to charm the fire out of the deceased; she attended and repeated some words and passed her hands over the injured places. In the opinion of the parents of the deceased good was done. The witness added that Mrs Brundish's power was generally believed in, in the village. Mr W. Cuthbert, surgeon, having given evidence, a verdict of 'accidental death' was returned.

As with much other reporting, failures were more likely to be recorded than successes. Nevertheless, in 1910 HMSO published a *Report on the Practice of Medicine and Surgery by Unqualified Persons*, in which it was revealed that there were:

> Old women called wise women who though as a class are rapidly in a state of dissolution, sold secret salves, ointment, charms etc often of a disgusting character for the treatment of abscesses, whitlows, gatherings and scalds.

For instance, in the 1890s a Mrs Goodby of Littleport cured a young man suffering from a chronic abscess in his back by daily application of a poultice made from fresh cow's dung and mare's urine. The man finally died, from old age, in 1931. Similarly, W. H. Barrett recalls a 'Granny' Gray (also of Littleport) who cured boils by rolling the tarry deposit left in the chimney after burning peat into little pills and prescribing that they be swallowed three times a day. The same old wife sold pills for anaemia at three for a penny, which contained iron filings crushed to a fine powder and mixed with honey, butter and dandelion root.[33]

A letter in the *East Anglian Magazine* in 1904 states:

> Your correspondent 'C. P.' shows how a belief in witchcraft still survives in Suffolk and it is sad to have to acknowledge its truth. In Stowmarket we have a woman who is said to have inherited the gift from her mother, who *cuts* for the *spleen*, an imaginary infection, the symptoms of which are probably attributable to indigestion or anaemia. Anyhow, the process of the cure is as follows: the woman cuts the back of the ear slightly with a razor, dips her finger into the exuding blood, marks the forehead with the sign of the cross, mutters an incantation, puts a plaster of the expressed oil of mace upon the pit of the stomach, orders them to chew rhubarb root before each meal and the *spleen* will be cured. She charges a fee of 5s, an important factor in the treatment.

Whatever the quality of diagnosis or the treatment, it is clear that many working people still resorted to the old wife. Indeed, it is likely that for abortion or the treatment of venereal diseases many of the middle classes would have chosen her services. Although it seems clear that abortions on therapeutic grounds were easier to obtain for the middle classes than the poorer classes, for a single woman, for instance, there would have been few doctors prepared to risk their reputation and livelihood by performing an abortion for purely 'social' reasons. Similarly, though venereal diseases required hospitalisation by law, the social stigma attached to the disease undoubtedly made many sufferers, poor and wealthy alike, reluctant to submit themselves for treatment. W. H. Barrett recalls such an instance, when

There were several wise women living around Sandringham when HRH the Prince of Wales bought it in 1863 . . . As the years passed by, His Royal Highness as a hobby built up a stud of thoroughbred horses. Inside Sandringham House he collected a number of thoroughbred ladies. As a result of having to keep one eye on the brood mares in the stables, and the other eye on the females inside the house, demanding a share of the royal favours, his health broke down; this in 1880. He was very ill for a considerable period . . . Discreet inquiries down the social scale revealed the fact that some of the kitchen staff had good cause to be grateful to an old woman, a supposed witch, living at Flitcham, for getting them out of a muddle due to wandering off the narrow way that single women were supposed to walk thereon.

In due course the old woman was commanded to appear before the Princess, who suggested perhaps that the old woman knew of some remedies that would help the Prince to recover. The old woman replied 'I can give you a bottle of wine which I have made myself. Give the Prince three glasses a day and within three days – unless he is in the undertaker's hands – he will be sitting up in bed.' Four days afterwards a groom from the royal stables brought the old woman the news that the Prince of Wales was getting better; also, would she give him three more bottles of wine to take back . . .[34]

The wine, apparently, was her own special mandrake root wine. The same woman was renowned for her rue tea. 'It was nothing less than liquid gunpowder, and everybody said it was so powerful it would shift a traction engine. She had a lot of cures in her house, some in jars, some in bottles . . .'

DOCTORS AND THE WORKING CLASS

Despite the very limited provision of personal health care, as far as the BMA was concerned there was too much free provision. The expansion of Poor Law infirmaries had increased the numbers of free patients. It had also expanded the rôle and numbers of hospital consultants who, by the mid 1880s, had succeeded in excluding the general practitioner from hospital service. Similarly, the increase in Friendly Society membership and the form-ation of Medical Aid Associations in the 1890s further increased the number of patients entitled to 'free' medical care.

The doctors, for the most part, were in a dilemma. Throughout the nineteenth century their numbers had steadily grown, and the middle-class market had become saturated. Many doctors were now forced into working-class practice in order to make a living. Yet working-class practices did not pay. Attempts to establish a scale of payment were thwarted by the recognition that allowances had to be made for the very poor, yet failure to treat this class of patient would simply drive them further into the hands of the unqualified practitioners. One 'means test' proposed (by the Manchester Medico-Ethical Association in 1879) was based not on the income of the patient but on the rental they paid, and on the thorny question of what was included in the fee the same Association recommended that doctors' fees were paid only for diagnosis and not for drugs, even if they were included. 'Of course', it continued, 'no extra charge for them is understood *as their cost is simply made up by the greater hold the practitioner has on his patient.*'[35] (my italics)

The doctor's dilemma was recognised and exploited, first by the Poor Law Board and then by the Local Government Board which, in 1879, commented that:

> the facility with which, when the office of medical officer becomes vacant, competent medical men are found to fill the vacancies, affords a strong presumption that on the whole remuneration is not deemed to be insufficient.[36]

Such attitudes did not incline the general practitioner to State employment, whether centrally or locally administered. Similar forms of exploitation were also employed by the Friendly Societies, who equally underpaid and overworked their medical officers.

Any moves which attempted to undercut private practice were likely, therefore, to be strongly opposed by the BMA. Their opposition to the registration of midwives is indicative of this. Similarly, moves to establish a

Central Board of Health were opposed.

> The bulk of the profession showed interest in the subject only
> when it held out hope of strengthening their economic position.
> What they wanted most of all was protection against the competition
> of unqualified practitioners. Here, however, the 1858 Medical Act
> and the 1911 National Health Insurance Act satisfied much of
> their needs – the former, by confining Friendly Society (as well as
> public) posts to registered doctors; the latter, by extending this
> protection from one-tenth to one-third of the population. After
> 1911, medical interest in a Ministry weakened and it revived in
> 1918 only after the profession saw how much protection could be
> extended further without running risk of bureaucratic control.[37]

Thus the 1911 National Insurance Act was bitterly
opposed by the BMA. It argued that the contributory
principle was a 'bare faced fraud' and that all that was
good in professional ethics would disappear, and refused
to co-operate with the scheme unless and until 'six
cardinal principles' had been conceded. These covered,
essentially, methods of payment and the scope of the
provision. They argued that to qualify for insurance an
income limit of £2 per week should be established, that
the patient have a free choice of doctor, that the medical
benefits be administered not by the Friendly Societies (or
Approved Societies) but by local 'Insurance Committees',
and that all administrative committees have a strong
medical representation. They further argued that payment of doctors on the scheme should be established by
capitation fee or by payment for individual services, but
always by agreement, and that stipends, where paid,
must be adequate. Indeed, throughout the negotiations
it was inevitable that, as the British Medical Journal noted
in 1909, 'what appear to be the selfish interests of the
profession will loom large in our debates'. Dependent on
the support of the medical profession, the Chancellor of
the Exchequer conceded every one of the doctor's
demands, but it was not until 1913 that the BMA withdrew
its formal opposition to the scheme, and lost many of its
members in the process.

Essentially, the National Insurance Act attempted to redress the inadequacies in personal medical provision. There were, nevertheless, enormous gaps in its provision. The Liberal Party did not accept that it was the duty of the State to provide benefits freely and for all. For instance, although maternity benefits had been included in the 1911 Act, they consisted of a cash payment only; and the cost of medical and other help at confinement was not included. Not surprisingly, many poor women used this benefit not to supply midwifery services but to supplement the family diet. Agitation from, among others, the Women's Cooperative Guild, resulted in pressure on local authorities to increase their provision for working-class women, and in 1918 the Maternity and Child Welfare Act was passed. For the first time, the mortality rate went down, from 151 per 1,000 live births in 1901 to 89 per 1,000 in 1919.

THE LIMITATIONS OF THE 1911 ACT, AND THE CONTINUATION OF OLD WIVES

Although the 1911 Act provided medical services for certain groups hitherto not entitled to or unable to afford a doctor, medical facilities still remained inadequate in terms of staffing and distribution of resources. Moreover, the doctor was not free. Although his fee was small, it represented for many a substantial sacrifice. The 'Shilling Doctor', as he became called, was still not always within financial reach.

> A shilling could go a long way then [in the 1920s]. You could get a good meal for a shilling. There were eight children in my family. You thought hard about getting a doctor – or going without a meal.[38]

> When it was a choice between the doctor and the meal, you had the meal.[39]

Services were also divided by a complicated administrative structure.

> For the patient a comprehensive service existed only for those who
> could pay and those who could satisfy the means test requirements
> of voluntary hospitals. The services as a whole represented a
> hotchpotch of entitlements and disqualifications with the result
> that many had to go without medical care or appropriate medical
> care.[40]

Although the Poor Law Authority had been abolished
in 1929 by a Ministry of Health created after the First
World War, and local authorities had been empowered
to provide many ancillary services as well as administer
medical provision locally, medical provision in the inter-
war period was by no means uniform. The hospitals, for
instance, were still divided in 1939 between those maintained by local authorities and the old voluntary hospitals
which, because they took 'paying' patients (either insured
or subscribers), discriminated against some patients. A
means test was applied. Even so, out-patient services
were sometimes cheaper than the doctor, and there was
also a sense of getting your money's worth.

> Most of the time we went to the hospital, and they decided how
> much you pay. They used to go through all how much – who
> earned this, and what this and that, and how much the income was
> of the family. They decided what you should pay. They were very
> fair. I liked going to the hospital (as a child). I had cake and tea
> there. Anything to eat we was after. But I don't think lots of people
> liked the hospital. We didn't mind going there because we'd be
> sitting down, all quiet, you know, and people talking about their
> complaints. Though we were only little, but we were interested.
> That was the outpatients. You were all mixed there . . .[41]
>
> People would go to the hospitals. They'd pay thruppence. For that
> thruppence you'd get yards of cotton wool, bandages, the lot. You
> used to come home well-loaded from there sometimes. Virol they
> used to give you . . . but if you needed an operation, that cost you
> money . . .[42]

Operations cost money and panel patients took low
priority. Those who could afford it paid into associations
like the HSA – the Hospital Savings Association. For
threepence a week contributors were entitled to hospital
consultation and, if necessary, an operation and stay in

hospital. Those on the HSA were 'treated like royalty'. Unlike the 'panel' and other patients, they could jump the queue and were placed in a ward of only four beds. But even threepence a week was beyond the reach of many poorer families. Many relied on what was known as 'cards'. Wealthy philanthropists might donate vouchers worth a certain amount for the use of poor patients requiring hospital treatment. Some kept the vouchers, others deposited them with the Hospital Almoner for her to distribute at her discretion. A patient who required treatment but could not pay would go to the Almoner for her to allocate the voucher(s) or else would receive from her a list of benefactors who held vouchers or 'cards'. The patient would then have to call on the benefactors personally and hope to collect sufficient 'cards' to cover their costs. It was a system that was both resented and inefficient for patients often failed to collect sufficient vouchers to cover costs and would therefore be forced to forego the required treatment.

On the whole, doctors and hospitals still remained the exception rather than the rule for many working families, and would only be brought in when all else had failed. People suffered and even died from lack of early medical help. One such incident is remembered by a woman from Lambeth, who talks of her mother's death from a relatively non-serious cause:

> She had a poisoned toe. My sister used to look after it and that, keep it clean and all that, and then it turned septic so she had to have the doctor in. He ordered her away, to the Hospital. She went in on the Saturday and on the Saturday she died. Had her leg off. My father – and I don't know come to that – don't know whether she had it off at the knee or at the ankle.

When asked why she had not got the doctor earlier, she replied:

> Well, my sister was more a nurse than anything else. She doctored us all mostly. Them times we had to, didn't we? Just had to use your own common sense.[43]

So the old wife was still employed though, perhaps, not as widely as she had been hitherto. The following extract from *Bristol As We Remember It* gives an impression of life in the 1920s and 1930s:

> *Bertha Milton* You never had a doctor unless you paid him. We never had a doctor. If you were ill mother rubbed your chest or put something in your ear. I can never remember a doctor coming to our house.
>
> *Ralph Bewley* You used to go down the Herbalist, down Stapleton Road.
>
> *Sid Stephens* I lived in Salisbury Street – it was a street of good neighbours. I well remember one lady 'Grannie Hedges', she was the street 'doctor'. Any young mother who had illness, especially with children, she could tell what was wrong and could give advice free. A doctor's fee was 3/- if you called to see him and if he had to call it was a charge of 6/-, a lot of money in those days.[44]

The first treatment of sickness for working-class people in the early twentieth century was always at home. There was often a weekly preventive regime of senna tea or brimstone and treacle:

> Every Saturday we'd have brimstone and treacle. We'd have a bath, a zinc bath on the floor. And there was eight of us, all ready for action. Number one went in. Out come a kettle of water and number two went in. And my father was lined up with the brimstone and treacle, ready. Every Friday we'd say 'oh, we've got to take all that medicine again'. I know I had one sister who objected to medicine of any sort. She could not take it. If they held her nose and poured it down, she poured it up again . . .[45]

There were three broad categories of home treatment which would be tried before a doctor was resorted to, if at all. The choice of treatment depended largely on what could be afforded. The most expensive home treatment was the use of prepared medicines bought from a chemist – Galloway's lung syrup ('I think my mother helped Galloway's make their fortune', commented one man), Friar's balsam and other such ready-made compounds. Next came the use of the local herbalist. The decision to frequent the herbalist was made partly for economic reasons but, in some instances, from preference.

> You used to nurse your own children. My mother, she used to have all old fashioned remedies, herbalists, and people believed in all those ointments what they used to make. Made out of herbs and that. If you had a bad sore, they used to put ointment on the sore. My mother used to buy this ointment off of this herbalist, in the East End, just round the corner from where she lived. All different kinds of things they made, and dandelion tea . . . they had to have a diploma to become herbalists. He was known as 'doctor' something – we used to call him doctor, but whether he was a proper doctor nobody knows.[46]

The most common form of treatment was home-doctoring, using 'common sense' and home-prepared medicaments. 'There was eight of us, so I don't suppose she (mother) had much time or money to go to the herbalists or anywhere else. When we was ill, she'd nurse herself. She couldn't afford to have the doctor out.'[47]

The basis of this 'common sense' was a store of knowledge and advice transmitted partly through many of the popular medical books of the nineteenth century (see Chapter 7) and partly through word of mouth, passed from mother to daughter or received from friends, relatives and neighbours. For measles, for instance:

> They used to pull the blinds down, if you had a blind, and bandage their eyes up. Because of the measles in the eye. A lot of people went blind. They don't do that now, do they?

Or for whooping cough:

> They used to take them to where the tar was, the hot tar in the road when they used to spread it, well the smell is sickly and it was supposed to loosen the mucous in the chest. Or over London Bridge or Tower Bridge, something in the tar on the bridges that was good for whooping cough.[48]

> I remember going down to the river side. I think it's Westminster Bridge where you can go down them steps right onto the river. And they used to take the children there. We went there as children. Walked all the way from Euston, two in the pram, two walking.

We'd play in the mud all day and they'd be saying "Breathe". We were there all day, and then go home. But now you don't see children whooping in the street.

Coughs? I can remember my mother now buying those large onions and slicing them up in a pan and sprinkling between the layers brown sugar – not this white refined stuff, that was too expensive. She'd cover it over with a cloth and leave it twenty-four hours and then we'd drink the syrup. She couldn't afford Galloway's or anything like that.[49]

For headaches, brown paper soaked in vinegar was placed on the forehead, for sore eyes a cold tea poultice would be applied. Other cheap and home-produced remedies took care of many common complaints:

They'd take an onion and put it on a bit of flannel and wrap it round your throat. If you had a quinsy and that, the strength of the onion used to flake it, all things like that. Mother Hubbard's tales, really, I mean how could an onion outside . . . Well, they said the stuff penetrates the throat. All sorts of things like that. And in winter, brown paper and tallow, it was like dripping. You spread it on the paper and put it on the back and front of your child's chest. Recommended by a fine old lady downstairs where I lived. And it was supposed to be very good. They called it Russian tallow – more like lard, wasn't it? And bread on the finger – to get splinters and that out, draw it out. Bread poultice. She was a fine old lady. They did, old people, they'd say 'Why don't you get some of this marvellous stuff?' They believed in them. Bread poultice. Hot bread on a piece of bandage, bind it round and that drew it out. And yellow basilica, that used to draw the pus. Very drawing stuff. If you had a whitlow, put it on and bandage it up . . .[50]

The emphasis was, necessarily, on nursing. Without the use of modern drugs many cures, particularly for more serious complaints, were brought about by a combination of luck and nursing skill. Many illnesses could not be cured, for they were the result of poor environment and poor diet. And if one child in the family went down with an infectious illness, the chances were that all would catch it. Many old people recall sleeping four to a bed, 'two at the top, two at the bottom', all the children and often the parents sleeping in the same room. (The sheets were sometimes pawned during the week too.) Once sickness struck the family, there was little that could be done to isolate the patient.

THE 1930s AND THE MOVE
TO A NATIONAL HEALTH SERVICE

By the 1930s demands began to be made not only for reform of State medical provision, but also for the principle of free medical provision. Inspired largely by the Socialist Medical Association, the Labour Party began to argue against the notion of medical care as a charity for the poor and instead to demand that it be considered a right, a national asset which must be redistributed more equitably. The old emphasis on preventive medicine – a Fabian principle – had to a great extent been replaced by an emphasis on curative medicine. The outbreak of war in 1939 led to the establishment of Emergency Medical Services, and throughout the war a series of plans, negotiations and White Papers ultimately resulted in the 1946 National Health Service (NHS) Bill and Act.

The BMA was essentially opposed to free medical provision for all, favouring what they termed the '90 per cent' principle whereby the richest 10 per cent of the population could still pay, thus ensuring the continuation of private practice. Indeed, prior to the NHS Bill the BMA put forward seven principles on which they would not waver, similar in many respects to the 'six principles' they insisted upon before accepting the 1911 National Insurance Act. The Socialist Medical Association described them as 'completely unprincipled', the Medical Practitioners Union as 'seven futile clauses'. Nevertheless, the BMA largely won their argument, and although general practitioners lost the right to sell their practices they did gain what they wanted in terms of payment, control and the continuation of private practice.

Nevertheless, by 1947 doctors had a monopoly in health care and, for the first time, free medical provision was largely ensured for the majority of the population. The *Survey of Sickness* reported that between 1947 and 1951 there was an increase of about 20 per cent in the frequency with which people consulted the doctor; the largest increases were found among the very old and among women up to 35 years of age, indicating precisely the kind of gaps which pre-NHS facilities had failed to fill.

Once medical care was freely provided, the old wife found her rôle usurped – except in the area of abortion. Through State intervention, the medical profession was now able to provide a far wider range of medical and ancillary services. Added to this were the dramatic, and effective developments in medical science made in the nineteenth and twentieth centuries. By the mid-twentieth century, traditional medicine was inferior to that provided by doctors. The gradual increase in their monopoly, especially in hospitals, had enabled doctors to refine their research and results were incontestable. At the same time, research and marketing of new drugs and medical technology in which, as always, large profits are to be made, progressed apace.

Nevertheless, the tradition of the old wife and home doctoring persisted and still persists. The tradition of the old wife remains in vestigial form in the one area in which she retained her position longest. Pregnancy and minor childhood complaints often remain the preserve of the grandmother, particularly in working-class communities: there is a reluctance to 'bother' the doctor when a neighbour or grandmother is thought to suffice. Nothing testifies to this more clearly than the recent Health Education Council birth control campaign with the slogan: 'How can another woman make you pregnant?'

CHAPTER SIX

Conclusions: perspectives on the medical profession and the old wife

Medicine, like war, is an extension of politics. The story of the old wife is not the story of an inferior practice losing ground with the advances of medical science and technology; rather, it is a story which concerns the politics of medicine – a story of control and access.

The medical system we have inherited today has certain intrinsic features which were accentuated in the struggle for dominance over what came to be termed 'illegitimate' practitioners. These practitioners were largely women and the struggle for dominance was, I believe, fundamentally a gender struggle. To that extent, modern medicine is 'masculine' medicine, and some of its most dominant features are reactions against healers' practice. What are these features?

MEDICINE AS INTERVENTION: (1) PHYSICAL

Modern medicine is interventionist by nature. It seeks to cure rather than to prevent, to engineer rather than to heal. This is based on a mechanistic view which sees the body as the sum of its moving parts rather than a being in tune or at variance with its environment. Doctors are educated 'to see their patients as examples of individual pathology rather than as products of pathology in the social structure.'[1]

We do not know for sure how women healers in

ancient societies regarded their patients. We do know that their explanation for disease included not only a malfunctioning of the body but also an understanding of broader environmental influences, which included demons who worked their ills in a variety of natural and supernatural ways. Cure involved prayer as well as practice, a process that was broader than the mere application of medicaments, which flowed from a wider cultural and social awareness.

The first departure from this practice arose with the development of surgery in ancient Egypt. As noted in Chapter 2, surgeons were male and it is no coincidence that their skills evolved from the practice of embalming in which the body shell, as repository for the soul, was immortalised, while the vital organs were treated as offal.

The second major departure came with the development of humoural pathology (see Chapter 2) as epitomised by the Hippocratic and Galenic schools of medicine which dominated European practice for so long. This tradition saw a causal relationship between the mechanics of the body and behaviour or temperament and disease. The parts of the body could be adjusted to secure equilibrium, though interest frequently centred on the imbalances – that is, on deviance. It anticipated the use of medicine for purposes of social engineering, an attitude which could only arise from a mechanistic view of the body.

The mechanistic approach to medicine vested control over healing with the practitioner and denied a social context to healing. If disease had a mechanical cause then it required a technician to solve the problems. This technician, moreover, did not need to refer to other 'authorities' and powers – such as the goddess or demons – to sanction his practice or explain the causes of sickness. Although the origins of this approach have long been forgotten, the approach itself still predominates in medical practice, albeit with more sophisticated tools and analysis.

The approach can be seen in the position of surgeons, the archdukes of intervention, who rank highest in medical hierarchies. The surgeon, moreover, is the hero – the individual who achieves miracles against the odds, who fights the lonely duel with the dragon of disease. The glamour of a transplant is matched by the glamour of the surgeon so that only the most churlish dare question the social ethics of surgery or indeed the medical value of much interventionist medicine. Yet the number of operations performed is not related to the health of the population but is in direct correlation to the number of surgeons. There are twice as many operations performed in the USA as in England and Wales – the USA has, proportionately to population, twice as many surgeons.

Willingness to intervene is not confined to surgery. It is often used in diagnosis too. For example, the use of lumbar puncture to confirm multiple sclerosis will only confirm with 100 per cent certainty what can be ascertained with 95 per cent certainty using less aggressive diagnostic tests which, apart from being painful and distressing to the patient, are likely to bring on another attack from the disease. Until a few years ago, x-rays were routinely used on pregnant women, and some doctors still use pills containing oestrogen and progestogen for detecting pregnancy despite the real dangers of this producing deformities in the foetus and the fact that a simple urine test is more accurate and harmless to both mother and foetus.

It is easy to exonerate doctors by arguing that these judgements can only be made with hindsight and that medical advance can only occur through experimentation. But it is this very perspective, and the eagerness with which new techniques and methods are embraced, which distinguishes the old wives' traditions from current medical orthodoxy. Medicine, despite huge advances, still operates in a world of uncertainty and ignorance. Experimentation is an attempt to conquer this ignorance. Although the old wife's methods may have been empirical, she was not an experimenter. She possessed a skill based on proven methods and practices. It was a conservative skill. Though diseases come and go the body has not changed and does not change, and while in no way advocating ignorance there is, nevertheless, an argument for conservatism: radicalism has certainly led in some areas to needless intervention in the name of progress (and often profit).

MEDICINE AS INTERVENTION:
(2) SOCIAL

Medical intervention also operates in relation to social behaviour. The mechanistic view which interprets all maladies as originating from the body, and denies the patient's social context, has led, for instance, to some well-documented excesses in the treatment of mental disorder (for a discussion of this topic see, for instance, the analysis of R. D. Laing or Irving Goffman). And failures to conform are frequently interpreted medically as physical failures in the individual. This implies a desire to control behaviour and tends to reduce variations in human behaviour to a standard model.

The old wife was not concerned with social behaviour. Her tradition was humanist and personal; she knew intimately the family and the community in which her 'patients' lived, and while she may have had views concerning the behaviour of individuals, these views had no place in her approach to medicine. Health was concerned not simply with controlling the body but with understanding the environment. Her aim was to assist rather than intervene; she did not judge.

This difference in approach is seen more clearly in the treatment of women. In terms of routine complaints the old wife did not treat women differently from men. But because old wives were often particularly concerned with women's health, which included pregnancy, childbirth and all that surrounded these events, women's medical problems were not treated as 'abnormalities' but as characteristics of women. A second major feature of 'masculine' medicine is the loss of this perspective.

MAN, THE MODEL FOR HEALTH

The Hippocratic tradition considered the male body to be the yardstick by which to measure normality. It argued that male behaviour was the norm and that women must, and did, behave differently not because society conditioned them to do so but because they possessed an extra (and, by implication, abnormal) organ, the womb, which governed their behaviour. It made women less reasonable – that is, less like men. Hippocratic attitudes have not altogether died. According to the *American Journal of Obstetrics and Gynaecology*, women have a pre-menstrual phase described as 'an oppressive cyclic cloud ... (which) stops them functioning in a logical, male fashion'.[2] 'Doing anatomy', commented Anne Scott, 'taught me a lot about the extent to which the human body has been defined as male. Women are described only when their anatomy differs from men's ...'[3]

More crucially, the social rôle and position of woman is determined and confirmed by her reproductive facilities. Failure to conform to this tends to be regarded by doctors as a medical rather than a social problem. One study, by Michelle Barrett and Helen Roberts, shows the depth and prevalence of this position among doctors: '... women were quite remorselessly confirmed in traditional family and domestic rôles and more than one instance of a woman's refusal to do housework resulted eventually in hospitalisation and ECT.'[4]

Old wives had a bi-modal view of the sexes: women were not fundamentally different from men, but there were specific differences. These differences were not denied or treated as deviant.

A clear example of the masculine perspective is provided by the current practice of obstetrics and gynaecology. Pregnancy is concerned with healthy women and natural processes, yet the process of pregnancy, labour and birth is seen not as a natural one in which nature should be helped to take its course but one which the medical authorities should 'actively manage'. This is inevitable in a mechanistic approach to medicine which cannot allow for too much individual variation, social or physical. Technology has considerable ability to standard-ise; it can also ensure that the doctor's authority and control remain paramount. For technology requires hospitalisation and the pressure to admit women to hospital for their confinement is strong. The rationale is that it is safer, and this is sometimes the case; but there is another reality – that once in hospital the woman is placed in the subservient rôle of patient and will behave accordingly.

But some women naturally have long labours, and some short. From my own experience, if labour is allowed to run its natural course the woman is in a strong position to control her own body for the first and subsequent births. But such control is not only a challenge to medical authority – it is also a challenge to men. The mechanisation of birth, as Jean Donnison suggests:

> the wiring up of the mother to the fetal monitor, routine episiotomy, increased use of the forceps, an epidural analgesia (already shown to have its dangers) all militate against the woman's control over her own body. All these interventions, along with a high rate of artificial induction – often associated with increased pain and trauma for the mother and adverse consequences for the infant (and used, say its critics, to ensure nine-to-five working for the obstetrician) increasingly combine to rob the mother of the experience of natural childbirth.[5]

A mechanistic view of medicine is mainly concerned not with health but with curing disease, so pregnancy is seen as an abnormality. Under present medical orthodoxy, and in our society, it is also seen as an abnormality because of doctors' prejudices regarding women and women's bodies. The willingness to intervene is essentially a form of social intervention and control. It attempts to annexe from women one of the major ways in which they demonstrate their sexuality.

THE INHUMAN FACE OF MEDICINE: SCIENCE

Medical science as we know it today developed with the professionalisation of doctors. It was not, however, the imperatives of science which encouraged doctors to institutionalise their knowledge and skills. Rather, the professional requirements of doctors led them to formulate a concept of science which could be used to justify their claims to exclusivity. From very early on physicians sought to limit those entitled to practise medicine to university graduates or those holding a bishop's licence. University knowledge was the exclusive prerogative of the rich and of men. The hierarchy of scholarship carefully selected its own entrants. Science became incorporated into a university culture. Indeed, it became defined as that which could conform to academic discipline. The knowledge and skills of a popular culture were by definition unscientific.

Skills capable of self-acquisition were not specialist skills – they were not subject to control and would cease, in the new ideology, to have a market value. Neither would they conform to the system of hierarchies ordained by a division of labour. Moreover, many of these skills were not only self-taught but intuitive. Intutive knowledge was subjective knowledge; such popular knowledge was rooted in popular culture. It was necessary to divorce science from popular knowledge – both its approach and its subject matter. Ironically, this may well have retarded the pace at which a systematic medical knowledge could develop, for the new system cut itself off from the old wife and her traditions and, in the process, from a great deal of empirical knowledge and experience.

The new medical science developed a language which differentiated it from other methods. The patient became the object and treatment a private and mechanical contract between practitioner and patient. The doctor had to be objective, as his science was 'neutral'. The body was a mechanism, and the doctor unconcerned with social processes. The body was dehumanised and the doctor impersonalised. A sense of remoteness was as important for the status of the 'professional' doctor as was his science.

THE INHUMAN FACE OF MEDICINE: EXPERTISE

Those who took up science, who entered the university, preserved the hierarchy of medical knowledge and its practitioners. The antagonism, from the seventeenth to the nineteenth centuries, of physicians to the surgeon/apothecaries, can be seen in this light. The latter came, on the whole, from an inferior class and challenged the exclusivity of the physicians. One can also see why physicians and surgeon/apothecaries were united in their opposition to old wives. In the making of this professional caste, the doctors were prepared to sink their intra-professional jealousies to defeat a rival tradition and practice. What is unique about this situation is the scale of the struggle it represented. For the attempt to eradicate the old wife's practice was not simply a question of the evolution of knowledge within a discipline, as was the move, for instance from Phlogiston to Newtonian physics. It was a move to outlaw a body of knowledge and its practitioners, involving the total defeat of a tradition which stood as a direct antithesis to it.

Moreover, this struggle was couched in terms of gender. Science came to be seen as a masculine concept – a rigorous, logical discipline ruthless in its pursuit of learning, Old wives' tales were seen as feminine, intellectually anarchic and conservative in their approach.

This struggle, eventually successful, was linked inseparably with the development of capitalism. A hierarchy of knowledge became established which paralleled the social hierarchies. Certain forms of knowledge were identified with class and gender. Medical science became male, bourgeois science.

The growth of the middle classes was a necessary requirement for the expansion of the doctors. The middle classes employed the new professionals as an indication of their status, but status was also necessary for doctors to ensure their acceptance as *bona fide* members of the bourgeoisie. As yet, science *qua* science had proved a questionable basis for their authority, whereas class membership provided a spurious legitimacy to their medical practice. The tradition of the old wife had included women from the lady of the manor to the cottager's wife. Their status, in other words, was not defined by class membership but was wholly related to skills and knowledge: recognition for the old wife depended on her competence.

By the eighteenth century some major advances in the physical sciences were providing an explanation for some areas of human experience free from religious, political or social connotations. By attempting to link themselves with these new developments, the newly professional doctors sought to place themselves above the political, religious and social disputes of the day. Confusingly, they were often opposed to scientific developments, for instance, Jenner's work on smallpox vaccine. (Intriguingly, the inspiration for Jenner's own work on smallpox vaccine was based on an 'old wives' tale', see Chapter 7). Nevertheless, they claimed the authority to set the parameters of orthodoxy – to define not only who could practise but what could be practised and on whom. Moreover, women had always been excluded from the universities and therefore membership of the medical profession. The growth of class stratification came to cut the poor off from this new medicine and, at the same time, denied the old wife the possibility of replenishing her ideas and treatments.

The creation of a 'doctor class' also created the expectation of payment in return for services, in contrast

to the informal economic relationship between the old
wife and her community. Moreover, it established a
private relationship between patient and practitioner
based partly on an approach to medicine which empha-
sised a one-dimensional approach to health and partly
on the needs of a professional. For the doctor had to be
unique in his authority and relationship with the patient.
In contrast, the old wife's practice was public. Not only
did she draw on many sources for her diagnosis, but the
prognosis itself was multi-dimensional. It was a public
affair involving not only the help of supernatural agents
but also the community as witnesses. Her knowledge was
popular knowledge accessible to all. She was *prima inter
pares*. Her surgery was the street; the doctor's was a
private room.

MEDICINE AS INTERVENTION:
(3) POLITICAL

The professionalisation of the doctor meant exclusivity
of a practice and a limitation of the field of operation.
And, as a private financial contract, it excluded all those
unable to fulfil their side of the bargain. The poor were
least able to afford the doctor's services although, as
always, they suffered the greatest incidence of sickness.
The method of remuneration crystallised the idea that
health was a bargain to be exacted rather than a process
which actively involved the sick as well as the doctor.

Even such a radically different form of medical
administration as the National Health Service in Britain,
though it altered the economic relationship between
doctor and patient, did not change the power relationship,
or the class and gender bias of medical science and its
particular application by doctors. In practice, it reinforced
it. First, it maintained the monopoly on medical orthodoxy. Choice of practitioners may (in theory) be provided, but not choice of method. If patients wish to avail
themselves of other approaches to medicine, they have to
pay. Osteopathy, homeopathy, acupuncture and herbal-

ism are all outside the National Health Service and regarded by most of the medical establishment as dubious. Abortion was illegal until the 1967 Act. Many doctors, and the medical establishment, viewed it as unethical, for it violated what doctors perceived as the natural rôle of women – to have babies. It was left, therefore, to the uncontrolled world of the medical market place.

The distribution of NHS resources is closely linked to the geography of class. Working-class inner city areas are less well provided in terms of medical resources (including ancillary services) than middle-class equivalents. Despite the introduction in 1966 of a 'designated area allowances' – cash inducement for doctors to practise in deprived and under-doctored areas,

> the belief appears to be widespread among the medical profession that the designated areas are, as it were, a kind of third world – worthy to receive general medical services, but scarcely fit places in which sensible people would voluntarily choose to live.[6]

The reluctance of general practitioners to work in deprived areas, especially in the inner city, is as much the fault of doctors as of public policy. With little or no central planning provision many general practitioners are attracted towards areas with high income groups offering the most attractive market in terms of class of patient and nature of ailments. The pre-NHS situation, described by Titmuss, in which 'the gross overcrowding of the London specialist population was accompanied by an abundance of GPs in the well-to-do and supposedly healthier areas'[7] still seems to prevail today.[8] The reluctance of the GP to practise in working-class areas has historical antecedents, but the ultimate responsibility today for an inequitable distribution of medical resources lies with the government.

The part played by politics in medicine is closely linked with the rôle of medicine in politics. The State has ultimately always supported the demands of the medical profession: the passing of the 1911 Insurance Act and the 1948 National Health Service Act took place with heavy compromises in favour of the BMA and its demands. In terms of who and what constitutes medical practice, the State has never challenged the doctors' definitions. Indeed, it has granted doctors an unequivocal right to choose in these matters.

Finally, the gender bias of modern practice is couched in terms of professional jurisdiction, competence and ethics. There are two major areas relating specifically to women's health issues where the tradition of the old wife remains strongest, and they have been associated with the most acute social and political conflicts – abortion, and obstetrics and gynaecology.

The Abortion Law Reform Association, founded in 1936, spent thirty years lobbying before the Abortion Act of 1967 was passed. This Act did not repeal previous legislation (which dated from the nineteenth century and made abortion a criminal offence), but only made abortion a non-criminal offence in certain specific instances. In the nineteenth century the BMA had lobbied for a tightening of the abortion laws. Its view was based on two principles. The first was the profession's need to dissociate itself from what it saw as disreputable groups and practitioners. The second was based on a clear view of the rôle of women, perceived in terms of a bourgeois ideal. The woman's duty was in the home, to husband and family. Her childbearing function was her primary rôle, and anything which interfered with this was, by definition, unnatural.

The BMA opposition to the 1967 Act was equally based on the requirements of professional status and centred on the fear that the Act, if passed, would require doctors to make a positive *social* judgement in referring a woman for abortion. They feared that this social judgement would replace strict medical criteria. No matter that a decision not to abort was also based on social criteria – in this case passive ones in favour of the *status quo*. Under the *status quo* social criteria and judgements were subsumed under the blanket of medical criteria, freedom and ethics.

Even after the passing and implementation of the 1967 Act, the distribution of abortion facilities is uneven and depends on the preparedness of individual practitioners to refer and on the willingness of area hospitals to provide adequate facilities. It is significant that the BMA is now opposed to moves to amend the existing legislation, for the post-1967 situation has become the new *status quo* and they fear that amendment of the Act would create a group of practitioners who would perform abortions beyond the control of the BMA, and thus threaten their new monopoly in this area of practice.

Obstetrics and gynaecology, for long ignored by the medical profession, is now an area where science and technology are playing a larger and larger part. New developments are often aggressively pursued while, at a 'professional' or occupational level, there is an attempt to denigrate the profession of midwifery and to reduce the status and rôle of the midwife to that of obstetric nurse.

Midwives are legally entitled to act without the presence of a doctor. Midwifery is still a practical craft and its approach, of necessity, empirical. No one birth is exactly the same as another and the midwife's skill lies in adapting her craft to meet each individual woman's labour and requirements. It still remains a 'democratic' job in that anyone can train to be a midwife without previous medical qualifications. (Indeed, assuming that there are no complications, in an emergency anyone can perform the functions of a midwife).

Midwifery still remains in some respects an implicit denial of medical science and the rôle of the medical profession. The uneasy coexistence between midwives and doctors is seen in the USA by the fact that midwifery is illegal, and in the United Kingdom by the difficulty of obtaining a home birth.

Technologised childbirth removes at a stroke the craft

skills from midwifery and diminishes the midwives' area of responsibility as practitioners in their own right. It makes childbirth a specialist area, requiring not only hospitals (where consultants reign unchallenged) but also teams of obstetricians, anaesthetists – and nurses. And, as Jean Donnison points out, it

> deprives a rising generation of midwives, medical students and mothers of the knowledge that such an event (natural childbirth) is even *possible* and the base line of *normality* by which we may still judge *abnormality* is in the process of being lost.[9]

This loss is the obstetrician's gain, one result of which is that 'a growing percentage of births is becoming "abnormal" and the incidence of technical interference with the birth experience is ever increasing.'[10]

Indeed, women in hospitals, especially the large teaching hospitals, are often viewed as teaching material. In America:

> In childbirth, patients are those on whom students and residents practise techniques such as episiotomies, forceps extractions and Caesarian sections and suturing, and their deliveries are tailored to meet the needs of training.
>
> In their first year of training residents used forceps for delivery more often than later on, since this was the special skill they wanted to learn at that time. As one put it: 'I used them a lot to gain the experience of using them. There is almost no time when you can't use them, unless the woman delivers before you can get the forceps on.'[11]

There is little indication that the situation in the United Kingdom is very different. As one student midwife at a large London teaching hospital commented, there will soon be a generation of midwives who qualify as such but are incapable of delivering babies on their own, or without the aid of machines.

It is perhaps inevitable that childbirth and areas related to women's sexuality should have become those areas most susceptible to aggressive medical techniques. For not only are these areas ones in which the old wife remained a challenge but they are also areas in which women, as women, remain a challenge to men.

OLD WIVES' TALES NOW

The question of whether a medical profession which had incorporated the old wife and her traditions into its system would respond differently to issues of health and sickness, especially in women, is impossible to answer. Nevertheless, there are some notable points of departure from modern medicine in relation to women's health which indicate that this may have been the case. It is here that the real significance of old wives' tales now rests.

Attitudes and techniques which made women's rôle in medicine important in the past have re-emerged in women's health groups, especially in countries with technologically advanced medical system. These groups, in America and Europe, began from the premise that medicine, as applied and experienced, is not 'neutral' or 'objective'. While not denying the real advances of medical science, they deny the benefit of its wholesale application in the forms currently experienced by women.

Women's health groups are informal gatherings of no more than approximately eight or nine women. Their size is important, for they exist to encourage an atmosphere of trust and friendship in which issues central to women's health can be comfortably explored. It is felt that large groups would inhibit this development and many women feel nervous about talking in front of many people. A group will meet regularly and attempt to share their experiences, feelings and knowledge and to talk about their bodies and their attitudes to themselves. This often involves rediscovering and redefining 'normality' both in health and behaviour.

The approach to health represented by women's groups is holistic. Women see themselves as part of a total environment rather than as isolated individuals. Indeed, collectives can reassure women that they are not isolated in their problems and experiences. They attempt to see women in the context of their lives – what is happening to them at home, at work and in the community. Many women, as part of their conditioning as women, have internalised masculine expectations of themselves, especially in health matters where the line between medical and social judgement has become thin and confused, and where access to knowledge is controlled by the doctor in an essentially unequal relationship. Patients in our society are required to be passive, and so are women: women as patients carry a double burden of expected behaviour. These health groups aim, as part of the process of exploring their health, to explore themselves: not only to externalise what women know and feel about their bodies and themselves, but also to externalise masculine attitudes to women and women's health.

Thus discussion centres around issues specific to women's health, such as menstruation, pregnancy and childbirth, certain cancers (such as cancer of the womb or breast), menopause, cystitis, thrush and VD. Some groups will explore a single issue which is of central concern or common experience, such as menopause or childbirth; others will cover the whole range of health issues. Their aim is one of discovery and education and the emphasis within this process is on self-taught knowledge. The group is essentially democratic in its power relationship. For here it is not 'services' rendered, but experience shared. Thus many of the groups encourage self-examination with the aid of a speculum with the intention, as Nancy MacKeith put it, of

> familiarising a woman with those parts of her body with which she has been denied familiarity. Underlying this is a responsibility for keeping her body healthy, a responsibility which a woman can choose to undertake herself, rather than abdicate to a doctor. This involves becoming conscious of the well body, so that she becomes sensitive to changes in her body which might indicate the development of sickness.[12]

These groups aim to assist rather than intervene.

Many of them have attempted to revive some of the herbal lore associated with traditional women's practice and to advocate, where possible, natural remedies – a pessary soaked in yogurt, for instance, as a cure for vaginal thrush rather than a course of antibiotics, or practical measures which can be taken to prevent cystitis or relieve period pains. They do not prescribe or diagnose, but simply draw attention to the alternatives available and question the experimental nature of much of modern medicine. The use of insufficiently tested drugs in the area of women's health – thalidomide and depo-provera are but two powerful examples – stands as a constant reminder of the need for caution in reassessing the rôle of drugs in medicine.

It is impossible to evaluate how widespread these groups are. Many have a natural life and disperse after the specific issues which brought the group together have been fully explored. Others, however, take on an educational rôle, either by setting up new groups or acting as a referral service, or by dispersing the information gathered by other means, such as publication. Examples are *Our Bodies Ourselves*, which came from theBoston women's Health Collective, and *The New Women's Health Handbook*, edited by Nancy MacKeith. In this way many women who might not be able to join a health group are able to avail themselves of much knowledge which is central to their lives.

Fundamentally, women's health groups aim to restore to women control over their bodies by establishing confidence through understanding, and to make what knowledge they have generally available. They aim to demystify science and the cloak of professional expertise. They aim to have a more eclectic approach to learning. For medical science, as much as tradition, can be understood and extended to the people: it does not have to be the prerogative of a few. They have resurrected a public approach to health rather than a private contract to cure.

Implicitly, however, self-help groups represent a

political challenge – to social attitudes to women, to authority and to the division and annexation of knowledge. It is a challenge that has not changed since early times. It is this challenge which is at the heart of old wives' tales.

PART TWO

TALES

CHAPTER SEVEN

Introduction to Remedies

The origins of old wives' tales are as varied as the tales themselves, for medical ideas and drugs have been exchanged and traded across and within cultures for thousands of years. Domestic medicine, therefore, is an interplay of influences – of pagan ritual, herbalism and outmoded medical orthodoxies. It is often difficult to distinguish between a medical 'orthodoxy' and an old wives' tale. Trotula, whose work on midwifery in the eleventh century became the model for most subsequent writings on the subject until at least the seventeenth century included, for instance, this advice for the newborn: 'In the beginning of his life the eyes should be covered and special care taken that he be not in a bright light.'[1] This advice, a medical 'orthodoxy', was still adhered to in popular form well into this century:

> . . . and veils, till they were three months old. In case they got too much daylight. You couldn't take them to the window or put them out. They used to say they can't see till they were three months old, and daylight was bad till they could see. So they kept veils over their eyes . . .[2]

(The Leboyer method of birth, now practised in many hospitals in full or modified form, advocates dimmed lights in the delivery room.)

In similar fashion the *London Pharmacopeia*, the official medical 'handbook' of 1650, included a recipe for a drug called Usnea, which was a moss gathered from the skull of a man who had died a horrible death. G. W. Black in *Folk Medicine*, published in the nineteenth century, included this remedy for a headache, directing that the sufferer take 'moss, growing on a human skull, dried and powdered, to be taken in the manner of snuff'.

Orthodox medicine incorporated as well as generated popular medical beliefs and practices. The most salient point about old wives' tales is their eclecticism, drawing as they did from whichever traditions and drugs appeared both relevant and accessible at any given point. This was inevitable when drugs and ideas were readily available and when the onus of responsibility for healing rested with the patient and not the practitioner, for the patient was then free to draw on favourite diagnoses and remedies. As Virginia Berridge comments:

> even though self-medication is still very much a feature of contemporary life – there are few families who do not take some form of non-medically prescribed patent preparations most weeks – reliance on professional and commercial guidance is now considerable, and preparations bought in this way are generally prepackaged commercial products. But at the turn of the century the balance was rather different, and it was often the customer rather than the seller who dictated the terms of the transaction. Families, like the North Kensington one, had their own opium recipes; a Hoxton woman recalled a family cough mixture based on laudanum and ipecacuanha.[3]

Most families had their own recipes and their own store of advice. The criteria for use were price and reputation. Few would have been aware of the origins of their preparations.

Nevertheless, it is useful to distinguish two broad traditions in domestic medicine – spells and remedies. Spells are premised on the idea that disease and sickness are controlled by agents. In other words, disease was anthropomorphised and spells contained a basic ritual designed to instruct, verbally or symbolically, the agent of disease. Remedies are practical measures, usually based on the application of a recipe containing herbal, mineral or other ingredients, to alleviate the symptoms of disease or arrest its development. In modern terminology, spells can be seen as analogous to treating the cause of disease, and remedies to obviating its effects. The division is, however, somewhat arbitrary. A spell would rarely have been used without a remedy, and it is doubtful whether the distinction between the two was, in any case, a conscious one in the minds of the practitioners. Moreover although spells were a feature of Anglo-Saxon and medieval practice lingering on in rural areas until the nineteenth century they were not a feature of urban twentieth century old wives' tales. Their interest and relevance is, in this sense, antiquarian.

SPELLS

Spells did not acquire their association with magic until Elizabethan times. Until then, they simply meant information or instruction. The suspicion which now surrounds spells is due partly to their obvious pagan origins and partly to the method by which they are transmitted. The spoken word is now devalued as a means of communication not only because it is thought to be unreliable, its accuracy dependent on the skill of the communicator, but also because its transmission cannot be controlled. In a literate society, access to the written word is relatively freely available, but access to a spoken message depends on personal contact.

The classification of 'spell' used here is based on the criterion of principle – those remedies which implicitly or explicitly contain reference to agents of disease. It is important to remember that all medical remedies would originally have been transmitted orally and were, as instructions, technically spells.

The notion that disease is caused by demons has already been discussed in Chapter 2. Its origins are found in pre-classical times. The Ancient Assyrians believed in disease demonology, as did the European Teutonic tribes with their notions of 'elves' who fired poison darts containing 'elf-shot' at potential victims. The instructions to the demons were converted by the early Christian Church into 'prayers' more in keeping with Christian practice. That this was a deliberate directive from the Church has been discussed in Chapter 3 and is further indicated by other signs, for instance, Pope Gregory's advice to the English missionaries that they should not destroy the old temples but only the idols, and that they should then sprinkle Holy Water in the old places of worship and altars and place relics there 'that the nation, seeing that their temples are not destroyed, may remove error from their hearts, and knowing and adoring the true God, may the more familiarly resort to the places to which they have been accustomed'.[4] This directive did not stop at places of worship, but also included methods of worship and other ancient practices. Although the Church was later less tolerant of these practices, at least in its early years it was prepared to utilise them as far as was expedient. This also applied to the incorporation and use of medical prescriptions.

An Anglo-Saxon spell against a 'dwarf' (elf) shows a spell in its transitional phase between pagan ritual and Christian prayer. It directs

> You must take seven little wafers, such as one used in worship, and write these names on each wafer: Maximianus, Malchus, Johannes, Martinianus, Dionysus, Constaninus, Serapion. Then afterwards you must sing the charm which is given below, first into the left ear, then over the man's head. And then let a maiden go to him and hang it upon his neck, and do this for three days; he will straightaway be better.

> Here came a spider creature stalking in;
> He had his dress in his hand.
> He said that thou wert his stead.
> He puts his bonds on thy neck.
> They begin to sail from the land.
> As soon as they left the land,
> They began then to cool.
> Then came the beast's sister stalking in,
> Then she made an end and swore these oaths:
> That this should never hurt the sick,
> Nor him who would acquire this charm,

Nor him who could chant this charm.
Amen, fiat.[5]

Most charms became totally Christianised. What is left is the pagan principle and form. Many, therefore, sound contrived, as, for instance, this spell for the ague:

> When Jesus went up to the cross to be crucified the Jews asked him saying 'Art Thou afraid, or has Thou the Ague?' Jesus answered and said 'I am not afraid, neither have I the ague.'
>
> All those who hear the name of Jesus about them shall not be afraid nor yet have the ague. Amen, sweet Jesus, amen sweet Jehovah.[6]

In other charms the transformation rests uneasily:

> Nail three horseshoes to a bed post with these words:
> Father Son and Holy Ghost
> Nail the devil to this post.
> Thrice I smite with Holy Crok,
> With this meil I thrice do knock,
> One for God,
> And one for Wod (Wodan)
> And one for Lok (Loki)[7]

The popularity and longevity of the belief in demons is exemplified by Eliza Vaughan who, in 1934, re-called:

> I once had an old cottage friend . . . she used to wake very early every morning with an attack of what she called the 'bad feels'. I was present when her doctor tried to explain to her, with much patience, that the cause was weakness; also perhaps, advancing years had something to answer for. She waited till he had finished talking and then, politely but firmly, pointed out the error of his opinion. Begging his pardon, she knew the cause. 'Well' said he 'What is it?' In a solemn voice the correct diagnosis was given. 'That's o'd Satan, a tryin' o' me'.[8]

The agents or demons of disease were considered as living beings and, as such, capable of being related to directly. Many spells, therefore, contain quite clear instructions to the agent. A spell for a tetter (a skin disease) clearly directs the agent to disappear. The structure of the spell is itself a ritual which enacts the future course of the agent's behaviour:

> Tetter, tetter, thou hast nine brothers
> God bless the flesh and preserve the bone;
> Perish thou tetter and be thou gone
> In the name (etc.)

> Tetter, tetter, thou hast eight brothers
> God bless the flesh and preserve the bone;
> Perish thou tetter and be thou gone
> In the name (etc.)

> Tetter, tetter thou hast seven brothers,
> God bless the flesh and preserve the bone (etc.)

> Till the last verse:
> Tetter, tetter, thou hast no brothers
> God bless the flesh and preserve the bone (etc.)[9]

Not all spells enacted the future. Some, like this one for St Vitus' dance, contained simple verbal instructions:

> Shake her, good Devil
> Shake her once well;
> Then shake her no more
> Till you shake her in hell.[10]

The agent was considered capable of taking orders. It was also considered capable of being tricked, of having its attention distracted or transferred on to some other person or object. This principle of transference is at the root of many spells. For ague, for instance, the sufferer is directed to 'catch a shrew, bore a hole in an ash tree, insert the animal and plug it up, alive. The ague will disappear as the shrew dies.' Many spells for warts also contain this principle:

> Steal a piece of meat, rub it over the warts, bury it in the ground, and as the meat decays, so the warts will go.[11]

> Rub the warts with the inside of bean pods, then bury the pod (secretly) and the warts will disappear.[12]

Important in these examples of transference is the

burying of the object on to which the disease has been transferred, for this symbolically suggests the course which the disease will follow.

The agent was also considered capable of taking some kind of responsibility for its actions, by offering the antidote. This is exemplified in spells which embody the principle of 'take the hair of the dog that bit you'. The cure, in other words, lies with the agent. A cure for the bite of a mad dog directs that the victim take the dog's heart, dry it over a fire and administer it (ground to a powder) to the patient. This principle was also extended to inanimate objects. If, for instance, a hook, a knife, a nail or anything else caused an injury, the instruction was to clean and anoint the offending weapon. An incident reported in the *East Anglian Magazine* of 1901 describes this principle in operation:

> A few years ago we went to make hay and have tea in a friend's meadow. My small brother was accidentally pricked with a hay fork. The wound was soon bound up; it was alright and we thought no more of it. At tea time the servant brought a message from the old coachman to say 'Please tell Master Willie that place will heal up right, for I have greased the fork and hung it up so that it keep bright till the place mend.'

Although this form of treatment may appear to have little practical significance, it did mean that the wound was left alone, for many wounds, if dealt with by unsterile dressings, are more likely to be aggravated than cured.

A closely related principle to that of the cause providing the cure is found in the notion of sympathetic magic or the 'doctrine of signatures' – of curing like with like. Many herbal cures are founded on this principle, where the plant resembles in shape or colour the affected part.

The colloquial names of many of our plants and herbs bear witness to this belief, for example liverwort, motherwort, etc. Similarly, other plants were used because they grew in the vicinity of the cause of an ailment and were therefore believed to contain the antidote. The most

commonly known example of this is the use of dock
leaves to relieve nettle stings. Another example is the
custom in the Fens of boiling the bark of the willow to
relieve symptoms of rheumatism, both being 'grown' in
damp locations. (For the chemical properties of the
willow, see later.) The principle also operated with
inactive or inanimate objects, often coupled with the
principle of transference. A cure for whooping cough
involved knotting a string nine times and hanging it
round the patient's neck. The knot 'sympathised' with
the cough and the disease was thereby transferred on to
it.

Many spells therefore contain either verbal or symbolic instructions. Amulets, crucifixes, and sometimes
written messages in the form of charms or prayers would
be worn to prevent the disease striking. Enid Porter, in
Cambridgeshire Customs and Folklore, records old Fenmen
wearing garters of eelskin to protect them against an
attack of 'ague' or marsh fever.

Other symbols included running water – one of the
three necessary elements for life. Springs and wells have
often been attributed or associated with cures, and water
itself is alleged to drive away the Devil. Baptism is the
epitome of this belief and its theological purposes have
often been obscured by the physical properties it was
believed to contain. A sickly child, one old wives' tale
directs, will never grow well until it has been baptised.
Similarly salt, a vital mineral, was believed to be anathema
to devils. It also has well established cleansing and
antiseptic properties.

Far more mystical in its origins and healing properties
was the use of colour. To a certain extent the principles
under which colour operates as a curative symbol were
similar to those of sympathetic magic. Red could represent heat. Thus red flannel was used to 'draw' out a fever.
Red flowers would be given for disorders of the blood,
yellow for those of the liver. Colours were also symbols of
more abstract objectives. Red, for instance, was symbolic

of victory and triumph. It was also a sacred Christian colour, being the colour of Christ's blood. Blue was the colour of the Druids and of the Virgin Mary, though it was thought to have few curative properties. Interestingly, however, brides were instructed to wear something blue on their wedding day, and a preventive measure for 'fevers while lactating' was to wear around the neck blue woollen threads or cords. Green was the ancient symbol of fertility and was once thought lucky; black symbolised darkness and night, evil and sin. Although these colours were not central to healing they represented omens – methods of warding off evil or ensuring good fortune. (The use of colour and other symbols, such as the sacred triangle, have been handed down to become popular 'superstition' but I do not propose to talk about such superstitions except where relevant to domestic medicine.)

Numbers figure strongly in many charms, partly because certain numbers were thought to contain an intrinsic value – three and multiples of three seemed to have a particular potency (the value of three is important in much religious symbolism), as did the number seven – and partly because they have a practical use in directing the quantity of ingredients in a remedy and the length of time remedial measures should be taken. A cure for whooping cough, for instance, directs:

> Pass the child nine times under and over a donkey three years old. Then take three spoonfuls of milk drawn from the teats of the animal, three hairs cut from its back, and three hairs cut from its belly. Place the hairs in the milk and let it stand for three hours. Then give it to the child in three doses, while the ceremony is to be repeated on three successive mornings.[13]

(This was likely to induce vomiting, which might cause momentary relief.)

In a letter written in 1827, the painter John Constable describes his son's whooping cough and comments: 'I find medical men know nothing of this terrible disorder and can afford it no relief . . . consequently it is in the hands of quacks. I have been advised to put him three times over and three times under a donkey as a perfect cure.'[14]

Many incantations involved the use of numbers, often structured so that the numbers diminished (see the spell for tetter, earlier). But the quaintness of the spells should not obscure their practical usage. For instance, elements from astrology were perceived as valuable symbols in healing. But more than that, the moon and sun directed not only the course of sickness but often the correct times for harvesting herbs and for administering treatment. Club moss, for instance, was believed to be effective for all diseases of the eye, and had to be gathered on the third day of the moon when it was seen for the first time. The gatherer was directed to take the knife with which it was to be cut in the hand, show it to the moon and repeat:

> As Christ healed the issue of blood
> Do thou cut what thou cuttest for good.

Then, when the moon was setting, the gatherer had to wash the hands and cut the club moss while kneeling and wrap it in a white cloth. Afterwards it had to be boiled in water taken from a spring nearest to the place of growth and then the decoction could be used as a fermentation for the eyes. Or it could be made into an ointment after it had been mixed with butter made from the milk of a new cow.

Although the ritual appears both elaborate and heavily symbolic, it contained important principles. For the efficacy of many herbs does in fact lie in the correct time of harvest. The active principle of a herb may vary according to its freshness and time of gathering. Modern research has demonstrated, for instance, that the yield of morphine from the poppy gathered at nine o'clock in the morning is often four times the yield obtained twelve hours later.

The ritual also conferred a legitimacy on the herb by calling on the deity to sanction its use. In the example of club moss, Christ was invoked. But the authority of pagan deities was also used, and many herbs had their efficacy sanctioned in this manner. The ash tree, from which the Celtic god Wodin was believed to have been formed, was a symbol of health and life, presumably because it grows long and straight and its branches, though slender, have both strength and elasticity. A popular cure for rickets and hernias involved passing the sufferer three times, with her or his head towards the rising sun, through a young ash which has been split down the middle. The tree would then be bound up and, as it recovered, so would the sufferer.

> These trees, when young and flexible, were severed and held open by wedges while ruptured children stripped naked were pushed through the apertures, under a persuasion that by such a process the poor babes would be cured of their infirmity. As soon as the operation was over the tree, in the suffering part was plastered with loam and carefully swathed up. If the part coalesced and soldered together, as usually fell out where the feat was performed with any adroitness at all, the party was cured: but where the cleft continued to gape the operation, it was supposed, would prove ineffectual. We have several persons now living in the village, who, in their childhood, were supposed to have been healed by this superstitious ceremony, derived perhaps from our Saxon ancestors, who practised it before their conversion to Christianity.[15]

Ash (along with oak) would often be tied to the delivery bed and newborn babies given a drop of ash sap to drink. But both the leaves and the bark of the ash were important in medicine. The bark was used principally as a remedy for fevers and rheumatism, for it is both a bitter and an astringent and was used as a precursor and a substitute for Peruvian Bark, from which quinine is extracted. The leaves were used as diuretics and laxatives and also as a cure for jaundice.

Deities, however, were not the only individuals believed to have control over the process of healing. Under certain circumstances, humans could inherit certain powers. The seventh daughter (or son) of a seventh daughter (or son), providing that the line was unbroken by members of the opposite sex, was particularly renowned for healing and psychic powers. The 'left' twin, that is, the child who has survived a fellow twin, was thought to be capable of curing thrush by blowing three times into the patient's mouth, providing the patient was of the opposite sex. And the touch of the king as a cure for the 'King's Evil', or scrofula, was legendary.

But if the living had powers, so too did the dead. A pre-Christian belief that was carried into medieval times and later held that the soul contained the life essences which were allocated to individuals in approximately equal proportions. If someone died, particularly prematurely, then his or her quota of life essence would not have been exhausted and was, in theory available to assist the sick whose own life essences were clearly waning. Many old wives' tales incorporate the use of the dead, or those associated with the dead. Hangmen used to charge a fee for the 'dead stroke', and sufferers from a variety of maladies would gather round a gallows. The Catholic Church incorporated the belief in the power of the dead into its use of relics of saints as curing agents.

But death was also used ritualistically. Some spells involved a symbolic acting out of sickness, of passing through death and being born again into health. Passing the patient through an arch or an aperture (as, for instance, in the cure for rickets and the use of ash, referred to earlier) symbolised this rebirth, while other spells, as in this one for whooping cough, involve the symbolic 'burying' of the patient:

> Lay the child face downwards on the turf of a meadow. Cut round the child in the shape of a coffin. Remove the child and turn the turf root upwards. As the turf withers so the cough disappears. This operation must, however, be done in secrecy.[16]

Secrecy is an element in many of these spells. Again,

this has practical origins. The soul or life essence was a vulnerable substance which could easily be extracted by demons or their agents and used against it. Spells which involved exposing the soul would need to be conducted in secret lest evil powers 'kidnapped' the soul and used it for maleficent purposes. Even if secrecy was not always involved, precautions would always be taken to safeguard the soul. Baptism, again, is one manifestation of this. An old wives' tale directs that a child under the age of one should never be shown its own reflection, for it was believed that reflections 'captured' the soul. When infant mortality was so high, you took few chances with the life of a newborn infant.

I have not attempted to unravel the origins of spells nor to give an exhaustive inventory of the principles under which they were believed to operate. All I have done is to indicate the variety of spells and point out that they should be seen within a context – not of magic and mysticism, as some writers on popular superstition indicate, but as a real method of controlling what otherwise might often appear a hostile and ungovernable environment. In any case, spells were rarely used in isolation but with an accompanying remedy, unless the remedy itself was intrinsic to the spell.

REMEDIES

The area of old wives' tales which is most familiar to us now is that of remedies – the practical measures taken in the event of sickness. They constitute the heart of traditional domestic medicine both in this country and elsewhere. Most traditional medicine relied on the use of indigenous herbs and spices, and this use is one of the defining features of the system. In Europe, however, trade in herbs and other drugs began early and was widespread, so although many traditional remedies contain instructions in the use of native herbs, this is not a distinguishing characteristic of European domestic medicine.[17]

In Britain, the Druids traded with the Egyptians, exchanging both recipes and ingredients, while gum arabic, obtained from a species of the acacia tree, has been imported into Europe from the Middle East for at least 2,000 years. As early as the eleventh century in Britain there were spicerers and pepperers who specialised in the import and retail of foreign spices used for both culinary and medicinal purposes. By the thirteenth century spicerers had begun to specialise, and those who sold spices for medicinal purposes were the forerunners of the apothecaries and pharmacists (which is why, until the seventeenth century, apothecaries were associated in trade with grocers). It was not until the sixteenth century that pharmacy in Britain began to come into its own, stimulated by the beginnings of exploration, the discovery of the new world and the import, from the new world, of new herbs, spices and drugs.

The most important of these new drugs imported in the sixteenth and seventeenth centuries was cinchona from Peru. Known as Peruvian or Jesuit's bark, it contained what has now been isolated as quinine. Other drugs included ipecac, guaiacum, sarsaparilla, curare, tobacco, cascara, sagrada and coco (from which cocaine is derived). These drugs, indigenous to the new world, were used in the traditional medicines of these lands and their effects and significance were not lost on the early explorers.

It is ironic that these 'old wives' tales' from the natives of the Americas and elsewhere, introduced into apothecaries' repertoires of England, undermined the traditional Galenic practices of the physicians and stimulated the development of the apothecary's trade and practice – to the extent that by 1617 the apothecaries successfully applied for a separation from the Grocer's Company and a charter was granted to the 'Apothecary's Company'. In 1618 the Royal College of Physicians, clearly alarmed by the growing strength of the apothecaries, published the first pharmacopeia, the *London Pharmacopeia* which by order of James I was to be obeyed by all apothecaries.

This first pharmacopeia contained no less thatn 1,028 simple drugs, 932 preparations and compounds, 91 animal drugs, 271 herbs, 138 roots and 138 seeds. In the list of preparations there were 213 distilled waters, 115 conserves, 58 electuaries, 45 lozenges, 53 ointments, 51 plasters and 17 chemicals.

In 1673 the first medicine was patented. Known as 'Goddard's Drops', the formula was bought by Charles II and subsequently published in *Bates Dispensary*, edited by Dr Salmon. The formula directed that you take

> Human bones or rather scales, well dryed, brake them into bits and put them in a retort, and joyn thereto a large receiver which lute well; and distil, first with a gentle fire, then with a stronger, increasing the fire graduation; so will you have in the recipient a flegm, spirit, oyle and volatile salt. Shake the receiver to loosen the volatile salt from the sides, then close your receiver and set it in the earth to digest for three months. After that digest it at a gentle heat for 14 days, then separate the oyle which keep for use.[18]

Dr Salmon adds that if you want to apply it to gout of a particular limb, it is best to make it from the bones of that limb. He warns that the smell is evil. Other formulae for Goddard's drops call for hartshorn (a source of ammonia), portion of skull of hung criminal, or dried vipers' bodies.

Throughout the seventeenth and eighteenth centuries more pharmaceutical preparations were prepared and marketed – Glauber's and Rochelle's salts, Gregory's powder (compound rhubarb powder), Palsy drops (compound tincture of lavender), compound tincture of benzoin, liquorice powder, compound pills of antimony (known as 'Plummer's Pills'), compound opium pills, Matthew's Pills, calamine, 'Stoughton's Great Cordial Elixir' (compound tincture of gentian), Godfrey's cordial (mixture of sassafras and opium), Huxham's tincture (compound tincture of cinchona) and Daffy's elixir (senna). In the nineteenth century, drugs such as iodine, morphine, emetine, hydrogen-dioxide, strychnine and quinine, to name but a few, were all added to the range of drugs and drug preparations, along with still-familiar brand names such as Beecham's Powders.

Initially, these new drugs were expensive and, therefore, like the services of the apothecary, beyond the reach of many. Most domestic medicine still relied on those herbs which could be obtained and prepared at home. But by the latter half of the nineteenth century (see Chapters 4 and 5) the costs of these preparations had fallen and an increase in working-class spending power meant that many more were available and incorporated in domestic medicine chests, either as patent medicines or in the form of basic ingredients for remedies prepared at home from people's own recipes. The *Morning Chronicle* of 15 November 1849 reports, for instance, a Manchester druggist who comments:

> Some use raw opium instead. They either chew it, or make it into pills and swallow it. The country people use laudanum as a stimulant, as well as the town people. On market days they come in from Lymm and Warrington, and buy the pure drug for themselves and 'Godfrey' or 'Quietness' for the children.[19]

Certainly, by the nineteenth and twentieth century – the period from which the majority of remedies and recipes given here were obtained – traditional medicine was a mixture of indigenous herbs and imported drugs, cost being the major determinant of use.

Although the use and efficacy of herbs and spices was originally established through trial and error, modern research indicates the current value of many traditional remedies and ingredients. Many of the drugs still used today in modern pharmacology owe their origins to 'old wives' tales', either from this country or abroad. Principal among these, and still featuring in the 1979 edition of the *British Pharmaceutical Codex* are the following. (The list is not exhaustive: it is merely an indication of modern application of traditional methods.) The uses outlined here are current, as given in the *British Pharmaceutical Codex*.

Gum arabic – used as a binder for slow-dissolving tablets
Almond oil – to soften ear wax

Aloes (Barbados, Cape or Socotrine) – purgatives

Aniseed oil – used in cough mixture

Belladonna – contains hyoscyamine and atropine and is used to decrease secretions of sweat, salivary and gastric glands; it is a powerful spasmolytic in intestinal colic and, given with purgatives, allays griping. It is also used for the relief of spasm associated with biliary and renal colic. Hyoscyamine is sometimes used in conjunction with pethidine during labour.

Belladonna was an old favourite with midwives.

Benzoin – an ingredient in inhalants

Caraway – used now mainly for flavouring and colouring

Coco – from which cocaine is derived

Digitalis (foxglove) – a source of digoxin used in treatment of heart complaints. William Witherington, a doctor, was the first to 'scientifically' investigate the use of foxglove for the heart and wrote of his discovery in *An Account of the Foxglove*:

> In the year 1775 my opinion was asked concerning a family receipt for the cure of dropsy. I was told that it had been kept a secret by an old woman from Shropshire who had sometimes made cures after the more regular practitioners had failed. I was informed also that the effects produced were violent vomiting and purging, for the diuretic effects seem to have been overlooked. This medicine was composed of 20 or more different herbs; but it was not very difficult for one conversant in these matters to perceive that the active herb could be no other than foxglove.

Dill – for the treatment of flatulence in infants

Caraway – used as a carminative

Cardamom – used as a carminative

Coriander – used as a carminative

Ergot – the active ingredient, ergometrine Maleate, is used for uterine contractions in expelling the placenta.[20] Other derivatives are also used in the treatment of migraine, to suppress lactation and to help in infertility. A further derivative, bromocriptine, is referred by the BPC for its action on pituitary. The hallucinogenic, LSD, also owes some of its ingredients to ergot.

Eucalyptus – an ingredient in inhalants, also used for relieving neuralgia and rheumatism

Gentian – a bitter, used to stimulate the appetite

Henbane – a source of hyscomine

Ipecacuanha – the actions are those of its principal alkaloids, emetine cephaëline. In small doses used as an expectorant.

Lavender oil – an ingredient of gamma benzoin hexachloride, used as an insecticide and larvicide

Liquorice – the important constituent is glycyrrhizin, used in cough medicine. Liquorice also contains saponins, which help break up mucus. It is good for stomach and gastric ulcers because carbenoxolene has been isolated and synthesised from glycyrrhizin and is used in the treatment of gastric ulcers.

Male fern – used in the treatment of worms

Meadow saffron or autumn crocus – used in the treatment of gout and, until recently, leukaemia

Nutmeg – contains hyristicin, which has an effect on the nervous system. Overdoses stimulate the cerebral cortex. Used also as a carminative.

Peppermint – a mild antiseptic and an ingredient of compound magnesium trisilicate tablets and sodium bicarbonate tablets.

Periwinkle – contains two alkaloids, vinblastine and vincristine used in the treatment of certain malignant conditions such as Hodgkin's disease or solid tumours or leukaemia

Podophyllum (Mandrake) – used as a purgative in Victorian times, and by the Indians to remove tumours. It is still used in the treatment of venereal warts.

Rhubarb – used as a purgative

Tar (pine, coal) – relieves itching

Willow – although willow does not feature, its active ingredient, salicin or salicylic acid, was isolated in 1899 and a derivative produced called acetylsalicylic acid. This derivative was given the trade name 'Aspirin'.

Other herbs, such as snakewort (used originally in childbirth) only disappeared from the *British Pharmaceutical Codex* twenty years ago as did, similarly, chamomile, aconite, coltsfoot and garlic (though garlic still features in the French and Spanish pharmacopeias as an expectorant, disinfectant and diuretic, and for the treatment of stomach disorders and blood pressure). Hawthorn and mistletoe, used in the treatment of blood pressure, still feature in some European pharmacopeias, and lily of the valley and hawthorn (for the treatment of heart complaints) appear in the Soviet pharmacopeia.

There are other remedies, now superseded by modern (often synthetic) drugs which, though not used or prescribed, nevertheless contain substances which appear to achieve the desired effect. Raspberry leaf tea, for example, widely advised by old wives to help allay the pains of labour as well as painful periods, contains an ingredient named 'fragarine' by Professor Burns who isolated it. In his tests it was shown to relax the uterus. Broom tops, used for the heart, have an active ingredient called sparteine. Nettles, thought 'good for the blood', contain (like spinach, cauliflower and most dark green vegetables) large doses of vitamin K and phytomenadione, which is important in preventing excessive bleeding.

Other old wives' tales which do not rely on herbal remedies provide some advice or code of practice, and many of these contain a medical 'truth' which has subsequently been validated by scientific experiment. Jenner, for instance, pursued his research into a smallpox vaccine after hearing the 'old wives' tale' that dairy maids who milk cows who have the cowpox will not themselves catch smallpox. The smallpox vaccine is a modified cowpox virus. Another tale advises the application of mouldy dung to an open wound or sore. The mould contains penicillin, the 'wonder drug' of the twentieth century. The old wives' tale which directs a dog to lick a wound may seem, by our standards, distinctly unhygienic, but a group at Harvard Medical School have recently discovered that there is a wound-healing agent in mouse saliva —called nerve growth factor (NGF) — which, in experiments, increased the rate at which wounds in mice healed. It seems highly probable that this healing agent is also present in other species, though as yet there have not been experiments to see if NGF operates across the species barrier. Such experiments, however, are due to begin.[21]

Similarly, the belief that breast milk can cure conjunctivitis in newborn babies may well contain a scientific truth. There is an antibody – immunoglobulin A (IgA) – which is present in high quantities in colostrum and in lesser amounts in human milk produced later by the mother.

> It seems that IgA is produced within the lactating breast and the antitoxic activity of breast milk against *Escherichia coli*, a common cause of infantile diarrhoea, correlates well with its IgA content. Thus, there may well be a scientific basis for the folk belief that the eye infection conjunctivitis can be cured in newborns by putting breast milk in the baby's eyes.[22]

TRANSMISSION OF REMEDIES

Just as the use of the ingredients of traditional medicine varied from herbal remedies through to patent medicines, so instructions on the use and efficacy of remedies were transmitted in an equally varied manner. The three basic methods of transmission were through oral, written and published sources.

Word-of-mouth transmission is the oldest method of transmission, as well as the simplest and the most common. Remedies were passed down through families, as were recipes. If they were seen to work within a family, they would be given a credence which defied any other evidence to the contrary. Opium and opium derivatives, for instance, were widely accepted as a 'cure-all', and disbelief was often shown of the narcotic effects of the drug. Virginia Berridge quotes the *Morning Chronicle* report on Manchester in 1849, in which a druggist comments:

... Recipes which had been handed down in families for generations, and which often contained dangerous quantities of laudanum, were occasionally brought to him to make up, but he found little difficulty in convincing their possessors of the noxious character of the ingredients, when he was sometimes allowed to change their proportions. Sometimes a half emptied bottle of cordial would be brought, in order that more laudanum might be put into it ...[23]

Families were not the only vehicles of oral transmission. Recipes would also be passed down among groups with a common interest as, for example, in the transmission of contraceptive and abortion advice and recipes among women, and information regarding abortionists themselves. In this instance, the use of word-of-mouth transmission was imperative, for the information could be passed only to those who were known to be genuine and trustworthy.

But recipes and remedies were also written down and circulated among friends, family and acquaintances. In 1464, for instance, John Paston, a member of a wealthy Norfolk family, wrote to his wife Margaret:

I pray yow in all hast possybyll to send me, by the next swer (sure) messenger that ye can gete, a large playster of your flose ungwentorum for Kynges Attorney, James Hobart, for all hys dysease is but an ache in hys knee. He is the man that brought yow and me togedyrs, and I had lever than xl li. ye koud with your playster depart hym and hys peyne. But when ye send me the playster, ye myst send me wryghtyng hough it shold be layd to and taykn from hys knee, and hough longe it shold abyd on hys knee unrenevyd, and hough longe the playster wyll laste good, and whethyr he must lape eny more clothys about the playster to kepe it warme or nought.[24]

Family prescriptions were not the only ones circulated. Prescriptions obtained from both apothecaries and physicians were copied by hand and circulated within and between households, written on scraps of paper or incorporated into domestic notebooks containing general recipes for food, cleaning materials and other domestic matters. In this way servants would often have vicarious access to the advice of physicians. Published sources would also be plagiarised, and the information transmitted.

The final method of transmission was through published sources, of which the earliest were in manuscript form. The Egyptian papyrus contains medical recipes, and Greek and Roman medical treatises form the basis of the physician's knowledge for many centuries. But the most popular of the published material was the herbal. Two herbals in particular, those of Dioscorides, a Greek of approximately the 4th century BC, and of a Roman, Apuleius, of 400 AD, had an enormous influence on European herbals for, unlike many other medical treatises, they were not 'lost' in the Dark Ages but preserved in Southern Italy by monks, especially those of the monastery of Squillace in Callabria. The monks copied out the codices and from there the manuscripts were disseminated to the rest of Europe. The influence of the classical herbals on Anglo-Saxon herbals was strong, to the extent that herbs not found in England but common to the Mediterranean would be faithfully replicated in the English herbals.

The advent of publishing increased the distribution of herbals, although England was relatively slow off the mark for printed herbals. Bancke's *Herball* was the first to be published in 1525 and was curiously, not illustrated. But it was swiftly followed by other herbals either written by English authors or translated from continental sources. *The Grete Herball* of 1523 was translated from the French *Le Grant Herbier*, and noted that the 'iuce of the leves of willows is good to delay the heate in fevers yf it be dronken'. The first edition of Gerard(e)'s *Herball* came out in 1597.

Throughout the seventeenth and eighteenth centuries herbals continued to be published, including many – like Elizabeth Blackwell's *Curious Herbal* – which came out in weekly parts and were later collected (1737 and 1739) into volumes. There was also Sir John Hill's *British Herbal* of 1756, and Timothy Sheldrake's *Botanicum Medicinale* or 'an herbal of medicinal plants in the College of Physician's list', which was published in parts in 1759. Although initially the market for these early part-works was limited to the middle classes, their popularity was great and they found their imitators in cheap bills and chapbooks.

By the end of the seventeenth century, the market for home remedy books which incorporated recipes not dependent on indigenous herbs had increased dramatically, coinciding with the expansion in the import, development and sale of new drugs. One of the first from this period was written by Elizabeth Grey, Countess of Kent, and entitled *A Choice Manual of rare and select Secrets in Physick and Chirurgerie. Collected and practised by the Countess of Kent* (late dec'd). The earliest surviving edition is the second, of 1653. It was followed by books of a similar character such as, in 1652, Leonard Sowerby's *The Ladies Dispensatory containing the Nature, Virtues, and Qualities of Herbs and Simples usefull in Physick, reduced into a Methodicall order, for their more ready use on any Sickness, or other accident of the Body, the like never published in English*. His claim was probably correct for, among other things, it contained remedies for the 'bitings of Crocodiles and Cockatrices' and the 'Venomes and poysons of Toads and Greene Frogs'!

Contemporary with Sowerby's publication was *The Ladies Cabinet, Enlarged and Opened*,

> containing many rare Secrets and Rich Ornaments of severall Kindes and Different uses, Comprised under three general heads – viz., 1) Preserving, conserving, candying etc.; 2) Physic and Chirurgerie; 3) Cookery and Housewifery; whereunto added Sundry experiments and choice extracts of Water Cycles etc. Collected and practised by the late Right Honourable and learned Chemist, the Lord Ruthven.

The 1696 edition of William Salmon's *The Family Dictionary or Household Companion* offered, for the treatment of consumption, a Snail Broth in which you were instructed to

> Take a Cock Chick and fill his Belly with Five-leav'd Grass, Bugloss, Egremony and Endive; when it is half-boil'd put in 100 snails, which must be slit, and the Guts taken out, but the Fat left in, and wash'd in several Waters and Salt, and wip'd very clean in a Cloath from Slime; then boil them in the Broath with a blade of Mace; drink this every morning for a Consumption or Weakness.[25]

Other recipes included that for 'oil of foxes' and a recipe for swallow water, which begins:

> take 12 swallows out of the Nest, cast them whole into a glass of Alembick, add thereto the Shavings of a Man's Skull three ounces, Castor one ounce and a half, pouder of Mistletoe one ounce . . .[26]

The tenth edition (1696) of the *Queen's Closet Opened* promised 'incomparable Secrets in Physick, Chyryrgery, preserving and candying etc which were presented to the Queen by the most experienced Persons of the times, many whereof were had in Esteem when she please to descend to private recreations', and quoted as its sources an impressive list of physicians, bishops, aristocrats and royalty. Although this was the seventeenth-century equivalent of the modern 'Doctors recommend . . .' it provides an indication not only of the market, but also of the classes who practised domestic medicine at that period. Among the recommendations was this one for the plague:

> there is no medicine more excellent than this when the sore doth appear, than to take a cock chick and pull it and let the Rump be bare, and hold the Rump of the said Chick to the sore, and it will gape and labour for life, and in the end die; then take another and third, so long as any one do die; for when the poyson is quite drawn out the chick will live, the sore will assuage and the party will recover.[27]

Although these editions were directed primarily at the monied middle and upper classes, by the eighteenth century there were medical remedy books on the market directed not only specifically at women, but at women from a wide social background. Hannah Wolley's *The Compleat Servant Maid* of 1704 contained, as well as general advice on housewifery, standard prescriptions for health, among them a recipe for Aqua Miravilis:

> take three pints of White wine; of Aqua-Vitae and juice of Celandine, of each a pint, one dram of Cardamom, one dram of Mellilor flower, Cubeds a dram; of Galingal, Nutmeg, Cloves, Mace, Ginger, of each of a dram; mingle all these together over night; the next Morning, set them a stilling in a glass Limbeck. This admirable Water dissolveth the swelling of the Lungs and restoreth them when perished. It suffereth not the Blood to putrifie, neither heed he or she to breath a Vein, that useth this excellent Water often. It cureth the Heartburn and expelleth Melancholy and Flegm, it expelleth Urine and preserveth a good Colour in the Face, and is an utter Enemy to the Palsie. Take three Spoonfuls of it at a time, Morning or Evening, twice a week.

The authors of these books varied from 'Ladies of Quality' to physicians and, in between, a group of more or less qualified authors. Those written by physicians, however, often contained an injunction that only 'qualified' people should prescribe and practise medication. Dr William Buchan's *Domestic Medicine* of 1789, for instance, while warning against unqualified practitioners, also included an interesting inventory of the eighteenth century domestic first aid cabinet:

Adhesive plaster
Agaric of the oak
Ash coloured
   ground liverwort
Burgundy pitch
Cinnamon water
Crabs claw prepared
Cream of Tartar
Elixir of vitriol
Flowers of sulphur
Gentian root

Olive oil
Pennyroyal water
Peppermint water
Rhubarb
Sal ammoniac
Sal prunell
Seneka root
Senna
Snake root
Spirits of hartshorn
Spirits of wine

Glauber's Salts
Gum ammoniac
Gum arabic
Gum asafoetida
Gum camphor
Ipecacuanha
Jalap
Jesuit's Bark
Liquid laudanum
Liquorice root
Magnesia alba
Manna
Nitre or Salt peter
Oil of almonds

Sweet spirits of nitrate
Sweet spirits of vitriol
Syrup of lemons
Syrup of oranges
Syrup of poppies
Tamarind
Turner's cerate
Vinegar of squills
Wax plaster
White ointment
Wild Valerian root
Yellow basilicum
    ointment

There are probably few twentieth century first aid cabinets that are so comprehensive.

Other authors were more forthright in their intentions. Sir Arthur Clarke wrote *The Mother's Medical Assistant* of 1820 as advice to mothers

> were it for no other purpose than to enable them to counteract the foolish and mischievous nostrums of ignorant nurses which bring thousands to an early grave, this consideration alone, should render the proposed inquiry worthy of their serious attention.

Nevertheless domestic remedy books written by non-medical men continued to be published and increased in popularity. Many were written to 'improve' the standards of the working-class housewife, and therefore contained cleaning tips as well as chapters on nutrition and home medication, but they were sufficiently cheap to allow a mass market sale. The medical recipes contained a mixture of traditional herbs as well as relatively 'modern' drugs obtainable from the druggist. The popularity of home medical books has not diminished; the major difference between a twentieth century one and an early edition of *Mrs Beeton* or the *Frugal Housewife* is that the latter contained recipes for practical measures as well as crude diagnostic guides. Modern books contain few or no guides to home cures.

The most important feature of these books was the use to which they were put and the rôle they played in the dissemination of popular domestic medicine. For they both incorporated and created conventional 'wisdoms': the interplay of the 'orthodox' and the 'popular' is a central feature of domestic medicine. Nowhere is this more true than in midwifery, where popular belief and practice were as much to do with custom as with learned theses. It is difficult to know the exact nature of the practice of early midwives. The Anglo-Saxon leechdoms, for instance, do not concern themselves with 'women's questions', although many of the 'classical' works contain references to gynaecological and obstetric matters. The Ebers Papyrus refers to a variety of complaints and offers this remedy

> when we wish to prevent a patient from suffering from fluor albus
> . . . We proceed as follows: the dried liver of a swallow is taken and
> rubbed up with some sour milk; this is then to be placed on breast,
> belly and joints.

And the works of Greek and Roman physicians such as Hippocrates, Pliny, Plautus and Galen contain similar references, though these were mainly obtained second-hand from the midwives of the day. Pliny provides a list of herbs useful for women's disorders, including rue and pennyroyal to 'bring away the afterbirth', mallow with goosegrease to produce abortion, leek, mint, heraclium, coriander and blite to 'arrest haemorrhage from the uterus', and elaterium, cabbage, parsley, rue and mallow to 'promote menstrual discharge'. The Mesopotamian physician Aetius of the sixteenth century AD recommends: 'to prevent conception the mouth of the womb may be smeared with various substances such as honey or balsam'. He later advises in the case of the failure of this method:

> that the second and fourth months are to be avoided, while the

third month should be chosen if we wish the patient to abort and this to be brought about by sitz-baths, external applications, bleeding and pessaries made of iris, galbanum, turpentine etc.

In this prescription he clearly acknowledges the second-century Roman midwife, Aspasia, as his source.

It was not until the eleventh century and the work of Trotula on midwifery that insights were provided into medieval beliefs and practices. But even Trotula referred and deferred to the authority of the ancients. She wrote:

If itching of the vulva occurs take camphor, spume of silver, cherry, laurel and white of egg and let a pessary or salve be made. Galen says that ground chick peas with blood of goose is useful for induration of the womb. This Hippocrates also testifies.[28]

Nevertheless, Trotula's work was also based on experience, both her own and that of others. In the chapter on the regulation for women about to give birth, she advises:

let an aromatic fumigation be made below the nostrils; it can also safely be applied at the mouth of the womb because then a fragrant womb follows and an evil smelling one is avoided . . . It is to be noted that there are certain physical remedies whose virtues are obscure to us, but which are advanced as done by midwives. They let the patient hold a magnet in her right hand and find it helpful. Likewise they let her drink a powder of ivory or they find that coral suspended on the neck is helpful. In similar fashion that white substance which is found in the dung of an eagle, when given in drinks is advantageous. Likewise give the dung of ladybirds which is found in the swallow's nest . . .[29]

Many of Trotula's remedies were essentially practical, as this one for engorgement of the breasts:

to some women there befalls pain of the breasts, from the milk. For this take potters earth blended with vinegar as a poultice. It alleviates the pain and regulates the milk if you first foment the breast with hot water.[30]

And she advocates the use of herbs and fumigations for a number of complaints, from excessive bleeding to 'suffocation of the womb'. Similarly for a prolapse she advises the midwife to

> restore it by a hand placed against it and push it back into place.
> Then let the women enter water in which has been cooked wild
> pomegranate flowers, roses, pomegranate bark, oak galls, sumac,
> myrtle, acorns, leaves and bark of live oak, cypress nuts and
> lentils.[31]

Nevertheless, the use of binders and stones to 'draw out' the child at the time of birth was also advocated by Trotula. The stones were held by the patient or tied to her so their application was external and largely symbolic. They were also a feature of medieval midwifery – the use of 'virgin's nuts' by medieval midwives has been referred to in Chapter 3. Trotula was not the only authority who advised their use. Jane Sharp, the seventeenth-century midwife, wrote of the virtues of the 'eagle stone': 'held near the privy parts will draw forth the child as the lodestone draws iron, but be sure so soon as the child and afterburthen are come away, that you hold the stone no longer, for fear of danger.'[32]

A Dr Hargrave, Dean of Christchurch, Canterbury, commented on his wife's stone:

> it is so useful that my wife can seldom keep it at home, and
> therefore she hath sewed the strings to the knitt purse in which the
> stone is, for the convenience of the tying it to the patient on
> occasion and hath a box to put the purse and stone in. It were fitt
> that either the Dean's (Canterbury) or vice-dean's wife (if they be
> marryed men) should have this stone in their custody for the
> public good as to neighbourhood; but still that they have a great
> care into whose hand it be committed and that the midwives have a
> care of it, so that it shall be the Cathedral's stone.[33]

In similar fashion a London physician, Richard Andrews, wrote to the Countess of Newcastle on 10 May 1633:

> I've also sent you an eagle stone which in the time of labour being
> tied about the thigh will make labour easier.[34]

Just as the use of the eagle stone was passed between

official and unofficial authorities, so too were other practices. In particular, the herbs used in labour as advocated by Pliny and Trotula were a formidable part of the medieval midwife's armoury. Ergot would be used to speed a difficult labour, as would darnel, poppy, henbane and bryony root. Belladonna and henbane would also have been used to ease labour pains and, as noted earlier, both belladonna and ergot are still used in modern midwifery practice. For abortion, pennyroyal and rue were familiar prescriptions and were still used in country areas for this purpose in this century.

Fundamentally, childbirth was a social event. The midwife would be called in, as would women relatives, neighbours and friends. Until the advent of the man-midwife in the seventeenth century, men were excluded from the process. Observation and participation in childbirth by women assured the continuation of tra-ditional practices and beliefs, and this information was transmitted verbally. Published works on midwifery did not appear until the sixteenth century, and then reflected the works of classical and medieval authorities and popular practice. It is difficult to differentiate the two, for popular ideas which showed a marked similarity to the works of Trotula, for instance, were clearly in circulation before the publication of later works which enshrined these same practices in print.

One of the earliest published works on midwifery was the sixteenth-century book *The Byrthe of Mankinde* by Rosslin, followed in the seventeenth century by books such as Percivall Willoughby's *Observations on Midwifery* and Jane Sharp *The Midwives Book* and *Compleat Midwife*. There was also the irrepressible Nicholas Culpeper who, having launched himself in the field of herbal remedies, now entered that of midwifery with his *A Directory for Midwives* in which he patronises and ingratiates his way into the subject:

Having served my own sex I shall see now if I can please the

> Women, who have no more cause than Men (that I know of) to be ashamed of what they have, and would be grieved (as they had cause for they could not live) if they were without, but have cause, if they rightly consider it, to thank me for telling them something they knew not before.[35]

These and later books, like Aristotle's *Book of Problems* of 1749 'wherein is contain'd divers Questions and Answers Touching the State of Man's body' and Sarah Stone's *A Complete Practice of Midwifery*, reflected the growing demand for information in this area. Aristotle's work, in particular, went through countless editions throughout the eighteenth and nineteenth centuries, each reflecting contemporary changes in information and attitudes and catering for what was perceived to be popular demand at any one time.

These books would probably not have been read by what Willughby called the 'meanest' sort who had taken up midwifery 'for the getting of a shilling or two'. And Jane Sharp who, in her introduction, remarked 'I have often sat down sad in the consideration of the many Miseries Women endure in the Hands of unskilful Midwives; many professing the Art (without any skill in Anatomy, which is the principal part effectually necessary for a Midwife) merely for lucres sake . . .', remained, presumably, sad. For although her book passed through several editions it was read almost entirely by the better educated midwife and the early man-midwives.

The assumption, however, that middle-class midwives were necessarily better than their working-class counterparts is not necessarily proven. Certainly book-learning on the subject of midwifery, for all Jane Sharp's claims, would not always have been enlightening. She might have owed a great deal to Trotula, who advocated similar practices and remedies,[36] but she also included much that was of dubious practicality and which owed nothing to a knowledge of anatomy. One of the causes of barrenness, for instance, was 'by Inchantment', for which she recommended 'the French in such a Case advise a Man to thread a needle Nouer O'equilliette, as much to say, to piss through his Wife's Wedding Ring and not to spill a Drop, and then he shall be perfectly cured.'[37]

Similarly, she advocated a number of tests for detecting the sex of the unborn child. To find out,

> observe these following Rules:
> 1) If it be a Boy, she is better Coloured, her Right Breast will swell more, for Males lie most on the right side and her Belly especially on that side lieth rounder and more tumified and the Child will be first felt to move on that side, the Woman is more cheerful and in better Health, her Pains are not so often nor so great; the right Breast is harder and more plump, the Nipple a more clear red and the whole visate clear, nor swarthy.
> 2) If the Marks before mentioned be more apparent on the left Side, it is a Girl that she goes withal.
> 3) If when she riseth from the Place she sits on, she move her Right foot first, and is more ready to lean on her right Hand when she reposeth, all signifies a Boy. Lastly Drop some Drops of Breast Milk into a Basin of Water, if it swim to the Top it is a Boy, if it sink in round Drops, judge the contrary.

These notions reflected both popular beliefs and conventional classical orthodoxy. Parmonides, of the sixth century BC, believed that male bodies formed on the right side of the mother's body. Hippocrates argued that if the child was a boy the right eye of the mother would be clearer and brighter, the right breast larger and the complexion clearer. Pliny believed that a woman pregnant with a boy had a better colour and Trotula insisted that the milk and water test was infallible. There was (and is) a popular belief that boys, being the 'stronger' sex, moved earlier and kicked more and that girls make the pregnant woman look and feel less healthy.

Jane Sharp's book, and others like it, reflected no more or less than the contemporary ideas on midwifery and related areas. Her practice probably differed little from that of working-class midwives whose 'qualifications' would have been experience, marriage and motherhood. Indeed, it is likely that in this period working-class women would have fared better than their middle-class counterparts, since they would have escaped the zealous activities of midwifery 'trendies' and man-midwives who were entering the field and who were over-keen to interfere in the natural processes of labour. Some of the advice contained in published works, like that of Nicholas Culpeper, was also far from sound. In cases of 'Falling out of the Womb' he advised:

> My own Magnetick Cure is this. Take a common Bur leaf (you may keep them dry if you please all the year) and apply to her Head, and that will draw the womb upwards . . . . whereas . . . . the vulgar way of Cure is: push it back, bind it in and fumigate.[38]

The 'vulgar way' was far more likely to have the desired effect than his own 'Magnetick' cures. Fumigations would have had both an antiseptic and soothing effect.

Throughout the subject of popular medicine the interchange of ideas and remedies is paramount. Herbs, drugs and ideas were traded and exchanged. The resemblance between the notions of demons and elves has been alluded to earlier. The idea of boys inducing a better 'complexion' in the pregnant woman is another instance of the exchange of ideas across cultures and through time. There is also a marked similarity between, for instance, the ancient Assyrian belief that a worm caused a toothache and the Anglo-Saxon leeches who diagnosed and prescribed:

> *If a worm eat the teeth*, take holly rind over a year old and root of arline thistle, boil in hot water, hold in the mouth as hot as thou hottest may.
> *For toothwark*, if a worm eats the tooth take an old holly leaf and one of the lower umbrels of hartwort, and the upward part of sage, boil two doles in water, pour into a bowl and yawn over it, then the worms shall fall into the bowl.
> *For toothworms*, take acorn meal and henbane seeds and wax, of equally much, mingle these together, work into a wax candle and burn it, let it reek into the mouth, put a black cloth under, then will the worms fall on it.[39]

And an English seventeenth-century version of the *Regimen Sanitatis*, which originated in Salerno in the eleventh century, stated:

> If in your teeth you hap to be tormented
> By meane some little worms therein do breed,
> Which pain, (if need be tane) may be prevented,
> By keeping cleane your teeth, when as you feede;
> Burn Francomscence (a gum not evil scented)
> Put henbane unto this, and Onyon seed,
> And with a tunnel to the tooth that's hollow,
> Convey the smoke thereof, and ease shall follow.

Popular traditions, from whatever source, were sometimes amazingly tough. The custom of putting ash on to the tongue of the newborn baby, for instance, may well have originated with the Aryans,

> Some thousands of years ago the ancestors of this (Highland) nurse had known the Fraximus Ornus in Arya or on their long journey thence through Persia, Asia Minor and the South of Europe and had given its honey like juice as divine food to their children; and now their descendants imitating their practice in the cold North, but totally ignorant of its true meaning, puts the nauseous sap of her native ash into the mouth of her hapless charge because her mother and her grandmother and her grandmother's grandmother had done the same thing before her.[40]

Traditional medicine may be viewed as nothing more than outdated orthodoxy. There was often little in medieval times and later to differentiate the practice of the physician from that of unlicensed practitioners. In many instances, their sources of both knowledge and drugs were similar. The significance of old wives' tales rests not in their content but in their social importance. However much traditional medicine may be viewed as archaic by medical authorities, for many it was the only form of medical treatment available. Recipes and ingredients were easily obtainable, and there was no established authority to shield sources or validate diagnosis or treatment. What was used was tried and tested and gave the practitioners a *de facto* authority. At the same time, they did not distance the patient from the practitioner. The healing process was one in which all could participate. Old wives' tales could not necessarily offer a cure, but they could offer an explanation and, in some instances, alleviation of the symptoms.

What follows is a compilation of some old wives' tales. It is not a comprehensive collection. I have relied for my sources primarily on oral or manuscript material because these indicate which tales were still held within living memory or, as in the case of manuscript material (from Suffolk County Archives) in the process of transmission or home recording. These are a few tales which come from published sources – herbals or domestic medical books – but these have been kept to a minimum. I have used my other source (folklore collections) in the manner of a primary source, since they are often a valuable (or only) record of many traditional medical practices, particularly those that employ the use of charms or spells. In the text I have marked the nature of the source with the following abbreviations:
O – indicates oral source
M – indicates manuscript source
P – indicates a published source
Further details of sources are given in the chapter notes.
   This section of the book is not a practical handbook. Many of the ingredients are unobtainable; some are fatal if used without skilled knowledge. The recipes obtained from either oral or manuscript sources have not been checked for accuracy of ingredients or proportions. They are merely duplicated as heard or found. In the case of recipes gleaned from manuscript material, the handwriting was sometimes indecipherable or spelling wrong. Unclear sections are marked with a '?' and the recipes left as deciphered. Nevertheless, I have tried in the case of some of the remedies to indicate which contain healing properties and which still figure in modern British

pharmacy. Those found in the *British Pharmacopoeia* or *Pharmaceutical Codex 1979* are marked with an asterisk.

Finally, the list is not, and cannot be, fully comprehensive. Diseases and particular treatments have disappeared over time and are now often lost. This is inevitable, for traditional medicine is a living tradition and subject to changes in the physical and intellectual environment. My sources provide remedies that are within or just beyond living memory. Early published material contains examples of medieval remedies but these are not included, for my purpose is not to portray the 'quaintness' of remedies but to demonstrate the variety and quantity of almost contemporary home preparations.

Included in this list are a number of old wives' tales relating to pregnancy and childbirth. Few relate to actual midwifery practice, for the simple reason that traditional domestic medicine is a method of controlling the uncontrollable and explaining the inexplicable. It therefore concentrates on the mystery of sickness and illness. The mechanics of childbirth require practical measures; the mystery is involved in conception and in sustaining the life of the newborn baby. And it is in those areas that old wives' tales abound.

CHAPTER EIGHT

Remedies

M=manuscript source
O=oral source
P=published source
*=found in the *British Pharmacopoeia* or the
Pharmaceutical Codex 1979

Abortion

To bring about abortion:
Decoctions of rue, pennyroyal, fennel,
hemp or savin (P)

To prevent abortion:
Belladonna (P)

Rest (O)

'Take of pure laudanum 2 drachms, of
aromatic calamus, Armenian bole,
dragon's blood, sealed earth, lodestone,
red coral, pomegranate rind, each 1½
drachms, of acacia cytinus each ½
drachm, of naval pitch and gum arabic
each ½ ounce, of turpentine as much as
suffices to make a plaster.' (P)

Adder bite

Head of the same that bit, bruised and
lay'd to the place (P)

The flesh of the Adder, given
inwardly (P)

A piece of hazelwood, fastened in the
shape of a cross, should be laid softly on
the wound and the following lines
repeated 'blowing out the words aloud,
like one of the commandments:

Underneath this hazelin mote
There's a braggoty worm with a
    speckled throat
Nine double is he;
Now from nine double to eight
    double
And from eight double to seven
    double
And from seven double to six double'
And so on until:
'And from one double to no double
No double hath he.' (P)

Aging   For old age take a decoction of nettles
                   morning and evening. (P)

Ague   Take an infusion made of marigold
                   flowers. (P)

                   Apply with an ointment made from the
                   leaves of elder. (P)

                   As a preventive:
                   scratch the legs with a holly branch.
                   wear a dock root strapped to the thighes.
                   wear a bag containing grated horseradish
                   round the neck. (P)

                   To cure children:
                   let them wear a waistcoat into which
                   bark has been quilted. (P)

                   Catch a spider, cover it with dough (or
                   place in a small piece of apple) and take
                   as a pill. (P)

                   The snuff of candle bruised – a teaspoon
                   taken mixed with treacle or jelly at
                   night (M)

                   One drachm of [Jesuit's] Bark, ½ drachm
                   of Venice treacle, the juice of ½ lemon,
                   one glass of wine, all these mixed
                   together to be taken going to bed
                   supperless. Take it three nights then

omit and soon for nine nights in ten days. Repeat it again in the same manner. A vomit should be first given, 30 or 25 grains of epechcune for a grown person, 20 only for one about 15 or 18 years old. (M)

30 drops of Balsam of Peru in a gill of white wine or brandy and water, to be taken one hour before the [sic] is expected and to go to bed immediately. If it fails the first time to be repeated with five drops more and five more for the third time, when it is hardly even been known to fail. (M)

Take of olibanum matick and Bole armenice of each ½ oz finely powdered, mix it in 2 oz of Venice Turpentine. Put as much as will spread the breadth of a shilling on glove leather and lay on the pulse to the wrist 2 hours before the fit is expected. If the ague is not gone in a fortnight put on a fresh pair of plaister which hardly ever fails. If the patient will take a vomit before they put on the plaisters they will be likely to have a quicker effect from them. (M)

¾ oz Jesuites Bark, a spoonful of Black pepper, ground, a spoonful of Brown sugar, a nutmeg* powdered, syrup of poppies sufficient to make it into an electuary. Take the quantity of a nutmeg every 3 hours, night and day when fit is off. Leave it off by degrees. (M)

Wear the chips of gallows in a bag round the neck. (P)

Catch a shrew, bore a hole in an ash tree, insert the animal and plug it up alive. The ague disappears as the shrew dies. (P)

To be said up the chimney by the eldest
female of the family on St Agnes' Eve:
'Tremble and go!
First day shiver and burn,
Tremble and quack!
Second day shiver and burn
Tremble and die
Third day never return.' (P)

When Jesus went up to the cross to be
crucified the Jews asked him, saying,
'Art thou afraid, or hast Thou the ague?'
Jesus answered and said 'I am not
afraid, neither have I the ague.' All those
who hear the name of Jesus about them
shall not be afraid nor yet have the ague.
Amen, sweet Jesus, amen sweet
Jehovah. (P)

Eat nine sage leaves fasting, nine
mornings in succession or go to an old
willow tree and after making three knots
in one of the branches say:
Good morning, old one,
I give thee cold; Good morning, old
one. (P)

Drink an infusion of willow bark. (P)

Anaemia   Dandelion tea (O)

Apoplexy   When the patient is in a fit take a
                  handful of salt and put it into a pint of
                  cold water and pour it down the
                  patient's throat, when he will quickly
                  come to himself if he's not already
                  dead. (P)

Appetite   Hops and caraway seeds* if used in
                  the manner of tea are good for the
                  appetite. (P)

Asthma   Smoking stramonium (thornapple) a
                  species of wild apple to be procured at
                  the chemist prepared for the pipe. Begin

with sufficient only to fill the end of the tobacco pipe, a *common* one and a double proportion may afterwards be used and only(?) when suffering under great irritation in the throat. The perfume is very strong and disagreeable to some persons. It should therefore not be smoked in bedrooms. (M)

Drink a pint of cold water every morning, washing the head therein immediately afterwards, and take a cold bath every fortnight. (P)

Babies

Never cut a baby's nails. (O)

Always put the new born baby in a drawer other wise it is unlucky, even if there is a cot there. (O)

'Good nut year, good baby year.' (O)

Birthmarks depend on what you eat, or what you see while pregnant (O)

If two women handle the teapot, one will give birth to ginger twins. (P)

Squeezing milk into a baby's eyes prevents sticky eyes. (P)

A donkey's hair worn round the baby's neck makes teething easier. (P)

A baby weaned when the birds are migrating will have a restless temperament. (P)

New born babies should go up before they go down. (P)

The length of the umbilical cord, after cut, will indicate the length of the penis for a boy and the length of the tongue if a girl. (P)

Babies born with the cawl will never die by drowning.

Babies born with the cawl will have the gift of the gab. (O)

Never show a child under the age of one its reflection in a mirror. (O)

Children are blind till they are three months old.
Bright lights are harmful to babies. (O)

It is unlucky for a baby to cut the upper teeth before the lower. (O)

It is unlucky to name the child before its baptism. (O)

Bathe the new born baby in salt water, and make it taste it three times. (P)

Backache   A poultice made from hot linseed, hot nettle leaves and pancakes (O)

Make a poultice from hot Juniper oil. (O)

The plant, golden rod, used in the manner of tea is a simple remedy for back pains. (P)

Take an ox-gall, pour into one pint of alcohol and apply frequently. (P)

Baldness   Apply a poultice made of chicken manure. (O)

Rub the part night and morning with a decoction of boxwood. (P)

Rub the part of the head morning and evening with onions till it is red and rub it afterwards with honey. (P)

Bee stings   Apply a marigold. (O)

Biliousness   Take 1½ oz of Aloes, ½ oz of Mastic powder, these ingredients separately incorporated then add a sufficient

quantity of syrup of wormwood to make
them into a mass, make it into pills
3 grains in each. Great care must be
taken to prepare the aloes either with
juice of violets or strong tincture of
liquorice.* The latter is generally used.
One or two of the pills to be taken
everyday during dinner or supper for
3 months and afterwards occasionally.
Half the above quantity makes
150 pills. (M)

1oz Socotrine aloes* beat fine from
the lum, 1oz fine powder of rhubarb,*
30 grains Emetic Tartar. Mix well tog.,
soften with syrup of Buckthorn and add
1oz of shavings of castille soap. Beat the
whole well into a mass and divide into
400 pills. 1, 2 or 3 to be taken at tea
time. (M)

Infusion of senna, 3 drachms,
compound infusion of gentian
10 drachms, take in draught night and
morning. (M)
(Infusion of senna: 1½ oz of senna leaves
in a pt. of boiling water, infuse the
leaves 3 or 4 hours then strain it.
Compound infusion of gentian:
1 drachm gentian root, 1½ drachms of
diced orange peel, ½ oz fresh lemon
peel, ¾ pt boiling water. Infuse for
2 hours then strain it.) (M)

1 gra. of Ipecacuana, 2 grms rhubarb,
made up with a little ginger into one
pill, to be taken constantly every night
for bilious complaints. (M)

Hot water drunk before breakfast is a
good remedy for bilious complaints; or
bilious attacks are prevented by taking
one teaspoonful of black currant

preserves before breakfast. (P)

Bites
Gnat bites: apply a mixture of
Laudanum and lemon juice, equal parts
constantly to the part affected. (M)

Bite from a mad dog:
Wash wound well with water poured from
the spout of a tea kettle or pump and rub it
with a linen rag, tied upon a stick; when
dry, put upon the wound as much gunpowder as will prime a gun and set fire to it
immediately, after which treat as a
common burn or scald. (M)

Bleeding
Charm to staunch bleeding:
'A soldier of old thrust a lance into the
side of the saviour; immediately there
flowed thence blood and water, the
blood of Redemption and the water of
baptism. In the name of the Father +
may the blood cease. In the name of the
Son + may the blood remain. In the
name of the Holy Ghost + may no more
blood flow from the mouth, the vein or
the nose.' (P)

'Christ was born in Bethlehem,
Baptised in the river Jordan
The river stood
So shall they blood (name of person)
In the name of the Father (etc.) (P)

Repeat these words three times:
Stand fast; lie as Christ did
When he was crucified upon the cross;
Blood, remain up in the veins,
As Christ's did in all his pains. (P)

Apply cobwebs. (O)

Apply dung. (O)

Apply mouldy leather strap. (O)

Blisters

To prevent inflammation of the skin and blisters:
Put a bread poultice in a bag and lay it over the blister plaster one hour before you take it off. Keep the blister plaster on 2½ hours, afterwards dress the blister with a plaster of spermaceti ointment. (M)

Blood

To cleanse blood: nettles or valerian (O)

One ounce of horehound, one ounce of burdock, one ounce of hops, one ounce of gentian, five ounces ginger, two ounces spanish juice, to five gallons of water. Boil one hour, strain through a cloth, ferment 24 hours, then bottle. For every impurity of the blood, or to keep a person in sound health. (P)

For all impurities of the blood the hop used as tea cannot be too highly recommended. (P)

Boils

Draw to a head by applying a poultice of soap and brown sugar. (P)

Apply a lily leaf. (O)

Cream of tartar made into a drink with 15 drops of sweet nitre to each tea cupful. (P)

Bowels

For bowel complaints:
5 grm. of nutmeg,* 5do. of Ippicachuna (sic), 5 do. rhubarb,* mix and use for all scorbutic or languid habits. (M)

Breasts

Breast cancer is a spinster's disease. (O)

To cure breast cancer, get a toad, rub its back till it is moist, then rub on the affected breast, until the toad is dry and the warts shrunk to pimples. Return the toad and bind the breast with a houseleek. (P)

Breathing

For difficult breathing a teaspoonful of cod liver oil night and morning. (P)

Bruises

Dissolve as much salt in water as it will, about to the amount of ½ pint then add ½ pint of spirits of wines, cork it in a bottle to keep and wash the hurt as required. (M)

(of the eye):
2 drams Rose leaves infused in ½ pint boiling water – let it stand till cold, pour off the infusion into a bottle and add 20 grms sugar of lead – shake it up and bathe the eye 3 or 4 times a day. It will keep. (M)

White of an egg beat up with a tsp of water or brandy rubbed into the bruise every morning (O)

A gill of linseed oil, ½ oz of yellow bees wax simmered together (M)

1 scruple salt tartar and one do. cochineal to ½ pint of water and a little sugar (M)

A poultice of flour of oatmeal and vinegar applied cold and renewed every 5 or 6 hours till the inflammation is gone (M)

Apply a treacle and brown paper plaster. (P)

Apply a vinegar and brown paper plaster. (O)

Bugs

To drive away bugs put under the pillow a bag of celery seed, the bag to be of muslin. (O)

Burns

For a burnt finger, place on the ear lobe to take out the sting. (O)

Charm for a burn:
'As I passed over the River Jordan I met
with Christ and He said to me "Woman,
what aileth thee?" "O, my Lord, my
flesh doth burn." The Lord said unto
me "Two angels cometh from the West,
one for Fire, one for Frost, Out Fire, In
Frost." In the name of the Father
(etc.)' (P)

The Middle finger of the right hand to
be wetted in the mouth and gently
rubbed over the burn or scald, and
repeat:

> There came two angels from the
>   Lord;
> One brought fire and one brought
>   frost.
> Out of fire into frost
> Praise Father, Son and Holy Ghost. (P)

If the skin is not off, apply cold
water. (M)

A pound of Litherge of gold to a quart
oz rather more of vinegar – shake it
when it is to be used and pour as much
into a tea cup as will be requisite for the
case, add to it as much sweet oil as will
make an ointment which may be spread
on a rag. Repeat the application as often
as appears necessary. (M)

Cancer

A carrot finely grated and made into a
poultice is good for a cancer or ulcer,
which both lessens the pain and
diminishes the smell. (P)

Red clover tops, to be used in the
manner of tea. (P)

Boil Turkey figs (the newest are best) in
new milk; when boiled thoroughly split

and apply them as warm as can be borne to the part affected whether broken or not; which must also be washed several times a day with some of the milk the figs were boiled in; the figs must be applied fresh morning and night and once or twice a day besides binding them gently on for some time. A ¼ pt of the milk they are boiled in should be drunk morning and night and frequently during the day. The quantity of figs to be boiled must be proportioned to the place they are to cover and the use of this method steadily observed for 3 or 4 months. The first application will be attended with pain, but after that relief will be found from it. (M)

Chapped hands   Rub on goose grease. (P)

Wash them with a mixture of bran and milk or potato water. (O)

Chilblains   If not broken rub them with flower of mustard and brandy; if broken wash them with tincture of myrrh and a little water. (P)

Put hot cinders in urine, when sizzling place on the chilblain. (O)

Rub on onions or a banana skin. (O)

1 pound of elderflower picked in bud on a dry sunny day, 1 pound of pig's lard. Boil the flowers and the lard together for one hour and strain. (O)

Take nine eggs and boil them hard and take the yolks and throw the white away and grease the yolks in a pan and wring out the liquor through a cloth and take as many drops of wine as there are eggs and as many drops of unhallowed oil and as many drops of honey, and as many drops from the root of fennel; then take and put all together and ouse it out through a cloth and give to the sufferer to eat. (P)

Cholera

Should the cholera show itself in the district to prevent its attack take a teaspoonful of cinnamon in hot water frequently; or, this simple remedy for cholera has never been known to fail – first, give the patient hot water to cause vomiting, which cleanses the stomach. Next, toast an oat cake and put it in a pint of boiling water and drink freely. (P)

An infusion of ginger, say a teaspoonful in ½ pint of boiling water, let it stand a few minutes to deposit the sediment. Pour the liquor off and sweeten it to taste. This is highly beneficial in numerous instances and is a specific in all cases of weakness of the stomach. (M)

1 tsp Salvolatile, 30 drops tincture of opium, 2 do. tincture of Cardamus, Cinnamon water, one ha. spoonful. 2 tbs make a draught. (M)

Colds

Garlic prevents colds. (O)

Cut and wash the hair, and the cold will 'bleed' away. (O)

Camphor and water snuffed up the nose will cure a cold in the head instantly. (P)

Fill washbasin with boiling water and add an ounce of flour of mustard. Inhale. (P)

Pare the yellow rind from an orange very thin, roll it up inside out and put a roll up each nostril. (P)

Rub oil of rosemary on the chest (oil

made from kidney fat of ewes, rendered down and pound to a paste with rosemary leaves and flowers). (O)

To prevent a cold: 2 tsp of spirit of Mindeum, 1 do. of Salvolatile, and 5 drops of Laudanum in a wine glass of Camphor Julep. (M)

Camphor bags or vinegar honey and brown sugar. (O)

Gargle with hot water and salt – good for catarrh and sore throats also. (O)

Rub goose grease or tallow on brown paper and wrap round the chest. (O)

Leaves of maram or Herb mastick, marjoram, Lily of the Valley of each one dram, atarabacca leaves (?) powdered two drams; mix and make the snuff. (M)

Constipation   Stewed prunes. (O)

Mandrake (white bryony) pessaries. (P)

Compound extract of colocynth, ½ drachm, compound Galbanum pills ½ drachm, Jacobs powders, 6 grains, Mix and divide into 12 pills. Take 2 to 3 every other night. (M)

Camphorated mixture one oz, infusion of senna 3–4 drachms, Carbonate of Ammonia, 4–8 grains, Compound spirit of ether 30 drops. Mix – this draught to be taken twice a day. (M)

Consumption   Cut up a little turf and the patient, lying down, should breathe into the hole for a quarter of an hour each day. (P)

Boil an egg in the patient's own urine. Bury the egg in an ant-hill and as the egg washes away, so will the disease. (P)

Take a brasse pot, fill it with water, set it on the fire and put a great earthen pot within that pot and then put in these parcels following: Take a cock and pull him alive, then flea off his skin, then beat him in pieces. Take dates, a pound and slit out the stone, and lay a layer of them in the bottom of the pot and then lay a piece of the cock and upon that some more of the dates and take succory, endive, and parsley roots and so every layer one upon another, and put in fine gold and some pearl and cover the pot as close as may bee with coarse dow and so let it distill a good while and so reserve it for your use till such time as you have need thereof. (P)

Consumptive persons will derive great benefit by the free use of mullen leaves, which are to be had from any chemist; use one ounce to a pint of boiling water; when cold strain and add one tablespoon of rum to preserve it; take a wineglassful 3 times a day, which both rectifies and makes new blood . . . consumption may be arrested by the free use of lemons, ground ivy, the lesser centaury and camomile flowers in equal quantities, made in the manner of tea in a quart of boiling water. (P)

(Pulmonary) consumption – immediately to be rubbed with vinegar and water, ½ vinegar ½ water, with a bath, both to be well rubbed in with the hand, beginning with the throat, neck, back etc. . . The washing with vinegar will cure the patient and strengthen the patient. (M)

Contraception   Sneezing at orgasm prevents conception. (O)

Corns

Apply the juice of an apple or carrot and salt. (P)

1 tsp of tar, one ditto of brown coarse sugar and one ditto of saltpetre. The whole to be warmed together and spread on kid leather the size of the corn and in two days it will be drawn out. (M)

Macerate the foot for ½ hour 2 or 3 nights successively in a pretty strong solution of soda or lees of potash. (M)

Corpse

The smell from a corpse is prevented by placing fresh ground coffee in the chamber. (P)

To prevent the smell from a corpse, place an onion in its mouth. (O)

Coughs

½ pint of treacle, ½ do. vinegar, 100 drops of laudanum, an ounce bottle of Friars Balsam mixed together. For internal use. (M)

An ounce of Newcastle coal, boiled in a pinch of milk till reduced to ½ pint. A teacupful to be taken warm night and morning. (M)

A pennyworth of each of the following mixed together: oil of aniseed,* oil of peppermint,* Ipecacuanha wine, laudanum, Paragoric, liquorice,* ½ pound of black treacle dissolved in 1 pint of boiling water, add the above and also a quartern of best vinegar. 1 tbs for a dose. (M)

Drops of ipecacuanha wine on sugar. (O)

Juice of ½ lemon, 1 small tsp glycerine, 1 dsp honey. Fill glass of hot water, stir and drink. (O)

Make medicine from the top of a swede,

fill it with brown sugar and take it morning and drink. Refill the swede. (O)

Cut an onion in half, scoop out the middle, fill with brown sugar, leave till liquid and drink. (O)

2 pennyworth of lint seed to a quart of water. Let it simmer over a fire and put some slices of lemon into it. Sip off it often whether hot or cold. (M)

Take a calves pluck (intestine) hot out of the calf with all the Blood about it, cut it into slices and divide it into half, putting each half into a separate still, to each still put one handful of the following herbs: Balm, mint, oak langs (?), unset (?), Hyssop and red sage; then put into each still a gallon of new Milk boiling hot and when you have got out of each Still about 3 quarts it is enough. You may drink it with sugar as they do milk. Water both morning and evening and at any time of the Day: When dry it may also be drank at meals mixed with wine. NB The top of the still must be taken off 2 or 3 times that it may be well stirr'd to prevent a burning. (M)

Charm for a cough: (with remedy incorporated)
> For the cough take Judas ear
> With the parynge of a Peare
> And drink them without feare.
> If you will have remedie
> The syppes are for the hyckocke
> And six more for the chyckocke
> Thus my pretty pyckocke
> Recover by and by. (P)

Cramp

Wear the patella of a sheep or a lamb during the day and as near to the skin as possible. (P)

Place a wine cork in the pillow slip, to prevent night cramp. (O)

Wear a finger ring made from a coffin handle. (P)

Hold a little flour of sulphur in the hand. (P)

Put your shoes and stockings in the shape of a cross at bedtime. (O)

Place under the bed a basin of cold water, which will 'draw' the cramp away. (O)

Cuts
Apply a bruised geranium leaf; or powdered rice sprinkled on a cut or wound stops bleeding at once. (P)

Bind on a dry oakleaf or put on a bit of white paper moistened with spittle. This also cures a cut. (P)

Apply lily leaves in brandy. (O)

Apply grated sugar. (O)

Get the dog to lick it clean. (O)

Dandruff
Make a solution of borax and use as a wash. (P)

Deafness
Put black wool in the ears as a preservative from deafness. (P)

Deafness, if it can be cured at all, is by equal parts of the oil of cloves, the juice from the foxglove flower and rum dropped on a little cotton and placed in the ears; or hot water used as a syringe with a pinch of carbonate of soda in. (P)

Death
When a cold dew falls on the skin of an invalid it is a sign that death is near. (O)

When the invalid picks at the blankets it

is a sign that death is near. (O)

No one can die on a feather bed. (O)

Debility and scurvy

1oz burnt sponge – pour upon it 1¼ pt boiling water. When cold strain it through filtered paper, take the solution thus strained and ½ oz of balm proply (sic) powdered and boil them 10 minutes and before it is cold, pour it off the dregs for use. Take 4 tablespoons 3 times a day adding to each dose one teaspoon of spirit of nutmeg.* (M)

½ pound treacle, 2oz cream of tartar, 2oz sulphur, take a teaspoon night and morning. (M)

Depression

Marigold tea is good for depression. (P)

Valerian, motherwort, yarrow tea are good for depression. (P)

The best comforter for a depressed or desponding mind is equal parts of agrimony and rosemary made and used in the manner of tea. (P)

Diabetes

Take a pint of new milk, put to it a quarter of an ounce of alom (?) powdered, boil and strain it from the curd, take a quarter of a wine pint of this whey every morning and night till you are well. (M)

Avoid sugar and prepare the following: peruvian bark, colomba root, summach berries and the plant known as queen of meadows, one ounce each; boil in 3 pints of water down to one quart and take a wineglassful 4 times a day. (P)

Diarrhoea

Powdered acorns, ½ oz rhubarb,* ½ oz ginger, ½ oz cinnamon, mixed in peppermint* water. If attended with much pain take 15 drops of laudanum in one of the doses which is one tablespoon as often as is required. (M)

Take raspberry leaf tea or flour and water. (O)

Digestion

One ½ pt. bottle of Right Acid Juice of Tar, prepared in Painter's Court, 5 doors from Jermyn St. 2 large tsp full in a gill of water may be taken nights and mornings and if you please an hour before dinner. (M)

36 gr. powdered rhubarb,* 48 gr. carbonate of soda, 12 gr. powdered ginger, 30 gr. castille soap, 5 drops oil of caraway,* syrup enough to form a mass – to be divided into 30 pills, 2 or 3 to be taken daily one hour before dinner. (M)

Nutmeg* aids digestion. (P)

Diphtheria

Cured by drinking the best olive oil freely. (P)

Distemper

Take one ounce of Jullips, 2oz Gamboge (?), 1oz nitre, 1oz of Aithiopothinerals (?), castille soap, a sufficient quantity to make them into a Ball. A piece to be given the size of a nut. (M)

Dizziness

For dizziness in the head drink sage tea sweetened to taste. (P)

Dropsy

Take of Broom Seed well powdered and sifted one drachm, let it steep 12 hours in a glass and a half of good rich white wine and take it in the morning, fasting, having first shaken it so that the whole may be swallowed. Walk after it, if you are able, or use what exercise you can without fatigue, for an hour and a half; after which you must be sure to take 2oz of olive oil; and you must not eat or drink any thing in less than ½ hour or an

hour after taking the oil. Repeat this
every other day or once in three days
and not oftener, till cured; and do not
let blood or use any other remedy
during the course. (M)

Drink 5 or 6 quarts of cider every day
for several weeks. (P)

1 pound of Julup in powder, 1 pound of
cream of tartar, one ounce of Arminian
Bole(?) in fine powder. Mix them all
together – the dose is from 30–40 grains
in broth or warm beer taken at bedtime.
It may be taken 2 or 3 successive nights
or longer if required. Good for the
watery or windy dropsy, provided the
patient has never been tapped. Very
valuable. (M)

Foxglove* and broom in small
quantities, make in the manner of tea.
Persevere with a wine glass full three
times a day. (P)

A decoction of the inside bark of the
elm, drunk freely, takes away water in
dropsy. (P)

earache

Take elder flowers, camomile flowers, St.
John's bark, Gentrey (Centre of?)
Mallowes, of each a handful, ½ oz of
anniseed boil^d in a quart of milk. Put it
in a jug and hold the steam to the
ear. (M)

Rub the ear well with a dry flannel. (P)

The ear should be bathed with a strong
decoction of camomile flowers and
poppy heads, as warm as it can be
borne. (P)

Boil a cockroach in oil and stuff it into

the ear. (P)

Place a clove of onion in the ear. (O)

Place drops of almond oil* in the ear. (O)

Epilepsy   The leaves of mistletoe, dried and made into an infusion. (P)

Wear on the fourth finger of the left hand a ring moulded by a silversmith from small pieces of coins, brooches, buckles, spoons, collected from 9 or 11 friends of the opposite sex to that of the patient. (P)

Take one ounce of mistletoe, valerian root, pellitory and black horehound, boil in 3 pints of water, clear off and when cold add one ounce of tincture of scullop. Dose – a wineglass-full four times a day. Used with good effect. (P)

Powder of man's bones, burnt, especially if it is made from a skull found in the earth. (P)

Gasper with his myrrh beganne
The presents to unfold
Then Melchior brought frankincense
And Balthasar brought gold,
Now he that of these holie kings
The names about shall beare
The fallyng ill by Grace of Christ
Shall never need to feare. (P)

Erysipelas   Well known deathly complaint, can be cured with 2 sprigs of wormwood, a quarter of an ounce of senna and a quarter of an ounce of camomile flowers to a pint of boiling water and drink freely. (P)

Excitement   The common meadow plant, Ladies' slipper, used as tea is good for spasms, hysteria, cramps, nervous headache, fits, neuralgia, hypochondria, fevers, colic, debility etc and wherever it is required to quiet the nervous system, is safer than opium and will act where opium fails. (P)

Exhaustion   An infusion of mugwort. (P)

Eyes   For weak eyes bathe them in cold water with a few drops of vinegar in it. (O)

For sore or tired eyes, a cold tea poultice. (O)

½ tsp of elderflower water and a tsp of Brandy and a tsp white vinegar. If it smarts, wash with water. (M)

1 grain of sulphate of zinc to each ounce of rose water (very good). (M)

3 grains of powdered alum in 2oz of water (M)

1 tbs of vinegar to ½ pt of water, the vinegar to be strained through muslin. (M)

3 grains of white vitrol to 5 tbs of rose water – an excellent receipt for inflammation of the eyes. (M)

Speedwell is good for the eyes. (O)

Hyssop, used as a bath, acts as a speedy cure for black eyes. (P)

Female disorders   An infusion of motherwort. (P)

Steel, quinine and pennyroyal pills answer for irregularities, hysteria, headache, costiveness, loss of appetite, pains, lassitude etc, sold at 7½d per bottle. (P)

Southernwood if used as tea is of great advantage for female complaints. (P)

To increase fertility, take mistletoe. (P)

Fever

4 oz of Nitre (?), 1 drachm Camphor, 30 grains of Saffron, 4 grains of Cochineal, all powdered and well mixed together. Keep it dry and close corked in a bottle, 10 grains or a small tsp every night till the fever is reduced. The best way of taking it is to put it in a spoon and just moisten it with water, put it far back on your tongue and drink a sip of water. (M)

Take an infusion of marigold. (P)

To burn rosemary in the rooms clears fever away; yet, if there be a spiders web in the house, the fever will linger in it. (P)

On attending fever cases, or any sick person wash the mouth, nostrils and hands with vinegar on leaving the sick room. (P)

Charm for a fever:
I forbid the quacking fevers, the sea fevers, the land fevers and all the fevers that ever God ordained; out of the head, out of the heart, out of the back, out of the sides, out of the knees, out of the thies (sic). Free the points of the fingers to the nebs of the toes. Out sail the fevers, go some to the ill, some to the hope, some to the stone, some to the stock. In St. Peter's name, St. Paul's name, and all the saints of heaven. In the name of the Father, Son and Holy Ghost. (P)

Fistulas

So painful, which to save the knife operation use Epsom salts and vegetable food freely; wash mussel shells, these burn to powder, sift them very fine and mix with lard spread on a wash leather, this apply night and morning which if persevered with, has cured the worst cases. (P)

Fits

Get a live mole, cut the tip off its nose, let 9 drops bleed on to a lump of sugar and give it to the patient. (P)

Those subject to fainting or other fits should use plenty of salt and water inwardly and outwardly; or, they will find great benefit by placing the feet in hot water up to the ankles. (P)

Flush

3oz mutton kidney meat shred very fine, add a tbs best starch boil them well together in a quart of milk till it is reduced to near a pint. Let a teacupful of this be taken warm 3 or 4 times a day. (M)

1 drachm of the seeds of Plantin (Sic) bruise them and take them in a draught of broth (which is best if a little tops of plantin be boiled with it) in the morning fasting; and continue it 3 mornings fasting. It never fails. (M)

Freckles

2 spoonfuls of fresh cream into half pint of new milk, squeeze into it juice of a lemon, add quarter glass of eau de cologne a little alum and some loaf sugar, boil, skim and bottle when cool. Wipe face every morning with this. (P)

Take two drachms of borax, one drachm of Roman alum, one drachm of camphor, half an ounce of sugar candy and one quart of ox-gall mix and stir well together, repeat the stirring three or four times a day, until the mixture becomes transparent; strain it through a filtering paper. Wash face with this before bed. (P)

Freezing

For a patient frozen: if a part be frozen and it is discovered before a person comes into a warm room the part may be exhacted (?) by plunging the part in cold water or rubbing it with snow till circulation returns and if this precaution has not been taken and the part be so frozen as to turn black and endanger the mortification all ill consequences may be prevented by covering the part with goose grease and never suffering it to get dry: by degrees the circulation will return and the blackness decrease till the person quite recovers. (M)

Gathering

When a gathering threatens a finger etc. dip it in scalding water. (O)

Goitre

15 nettle seeds, bruised into a powder and taken daily will cure goitre. (P)

Gout

For gout, bind the plant ground ash on the afflicted part. (P)

Boil 2 poppy seeds with 2ozs of Camomiles in 3 pts of water, until reduced to 1 quart then mix as much linseed meal with some of the liquor as will make a stiff poultice then add a small juice of lemon (?) to each poultice which must be applied quite hot. (M)

For the gout in the stomach
Take snake root, saffron, seville orange – of each an equal quantity, beat them in a mortar with a little brandy and as much fine sugar as will make a conserve. Take the quantity of an horse bean when you feel the pain in the stomach. (M)

Steep a piece of linen in salted water and apply it to the painful part. (P)

Gravel (or stone) No acids, no spirits allowed, neither high living; milk diet attend to. (P)

A decoction from the root called Best Harrow – after washing the roots as clean as may be from dirt without scraping the rind, slice 4 ounces of it into a gallon of water which is to be boiled till wasted to 3 quarts; then, drain it off and drink of it, when made as warm as milk from the cow, a pint and half in a day. (M)

Take of the pods of the Horse Bean, 10 or 12 either green or dry put them into a tea pot and pour thereon about ½ pint of boiling water, let it stand about ¼ hour, then pour it off and drink about ½ pint a day warm and sweetened to your liking. (M)

Drink freely on agrimony tea, sweetened with sugar candy; or, a little garlic extract, taken in brandy, is a cure for gravel, or take a teaspoonful of magnesia 3 times a day. (P)

Put a whole hare, skin and all, in an earthen ware pot close stopped and bake in an oven to dry so that it can be made into a powder, being given in white wine. (P)

Graze Plantain leaves, hit with back of a knife and apply. (O)

Hair *Pills for a hair complaint:*
1oz of Hiasapina (or Aiasapina?)
1oz Socotrine aloes powdered fine
1oz Castille soap
½ oz best powder of Rhubarb
14 oz best magnesia
– the soap to be scraped and mixed with

water till it becomes a paste. (M)

To free the hair from dandruff wash the head with hot water and a little borax in it occasionally. (P)

If hair is falling off, apply the lotion made from vinegar of cantharides half an ounce, Eau de Cologne one ounce, rose water one ounce. First well brush the hair. Vaseline ointment is also a good restorative. (P)

When the hair falls off, damp it frequently with sage tea; or equal parts of rosemary, boxwood and marshmallow to a quart of boiling water, and when cold use as a bath.

Rum applied to the hair keeps it exceedingly clean and promotes its growth more than oil or anything known. (P)

Hair dye:
The simplest hair dye is the shells of green walnuts boiled in as much water as will cover them, strain off and apply to the hair only, and a beautiful brown or auburn is the result. (P)

Headache

Fix around the head a halter with which one had been hanged. (P)

Moss, found growing on a human skull, dried and powdered and taken as snuff. (P)

Bathe the forehead and temples with hot water in which mint or sage has been added. (O)

Soak the feet in a hot mustard bath. (O)

Cured by grains of paradise, used as snuff. (M)

Nutmeg answers for violent headache, to be used in a little water, or one thimblefull of whisky rubbed sharply in the hands and held to the nose, cures headache at once, or mix one drachm of sweet nitre, one drachm of sal volatile and two drachms of carbonate soda, in a tea cupful of cold water; 2tbs to be taken three times a day. (P)

Pipe tobacco smoke, inhaled. (O)

Woodlice, taken as a pill, are good for headaches. (O) (P)

Apply vinegar and brown paper to the head. (O)

Health

One tbs of lime water taken in a little milk in a morning keeps a person in good health; or to look well and keep well, simply boil one pennyworth of watercress in ten minutes in one pint of water, the water to be drunk in milk in equal parts; to each cupful add one tablespoon of lime water and the best of health is the result. (P)

Heart

'Drink of black henis aiges and aquavite to sundrie persons that had the hert aikandes.' (P)

Lily of the valley, or mistletoe. (P)

Heart disease is greatly relieved by taking a tbs of whisky in a little milk. (P)

Avoid steps or stairs as much as possible. One teaspoonful of salvolatile, taken in a wineglass of water, is a most excellent remedy. (P)

Take eight drops of oil of carraway on a little lump of sugar. (P)

An infusion of the leaves of foxglove.* (O)

Hiccup	Hiccup is speedily cured by placing the fingers in the ears whilst drinking freely of cold water, or take a pinch of snuff. (P)
	Drink a glass of water backwards. (O)
Hoarseness	Hoarseness is speedily cured by placing a piece of sugar candy in the mouth before going to bed. (P)
Humour in the mouth	Of white vitriol, alum, Bol ammoniac, each equal quantities. Camphor – a fourth part. Powder all very fine then put as much as will lie on a shilling to a pint of boiling water, keep it close stopped till cold, then strain it for use. Use it as often as occasion requires and rub'd well on the part except an hour before or after eating. (M)
Hysteric fits	A cold bath with an ounce of quicksilver every morning and 15 drops of elixir of vitriol in the afternoon. (P)
	The smell of spirits of hartshorn is good for those subject to hysteric fits or a drowsy feeling. (P)
Incontinence	*To avoid*: Dandelions make you wet the bed. (O)
Indigestion	Rise early and eat a crust of bread about the size of your thumb. (P)
	A little Turkey rhubarb* chewed in the forenoon. (P)
	Mix one drachm of powdered colomba root, one drachm of ground ginger and half a drachm of carbonate of soda; this divide into twelve powders and take one in a little milk three times a day; or, one pennyworth of colomba root to a pint of boiling water is a most excellent and

cheap remedy for indigestion. Take a wineglassful three times a day. (P)

Infection

Infection first attacks the stomach. Remember whilst in a sick room do not swallow your spittle in a case of fever; on retiring wash hands in a little vinegar and water. (P)

An infusion against infection (plague or distemper)
Take rue, sage, mint, rosemary, wormwood and lavender a handful of each. Infuse them together in a gallon of white wine vinegar, put the whole into a stone pot closely covered up and passed over the cover, set the pot thus closed upon warm wood ashes for 8 days after which draw off or strain through fine flannel the liquor and put into bottles well corked and into every quart bottle put a ¼ oz of camphire. With this preparation wash your mouth and rub your loins and temples every day, sniff a little up your nostrils when you go into the air and carry about with you a bit of sponge dipped in the same in order to smell upon all occasions especially when you are near any place or person that is infected. (M)

Infertility

Drinks made from mistletoe will cure it. (Hence, a kiss under the mistletoe.) (P)

Inflammations

Clothes wrung out in very hot water and applied to the neck, changed as often as they begin to cool, is the best for removing inflammation ever tried. (P)

Influenza

Carbonate of Potash – 1 drachm
Nitrate of Potash – 12 grains
Infusion of senna – 2 ounces
Rose water – 2 ounces
Syrup of poppies – 2 drachms

To be mixed together and take
2 tablespoons with 1 tablespoon of
lemon juice whilst in a state of
effurescence every 4 hours. (very
good) (M)

Take 10 drops of elixir of vitriol in a
little water twice a day. (P)

Influenza runs its course in five or eight
days. Diet of beef tea, with raw eggs and
milk answers better than medicine. (P)

Insanity

Remedy in cases of Partial Insanity:
Expressed juice of Ground Ivy and
Asafoedita pills. 3 tablespoons of ground
ivy juice to be taken every morning,
fasting and pill every evening. (M)

Itch (ringworm)

Sulphur baths. (P)

Coal tar.* (P) (O)

Jaundice

A quarter pound of Venice soap, made
into moderate sized pills with eighteen
drops of the oil of aniseed; three of
these pills to be taken night and
morning.
A sudden shock will cause jaundice. (P)

*The following are good for jaundice and liver
complaints*:
Celandine (P)
Dandelion (O)
Nettles (O)
Sarsaparilla (O)
Juniper (P)

Fill a bladder with the patient's urine
and place near a fire. As the urine dries
up, so the jaundice will go. (P)

Kidney

The following are good for the kidney (and bladder)
Broom (P)
Dandelion (O)
Marshmallow (P)
Parsley (O)
A decoction of the leaves of plantain (P)

Nettle beer – boil the leaves, strain through muslin, ferment. Add honey or brown sugar, cloves, ginger root for flavour. (O)

Drink equal parts of lime water and pearl barley water, take a teacupful three times a day; or, lemon water mixed with salts is good for diseased kidneys – take a wineglassful in the morning; or, comfrey acts on the kidneys direct, to be used in the manner of tea. (P)

Labour

A charm for an easy deliverance:
'Thus said Christ: I received 102 blows on the mouth from the Jews in the Court, and 30 times was I struck in the garden. I was beaten on head, arm and breast 40 times, on shoulders and legs 30 times; 30 times was my hair plucked and I sighed 127 times. My beard was pulled 72 times and I was scourged with 6,666 strokes. A thousand blows were rained on my head with the reed, smiting the thorny crown. 73 times was I spat in the face and I had in my body 5,475 wounds. From my body flowed 30,430 blood drops. All who daily say seven Our Fathers and seven Hail Maries, till they have made up the number of my blood drops, shall be relieved of pain in childbirth. (P)

Midwives' prayer:
Mark each corner of the house with a

cross and before crossing the threshold, and repeat:

> There are four corners to her bed
> Four angels at her head:
> Matthew, Mark, Luke and John;
> God bless the bed that she lies on.
> New moon, new moon, God bless me.
> God bless this house and family. (P)

Herbs for an easy delivery:
Raspberry leaf tea, sage, dandelion, tansy. (O) (P)

For a difficult labour:
Borax very finely powdered 1 dram in Mugwort or Savin water 4 ounces or in some strong wine, or some opening decoction or mixed with an ounce of syrup of mugwort (P)

Liver of an eel, given in powder (P)

Belladonna* (P)

To stop excessive bleeding:
Basil, beet, Holy Rose, Dead nettle, Lesser Periwinkle, greater plantain, Savin, Shepherd's purse, silverweed, Yarrow. (P)

For cleansing the mother:
Make a suppository of cotton and anoint it with turpentine. (P)

The midwife to announce the confinement to the husband and threaten a transfer of labour pains. (P)

To speed delivery and expulsion of the placenta:
Ergot.* (P)

Lactation

Horseradish applied to the breast prevents excessive lactation. (O)

Lactating mothers should not put their

hands in cold water, otherwise they will lose their milk. (O)

Bathe breasts alternately with hot or cold water. (O)

Seethe mint in wine and oil and lay upon the teats in a plaster (for painful lactation). (P)

To prevent ephemeral fevers while lactating, wear around the neck blue woollen threads or cords. The cords are better inherited from your mother – and the older they are, the greater their powers. (P)

Lances

Take a common mercurial appelliant (?). Abstain from salt meat and use a thin diet – twice a day between meals drink about ¼ pint of juice of chives, which is got by pounding and squeezing them, take some of the juice, boiled and mixed with hog's lard, so as to make a very soft ointment and apply it constantly to wound, laying also the bruised chives onto it and to refresh it as often as it drys, taking particular care to keep the wound clean – this was continued 6 months – the benefit will be gradual – in 3 months more the wound was perfectly healed. Take the juice spring and fall. (M)

Take a cupful of bepel (?) newly mixed (?) and the inside (an essential circumstance). Pour in a certain quantity of wine oil, boil it over a small fire so as to keep it gently agitated. Do so 3 times in 24 hours – the oil will become the consistency of ointment. Rub the part affected for about 14 days. (M)

One part of used (?) lead, 2 parts of

Hog's lard, mixed together. Spread it on lint twice a day. (M)

Lice and nits   Apply rosemary salve. (O)

Liver complaints   Boil gently a quarter of a pound of stone brimstone in a quart of water, when cold bottle it, and take wineglassful twice a day —those subject to this complaint could have no better remedy; or, another active remedy for liver complaint is dandelion coffee, simply made from the dried root, roasted and ground, and used the same as coffee. (P)

Enlarged liver
Enlargement of the liver is dangerous. If the disease is severe the diet should be of the simplest; drink nothing very hot and make free use of stewed prunes for a fortnight. (P)

Sluggish liver
Equal parts of hops and dandelion tea is a cure for a sluggish liver, to be used as tea. (P)

Lumbago   Apply crushed linseed on brown paper, which has a wonderful effect. (P)

Lungs   Plenty of fresh air is most important. (O)

Iceland moss or seaweed made into a jelly with boiling water and sweetened with sugar candy is good for diseased lungs; or, the free use of sugar is good for diseased lungs. (P)

When damaged lungs should reach an inveterate cough the best healing remedy will be found in equal parts of cod liver oil and syrup of horehound, two pennyworth of each, with one drachm of paregoric and the juice of a lemon, shake all well up and take a tablespoon twice a day. (P)

Madness
Causes of madness:
Mandrake (O) (P)
Stamonium or Solanum Manicum (P)
Belladonna (O) (P)

Melancholy
For melancholy, stupor and insanity:
Expulse juice of ground ivy and
asafoetida pills – 3tbs of juice every
morning fasting and one pill every
evening. At their expiration 9 days a
patient was restored to health and
continued so ever after. (M)

Memory
For a bad memory, drink sage tea,
sweetened to taste. (P)

Menstruation
Menstruating women should never salt
pigs. (O)

Menstruating women must never enter a
dairy or the butter will not churn/the
cream will not rise/the cheese will not
set. (O)

If you wash your hair while
menstruating, you will get brain
fever. (O)

Menstruating women should not put
their feet in cold water, or even their
hands, in case it 'sent the blood to your
head.' (O) (P)

Menstruating women should not go
swimming. (O)

Miscellaneous
Aperient draught
Infusion of senna, 10 drams
Tincture of do. 4 do.
Sulphate of Magnesium, 4 do.
Oil of peppermint,* 1 drop
To be taken night and morning. (M)

Good Friday Loaf
Good Friday bread, a small quantity of
this dried, grated and given to the

patient will work when all other
remedies fail (P)

Herb snuff
Leaves of maram or Herb mastick,
majoram, Lily of the Valley of each
one dram, atarabacca leaves (?) powdered
two drams; mix and make the snuff.

Hops
Less medicine would be used if the
value of hops were more known. Use a
quarter of an ounce to a pint of boiling
water, and all the better with a
teaspoonful of Epsom salts in it; take a
wineglassful in the morning which will
not only restore but will keep anyone in
the best of health at little expense. (P)

Hot water
Hot water is a medicine within the reach
of everyone and if taken with a little salt
in it is one of the best gargles for
catarrhal troubles and if taken at the
beginning of a cold will break it up;
used as a gargle for sore throat no better
remedy need be which stays
inflammation; when the stomach is out
of order, hot water will soon set it right
again, such simple cures are neither far
to seek nor ill to find. Half a cupful as
hot as can be drunk comfortably taken
half an hour before every meal is a great
preventive for indigestion; or, if used
with the food will assist the stomach to
do its works well. It is good for
constipation if the use of it is followed
for a few months, works wonders with
the most delicate constitutions. Use hot
water and lemons for a bilious liver. (P)

Imbrocation
    2oz of Samphire (Camphor?)

1 pound spirits of wine.
Put them into a quart bottle filled up
with Bullocks gall and it will be fit for
use in 20 hours. (M)

Invalids' food
Slippery elm is invaluable food for
invalids or delicate persons – good for
inward or outward application for any
complaint. Some families feed their
infants with it and finer infants need not
be sought. Simply mix one teaspoonful
of elm with one teaspoonful of sugar
add a little milk to make it into a
smooth paste, then add hot water,
stirring quickly, till it becomes a proper
consistency. (P)

Lavender water (disinfectant)
   1 pint of best spirits of wine
   One shilling worth of oil of lavender*
   Sixpennyworth of essence of Amber
   grease
Shake them well together let them stand
all Night – put it in small bottles tied
down close. (M)

Laxative
One teaspoon of Brewer's yeast at
bedtime. (O)

Mandrake
Its properties for exciting the liver to
healthy action have few equals; good for
biliousness, dropsies, venereal, whites,
piles, gravel, jaundice, scrofula, impure
blood, rheumatism, pneumonia, croup,
sore eyes. In root or powder. The
chemist will tell what quantity to take.
4d an ounce. (P)

Medicine
Take the roots of elecampane florentine
orrice, liqerice [sic] of Tallop each an

ounce, seeds of anise of carraway each an
ounce, stoned raisins of the best, senna
each 4oz, best aniseed water 2 quarts.
Digest them 12 days pour it off, strain it
and take 4 spoonfuls at night going to
bed and as much more the next
morning. (M)

Restorative medicine: Extract of Bark,
powder of Green Alibanum, white
ambers prepared Myrrh in powder, of
each 4 grains, oil of mint one drop – a
small quantity of any syrup to make
them into 4 pills. This is one dose to be
repeated twice a Day. (M)

Mustard plaster

In making a mustard plaster, mix with
the mustard the white of an egg, instead
of water, which will not blister the most
tender skin. (P)

Oak

A decoction made from the oak is good
to use as a wash for offensive ulcers,
putrid sore throats, bleeding piles and
bloody flux. (P)

Ointment

The best ointment is made from cream
buried a day or two in a cloth in the
garden.

Pills

The best pills are made from equal parts
of bitter aloes, Turkish rhubarb, and
senna leaves, dried in the oven and
rubbed to powder; these to be mixed in
a little whisky to form a paste.

Pills (said to be Holloway's): aloes
36 grains, jalap 18 grains, myrrh
18 grains, all in fine powder, mix and
make into pills. (M)

Purge

Purging flax is a plant to use as a safe

and excellent purge. (P)

Senna tea or brimstone and treacle. (O)

Quinine
Quinine is a very valuable drug, yet the bark from the young twigs of oak well dried answers as well, used in the manner of tea. (P)

Rhubarb*
Dr Combes tincture of rhubarb: Rhubarb fluid 1½ ounce, virginian snake root Ledoary (?) bruised, coriander seed of each one dram. Salt of wormwood ½ dram. Steep all in a quart of mountain white wine close stoped for 8 days then strain and keep it close stoped [sic]. Take 5 spoonfuls (more or less) as you find it operates in a morning fasting and repeat the same as you find occasion one or 2 spoonfuls in a dose for a child. (M)

Roses
Compound infusion of roses (½ pint to be made): 1 drachm of dried Rose leaves, 40 drops of diluted sulphuric acid, 3 drachms of white sugar, ½ pint of water (boiling). Pour the boiling water upon the leaves in a bag then add the acid, let them infuse during one hour, stirring now and then with a glass rod or find a stick/bark with a metallic influence (?). Strain off the liquid and add the sugar afterwards. (M)

The rose mixture: 4 grains of Sulphate of Quinine, ½ pint of Infusion of Roses. To be mixed. 2 large tablespoons at each time twice or thrice a day. Syrup of poppies is liable to ferment – 10 drops of Laudanum may be used instead and one dram of sugar add to the above ½ pint mixture. (M)

Styptic
For a styptic: lint and brandy with common stinging nettle pounded to a paste in a mortar, bound on the part for 24 hours. (M)

Tonic
To each parcel of bruised Peruvian Bark put a pint of water. Boil for 10 minutes in a closely covered vessel then strain the liquor whilst hot and the compound tincture of laudanum to be added and directed upon the label of the phial – about a wine glassful of this tonic mixture should be given twice or thrice a day. A saline draught ought to be given occasionally whilst taking the bark. (M)

Mortification
Apply a poultice of flour and marshmallow water, sweetened well with brown candy, to which add a little yeast. (P)

Dust the part with lump, sugar or a little blue stone. (P)

Mouth
For a sore mouth apply the white of an egg, beaten in vinegar and lump sugar. (P)

Mouthwash:
To a quart of spring water, gr. of an oz of Boll-Allmaneck (?), ½ oz myrrh, qr.pd. currants, piece of alom, as big as a wallnut, boil these till a qr of a pint is wasted. When taken off the fire strain it through a sieve, put into it ½ pt red wine and 2 spoonfulls of honey. Warm it, when you wash your mouth. (P)

Mumps
Keep the head and face warm and guard against taking cold. Should the tumour on the neck suddenly disappear, its

return must be promoted by warm fomentations. To abate the fever take of nitrate of potass 1 drachm, tartarised antimony 1½ grains. Mix together, divide into 6 powders, one to be taken every four hours. (P)

Take the child to a river, cross the river and bend lips to drink. Do this three times. (P)

Nerves

To strengthen:
A diet of pea meal and treacle. (P)

Nervousness:
Nervous people will find that sage and thyme, used as tea, will give them relief. (P)

Nervous debility:
Nervous debility and palpitation is greatly relieved by mixing two drachms of chloric ether two drachms of tincture of gentian, two drachms of sal volatile, two grains of iodine of potassium to each half pint of cold water (first boiled) take a tablespoon 3 times a day. (P)

Neuralgia

Wear well pounded brimstone on the sole of the foot contrary to the pain side. (P)

Cayenne, sprinkled on hot flannels, affords instant relief to persons troubled with neuralgia. (P)

Very hot hops applied in a bag. (P)

Nosebleeds

Wear round the neck a skein of scarlet silk tied with 9 knots down the front. Male patients should be decorated by a female and vice versa. (P)

Place a cold key down the back. (O)

Nettle juice, steeped on a little lint and put up the nostrils will stay bleeding of the nose. (P)

Pain

A bag of hot moist bran gives relief. (P)

Thorn apple – cut off the top of the fruit in the green stage, pulp the inside, add a teaspoon of vinegar and inhale the fumes. (P)

Pain in the back
Take from 15 to 20 drops of oil of turpentine in a little peppermint; or flannels wrung out in hot water and sprinkled with turpentine and applied gives immediate relief. (P)

Palpitations

When very troublesome take 8 drops of oil of carraway on a little lump of sugar and use the stairs or steps as little as possible. (P)

A drink of cold water with a pinch of salt in it. (P)

Perspiring feet

The odour can be removed by sprinkling bran or oatmeal in the socks frequently. (P)

Piles

The herb pilewort, either applied to the place in an ointment or taken inwardly. (P)

Take a large handful of red nettles (red hemp nettle) and infuse in a quart of white wine in a jug on a hot hearth for 1 hour. Let the patient take a wineglassfull 2 or 3 times a day. (M)

Pile ointment should be made from two ounces of lard, one pennyworth of opium, half an ounce of gall; these mix and apply night and morning for a cure. (P)

Apply gall ointment at night and take one tsp of electuary of senna at the same time. (P)

Pimples

Every blotch or pimple speedily disappears by taking flour of sulphur before breakfast. (P)

Pins and needles

When you have pins and needles in your feet, bend down and make the sign of the cross on the toe of your shoe. (P)

Plague

To prevent the plague: Eat marigold flowers daily as salad with oil and vinegar. Or infuse rue, sage, mint, rosemary and wormwood, of each a handful, in 2 quarts of sharpest vinegar over warm embers for 8 days, strain it through flannel and add ½ ounce of Camphor dissolved in 3 ounces of rectified spirits of wine. With this wash the legs, face and mouth and sniff a little up the nose when you go abroad. Smell of a sponge dipped therein when you approach infected persons or places. (P)

Plague water: for smallpox surfeit and other diseases. 3 pints of Balmsey (?) or Muskadine (?), boil them in red sage and rue, of each a handful till reduced to 2 pints –strain it on the fire again, put to it a ¼ ounce long pepper, ½ ounce of ginger, ¼ ounce of nutmeg – beaten to a powder, let them boil a little then put to them 2½ drachms Mithridate 1 drachm benice (sic) treacle, ¼ pint angelica water, take it always warm in a morning fasting and in the evening if you be infected – a spoonful or two and sweat – if not one spoonful a day will do – half in the morning and half when you go to bed. (M)

Wear a dried toad on the chest – this is

supposed to draw out all poisons and is a precaution against the plague. (P)

Pleurisy

Take ½ drachm of soot. Or take out the core of an apple, stop it close with white frankincense and close with the piece you took out. Then roast it in ashes, mash it and eat it. (P)

Pleurisy is cured by the use of elder flowers used in the manner of tea. To be had from any chemist; or take seven drops of laudanum in a little cold water on going to bed. (P)

Pregnancy

If a pregnant woman sees a hare, the child will have a hare lip. (O)

Pickled onions give birthmarks if eaten while pregnant. (O)

Heartburn in pregnancy means the baby will have a lot of hair. (O)

Heartburn means a girl. (O)

Take bicarbonate of soda to ensure a boy child. (P)

Any bleeding in pregnancy will result in a deformed child. (P)

If the membranes rupture early, labour will be prolonged. (P) (O)

Do not stretch when pregnant or the cord will go round the baby's neck. (O)

If you see a snake when pregnant, the baby will have green eyes. (P)

Lose a tooth for every child you bear. (O)

A pregnant woman must eat for two. (O)

Women's gums should bleed during pregnancy. (P)

Tiptoe through the Maydew and you will miscarry. (P)

Sexual intercourse during pregnancy will make the child sensual. (P)

If you long for sweet foods during pregnancy you will have a girl, if you long for sour things, a boy. (P)

If you don't feel much movement from the baby it is a boy. (O) (P)

A lot of vomiting in pregnancy means an easy confinement. (O)

Nausea early in pregnancy means it will be a girl. (O)

Unless a woman gives way to her food cravings her baby will be discontented or minus some vital organ. (P)

You can't conceive as long as you are lactating. (O)

If the baby's late, it will be a boy. (O)

Swing a wedding ring suspended on a cotton over the pregnant woman's stomach; if it goes in a circle it will be a girl, if it swings to and fro, it will be a boy. (O)

A woman who eats strawberries while pregnant will have a baby with a strawberry mark. (O)

Prickly heat   A large portion of wheat bran mixed with cold or lukewarm water, bath two or three times a day. (P)

Quinsy   Toast one side of bread and on the other side put chewed tobacco, and place on the quinsy. (O)

Boil figs in milk and hot water with a little salamonica in it. This is to be used as a gargle and some of it drunk, which acts on the glands with wonderful effect. (P)

Rabies

4 ounces Tormentil roots, assafoetida ½ ounce, Rufoia (?) castor 2 drams, agrimony roots, primrose roots, single peony roots, leaves of box of each one handful; the Star of the earth 2 handful, the black of crab's claws prepared 1 ounce, Venice treacle 1 ounce, one root of Garlick [sic] or a handful of pine to be infused in 1 gallon of milk, 4 spoonfuls thereof to be given 3 days successively before and 3 days successively after the full and change of the moon. NB Boil the herbs and roots being first bruised in a mortar a quarter of an hour in the milk and then strain it off and mix the powders and Venice treacle with the liquor. It is best repeated 2 or 3 moons for greater safety. (M)

Eat the mad dog's liver, fried. (P)

1 pound of common salt to a quart of water, then squeezing bathing and washing the wound with it for an hour and not drinking any of it; then bind a little more salt to the part affected for 12 hours. (M)

Rheumatism

It was agreed at a meeting of the chief medical doctors of London that one ounce of Peruvian bark, used to a pint of boiling water, and when cold take a wineglassful three times a day with ten to 15 drops of oil of turpentine to each glass gives positive relief in the worst cases; or, rheumatism is greatly relieved by wearing a wash leather over the afflicted part; or, common soda dissolved in hot water is one of the best cures for rheumatism, which has to be well rubbed on the afflicted part. (P)

½ ounce of volatile tincture of guiacum, ½ ounce of antimony. Mix well together, first take 15 drops and if (it doesn't work?) increase to 21 in warm water. (M)

Rhubarb in powder, Nithe (?), flowers of sulphur, Gum Giacum each ½ ounce. To be mixed with 6 ounces of common treacle, the quantity to be taken each night going to bed, a large teaspoon. (M)

1tbs tincture of opium (otherwise laudanum), 4tbs eau de cologne, mixed as a liniment (sic). (M)

1 ounce of Gumquacum, ½ ounce salt petre, both to be well pounded, ½ pint of old rum, put the above ingredients into a bottle and let it stand in a warm place two or three days straining it very often. A tsp and half to be taken in a cup of warm water or barley water going to bed. Increase ½ a tsp at a time for 3 or 4 nights then continue the quantity till aired; if it affects the bowels take rather less – should it create a great heat it is not to be regarded (?) NB This medicine must not be taken in inflammatory cases. (M)

Take hyssop, or opium (make poppy tea from white poppies), or willow bark infused in boiling water. (P)

Soak a dubble Handful of Eldor [sic] flowers. Boil them in a pint and a half of milk and a pint of water. Boil it ½ an hour, then strain it off, them moak [sic] it boil up then put a pint of Muntin wine in it strain the curd from it, toak [sic] it in the morning fasting and last at nite. Pass ten drops of Turpentine upon a little nobb of lofe sugar ad 5 drops eatch time put the lofe sugar in first then drink ½ pint of the lier. It may be repeated in three or five days. (M)

Grind up fresh horseradish, place between two pieces of lint and place on the joint. (O)

Bee stings, relieve rheumatism, or cider vinegar. As a preventative, wear a copper bracelet. (O)

Carry in your pocket a stolen potato: its healing property leaves it as it becomes hard and another must be substituted. (P)

Carry in the pocket of your trousers 4 moles feet. (P)

A tonic after rheumatism: to restore the strength after rheumatism make a strong bath of cow heels and wash the parts affected with it warm twice a day. (P)

Crawl under a bramble which has formed a second root. The arch must be complete. (P)

Rheumatic gout:
Hot water drunk frequently is a good cure. (P)

Swallow a spider, preferably live. (P)

Rickets

Bury a lock of the child's hair at a cross road. It will work all the better if a full moon is shining. (P)

Split a young ash tree down the middle, hold it open and pass the child through it three times with its head towards the rising sun. Bind up the tree with pack thread and as the bark heals so the child recovers. (P)

Rickets is a disease peculiar to children, resulting from foul air, damp cold rooms, want of sunlight, exercise or cleanliness. Ablutions is a very important preventive. (P)

Ringworm

2 oz Tobacco, 1½ oz pepper, 2 oz black pepper. Boil them in 3 pints of water till reduced to a quart. A small quantity at a time every day or two dubbed on the head. (O)

Apply rotten apples or pounded garlic. (P)

Citrine ointment is a quick cure for ringworms; or, common soda dissolved in hot water and applied to the ring worms or lime water from the gas works, used in the same manner; or, the ends of matches applied, dipped in water. (P)

Charm for ringworm:
Take some ashes between the forefinger and thumb and hold it against the affected part, before each meal, and say:
  Ringworm, ringworm, red!
  Never mayst thou spread or speed
  But aye grow less and less
  And die away among the ashes. (P)

St Vitus' dance

Mistletoe tea is a cure, so also is quinine wine. (P)

Write the following and use as an amulet:
  'shake her, good Devil,
  Shake her once well;
  Then shake her no more
  Till you shake her in hell.' (P)

Scalds

Place the part in lime water. (P)

Put immediately under cold running water. (O)

Scarlet fever   Tie a tongue of red cloth around the neck of the patient. (P)

Sciatica   Sciatica is speedily relieved by two pennyworth of camphor dissolved in a pint of boiling water; a wineglassful to be taken three times a day. (P)

Sciatica is cured by a patient lying on the back by the side of a river or brook with a stick between the patient and the water, while one repeats:
  'Boneshave right
  Boneshave straight
  As the water runs by the stave
  Good for boneshave.' (P)

Scrofula   The touch of the monarch will cure the complaint. (P)

Rub a toad on the diseased gland. The toad should afterwards be kept up the chimney. (P)

Scurvy   Live on turnips for a month. (P)

For scurvy, the free use of lemon and cream of tartar made into a drink. (P)

For any swelling of the Gummes or the Canker or Scurvie: Wash and pick a quantity of Sorrell, boile it of itselfe without water, then rub it through a sieve; then clarifye a little honey, to w^h put a little red Saunders and a little alom and boile these together to a sirrup; keep ye sorrell by itselfe and the sirrup also; when you use this, mix them together scrape some lint, lay this medicine upon the lint and to ye swellings and at your pleasure rub the gummes with it. (P)

Shingles	Drink sea water every morning for a week. Towards the end of the week, bath. (P)
	Either paint with ink or burn a quantity of clean oat-straw, mingle the ashes with the best pork lard and lay it on the parts affected. (P)
Sick	For sick people: great nourishment from half an ounce of isinglass in half a pint of milk and sweetened to taste. (P)
	Sick rooms: On visiting a sick chamber chew a little ginger which prevents contagion. (P)
	To keep the air in a sick room pure, wet a cloth in lime water and hang it in the room. (P)
Skin	For spots and blemishes on the skin apply the juice of onions mixed with vinegar. (P)
	Roughness of the skin is cured by one ounce of olive oil to one ounce of white wax melted in it. Mix, when near cold, with one pennyworth of white precipitate and use as an ointment or scorbutic persons will find the free use of celery invaluable. (P)
	Apply chopped nettles for getting rid of pimples. (O)
	For sore hands: Apply finely pounded parsley mixed with the fat from a chicken roast. (O)
Smallpox	Drink toast and water, also milk and apples. For violent cases bleed the feet, bathe the legs with warm water 2 or 3 times a day. Apply boiled turnips to the feet. (P)

Smallpox is mastered by one teaspoon
of cream of tartar to each half pint of
hot water. Drink freely. (P)

Eat fried mice. (P)

Cover in red flannel to prevent the light
penetrating – this prevents scarring. (O)

Charm for the smallpox:
'In the name of our Lord Jesus Christ,
may the Lord protect these persons and
may the work of these virgins ward off
the smallpox. St. Nacaise had the
smallpox and he asked the Lord (to
preserve) whoever carried his name
inscribed, O, St. Nacaise! thou illustrious
bishop and martyr, pray for me a sinner
and defend me by they intercession
from this disease. Amen.' (P)

Snake bites   Apply the warm entrails of a newly
killed fowl to the poisoned part. (P)

Apply mistletoe. (P)

Sores   Ivy leaf is good for sores: the underside
draws, the top side heals any old sore. (P)

Marshmallow ointment cures the worst
of sores. (P)

A receipt to wash sores: It is good for
human people and all beasts. A pint and
½ of spring water put in a good handful
of lavender flowers,* let it boil till a
quarter pint is wasted, then strain it off
and set by ye fire again and put on a
¼ pint of white wine and a piece of alom
as big as an egg beat fine, add a good
spoonful of honey, stir it well together
and when it is cold bottle it up for use;
and tis better used warm and upon fine
rag. (Mrs Cage's) (P)

The touch of a suicide's hand. (P)

Sore throat:
Tie an old sock around the throat. (O)

Take a pint of cold water lying down in
bed or apply a chin-stay of roasted
figs. (P)

Charm for a sore:
>   Thir sores are risen thru' God's wark
>   And must be laid thru' God's help;
>   The mother Mary and her dear Son
>   Lay thir sores that are begun. (P)

Spirits

Suitable for disruption of the spirits:
1 ounce tincture of Balm
1 ounce tincture of Balinian (?)
60 drops spirits of lavender
– take a teaspoon in a glass twice a day
for in continuance. (M)

Sprain

For a most violent sprain:
3 ounces of camphor dissolved in ½ pint
spirits of wine. Add a bullocks gall, rub
it well (about 3 tablespoons twice and
three times a day). (M)

The best remedy for a sprain is a bran
and vinegar poultice. (P)

Charm against a sprain and a bruise:
'As our Blessed Lord and Saviour Jesus
Christ was riding into Jerusalem, His
horse tripped and sprained his leg. Our
blessed Lord and Saviour blessed it, and
said:
>   "Bone to bone and vein to vein,
>   O vein turn to thy rest again.
>   M.N. so shall thine. In the name of
>   the father (etc.)" '

Stings

For wasps:
Vinegar and alum. First applying steel –
a key – to the part to extract the sting. (If
this doesn't succeed, laudanum.) (M)

Rub with the bruised leaves of a house-leek, watercress or rue. (P)

For bee stings:
Apply honey (apple honey). (P)

For nettle stings:
Rub with a dock leaf. (O)

Rub with the juice of nettle. (P)

For wasp stings:
Common salt and salad oil. If the wasp is swallowed, put a teaspoon of salt in the mouth. Salt kills the wasp and heals the sting. (P)

For beetle sting:
Any aromatic herb or common dock leaf applied. (P)

Stitch

Apply treacle spread on hot toast, or a potatoe [sic]. (P)

Charm against a stitch:
Make a cross and sing over the place thrice:
Stand fast; lie as Christ did
When he was crucified upon the tree.
Blood remain up in the veins,
As Christ did in all his pains.
Or:
Christ he walketh over the land
Carried the wild fire in his hand
He rebuked the fire and bid it stand,
Stand wildfire, stand.
In the name of the Father (etc.) (P)

Stomach

Medicine to strengthen the stomach:
Put ½ ounce of camomile flowers, the rind of ½ a fresh lemon cut thin, as much grated ginger as can be taken upon a shilling, all together in a quart white jug with a sprout of corn. Pour a pint and a half of boiling water *measured*

upon these ingredients and let them infuse until cold – or during the night – when cold add tablespoon of brandy to the Infusion. Stir it well and leave covered in the jug without straining off the liquor. If the camomile flowers are of last year fresh dried the infusion will be a good better. A small sized wine glass or 4 large tablespoons, the quantity to be taken at each time. (M)

Stomach complaints may be overcome by the use of camomile tea. (P)

For a disordered stomach, the simplest remedy is salt and water. (P)

Stye	Rub with a gold wedding ring. (O)
	Rub with the hair of a black cat's tail. (O)
Suffocation	For one seemingly killed by lightning or suffocated: Plunge him into cold water or blow strongly with bellows down his throat. (M)
Sunburn	Wash the face in sage tea. (P)
Swellings of the leg	Place bandages around the swollen limb and while this is being done repeat the following charm nine times, to be followed by the Lord's prayer: As Christ was walking he saw the Virgin Mary sitting on a cold marble stone. He said unto her: 'If it is a white ill-thing or a red ill-thing or a black ill-thing or a rotten ill-thing or a cold creeping ill-thing or a sore ill-thing or a smarting ill-thing, or a swelling ill-thing, let it fall from thee to earth in My name and the Name of the Father, Son and Holy Ghost. Amen.' (P)

Tapeworm

The tapeworm alone will produce all the symptoms of every known disease and are often the direct cause of consumption, fits, insanity and death. They are killed in a grown up person by first taking a little opening medicine, next fast for a day or even two, then take a thimbleful of the oil of male fern* in a tablespoon of water before breakfast and this repeat. (P)

Teeth

To clean the teeth:
½ ounce tincture of myrrh
½ ounce tincture of Bark
¼ ounce Gum Benzoin
2 ounce best cinnamon water.
It must be well mixed and laid by before use. (M)

Rub with the ashes of burnt bread. (P)

Rub with bi-carbonate of soda. (O)

Thorn

For getting out a thorn:
Castile soap and musty bacon. (O) (P)

Charm for the prick of a thorn:
    Christ was of a virgin born
    And he was prick'd by a thorn
    And it did never bell (throb) nor swell
    As I trust in Jesus this never will. (P)

Let the middle finger of the right hand keep in motion round the thorn and at the end of the following words, three times repeated, touch it every time with the tip of your finger and with God's blessing you will find no further trouble:
    Christ was of a virgin born,
    And crowned was with a crown of
        thorns;
    He did neither swell nor rebel,
    And I hope this never will.
    Jesus of a maid was born,

He was pricked with nails and thorn;
Neither blains nor boils did fetch at
   the bone,
No more shall this, by Christ our
Lord. Amen,
Lord bless what I have said. Amen
So be it unto thee as I have said. (P)

Happy man that Christ was born
He was crowned with a thorn;
He was pierced thru' the skin,
For to let the poison in;
But his poor wounds, so they say
Closed before he passed away.
In with healing, out with thorn.
Happy man that Christ was born. (P)

Throats (sore)
and thrush

Wrap around the neck a red rag. (O)

2 wine glasses of sage tea – cold, 1
wineglass of port wine, ½ wine glass of
vinegar, or vinegars to the tast [sic]. All
to be bottled up and used cold – the
throat to be gargled 3 or 4 times a
day. (M)

Roast a potatoe [sic] then crack it, place
it in a piece of flannel and apply it very
hot, when the steam from it will be
found to have made a cure in one
night.(P)

Wrap a frog in pure white linen cloth
and let the baby suck it. (O)

The leaves of the Viburnum or
Wayfaring tree make an excellent
gargle. (O)

Repeat the 8th psalm over the patient 7
times on 3 mornings. If said 'with the
virtue' it is an unfailing cure. (P)

Toothache

Salvolatile 3 parts, Laudanum 1 part and
rub the part affected frequently or if the

tooth be hollow drop some of this on a
piece of cotton and put it with the tooth.
For a small face-ache sore throat
moisten a bit of flannel with spirits at
night to the part affected. (M)

Wash the mouth with volatile tincture of
Guiacum in water every morning. (M)

Charm for toothache:
> Christ pass'd by His brother's door,
> Saw His brother lying on the floor.
> What aileth thee, brother?
> Pain in the teeth?
> Thy teeth shall pain thee no more.
> In the name of the Father (etc.) (P)

This cure is impossible if other remedies
are taken or other advice sought. The
Patient must not allow another of the
same sex to repeat the incantation or to
perform the cure. One from the
opposite sex must do it. Rub the gums
and repeat:
> As Thomas sat upon a marble stone
> Jesus came unto him all alone
> And said 'Thomas, swear now for my
> sake,
> And you shall never have
> toothache.' (P)

Pierce the gums with a piece of bark
from a tree; return the bark to the tree,
covered in blood. (P)

Rub with oil of cloves. (O)

Typhus fever Take yeast in a spoon diluted with warm
water and coarse sugar. (M)

Apply the spleen of a cow to the soles of
the patient's feet. This draws the fever
away from the head. (P)

U lcers   Dry and pound a walnut leaf and strew it on, and lay another walnut leaf over that. (P)

In April gather oken buds, bramble buds, hawthorne buds, the following herbs as they flower, strip their stalks, southernwood, mugwort, anicle, dandelion, agrimony, scab, violett leaves, patling, popies, wormwood, wood bithony, avens, wilde angel, comfrey, arabery leaves, dayseyes roots and leaves, sweet madelon, bugle eye, eyewort, playnton and ribwort, mints, sinksale, honysoikell – 25. Dry all the herbs free from dust, then take of each like quantities and put them into papor baggs and hang them up in a drie room for use, they may be used greene as well as drie, but there mus be equal parts eyther wayes – 3 handfulls thus mixt is to be put into a potte of spring water and a quart of white wine to stew together until halfe be consumed. Then straine it and put to it a poynt of hony, boyle it and scum it, when it is cold put it up into some convent (convenient) vessell, jugg or glass and stop it up close. 6 spunfulls is to be taken every morning fasting and to fast 2 hours after it, or 3 in ye morning and 3 at 4 of ye clock in ye afternoon and to fast 2 hours after eyther taking it. It cureth fistulas, scaleth bones inflammations, agues inward and outward wounds, the bones comonly scaleth within 30 dayes or 6 weekes, follow the other directions with this, that is abstaine salt meat or pye crust or sharp drinks. (c.1700) (P)

Urinary diseases   Juniper, used as tea in a weak form, is good for urinary diseases.

Viper bite

Rub the part well with sweet oil and take at the same time a tea cupful of oil and milk warm mixed thus: about 2 tablespoons of oil to ½ pint of milk, frequently. (M)

arts

Take some elder and knotch it with the number of warts, then bury. (O)

Break twig off a willow tree, let it hang by the peel and rub the wart on the peel. As the twig and peel withers, so the wart will go away. (P)

Gather a green sloe, rub on warts and throw it over your left shoulder. (P)

Rub with salt bacon, then bury. (O)

Rub with 7 white stones. (O)

Rub with dandelion juice. (O)

Steel the hair from the tail of a piebald horse and tie round. (O)

Rub with the inside of a broad bean, then bury. (O)

Buy the warts with a coin, then rub the coin over the warts. (O)

Apply washing soda. (O)

Rub with raw meat, then bury. (O)

Place in the water that the blacksmith uses to cool horses' shoes. (O)

Apply castor oil. (O)

Apply either aromatic vinegar or steep in the vinegar the inner rind of a lemon for 24 hours and apply to the wart. The lemon must not remain on for more than 3 hours. (P)

Wen

Apply sunlight soap and sugar. (O)

Pass the hand of a dead body on 3 successive days over the part affected. For preference, the hand should be that of a man who's been hanged. (P)

(Hunt says that he once saw a young woman led onto the scaffold in the Old Bailey for the purpose of having a wen touched with the hand of a man who had just been executed. 'Notes and Queries', quoted by Black, *Domestic Folk Medicine*.)

Whooping cough

Drink thyme tea. (O)

Wrap around the throat garlic crushed in linen and placed in a sock. (O)

Dissolve a scruple of salt of tartar in a ¼ pint of water and add to it ten grains of cochineal finely powdered, boil it 6 minutes, put in a lump or 2 of sugar. Give it to an infant a teaspoon 4 times a day – to a child 2 or 3 years old a desertspoon at a time – 4 years old and upwards a tablespoon. (M)

Boil a mouse and make mouse tea. (P)

Eat a fried mouse. (P) (M)

Visit the sea. As the tide recedes, so will the cough. (O)

Place a live flat fish on the bare chest of the patient and keep it there till it is dead. (P)

Let the parent of the afflicted child find a dark spider in her own house and hold it over the head of the child, repeating 3 times: Spider as you waste away/Whooping cough no longer stay. The spider should then be hung up in a bag over the mantelpiece and when the spider has dried up the cough will be gone. (P)

Put in a small muslin bag as many large spiders as the patient has years. Hold the bag in the patient's mouth for a few moments then hang it at the head of the bed for the remainder of the night. (P)

Lay the child face downwards on the turf of a meadow. Cut round the child in the shape of a coffin. Remove the child and turn the turf root upwards. As the turf withers, the cough disappears. (P)

Pass the child 9 times under and over a donkey 3 years old. Then 3 spoonfuls of milk drawn from the teats of the animal, 3 hairs cut from the back and 3 hairs cut from the belly placed in it. After the milk has stood for 3 hours, it should be drunk by the child in 3 doses, the whole ceremony being repeated on 3 successive mornings. (P)

Make nine knots in a string and hang round the patient's neck. (P)

Hot cross buns, if kept from one Good Friday to another will prevent an attack of whooping cough. (P)

Worms   For tape worms, take male fern.* (P) (O)

2/3 lavender cotton, 1/3 rue. Pounded in a mortar with a little sugar to make it moist – to be made as big as a marble, one to be taken every morning for 9 days. Leave off for 9 and then begin again. (M)

Soak raisins in brandy. Then give the child the raisins 3 mornings running, then leave for three. (O)

The receipt for worms or worm fever:
Take of senna 2½ drams, wormseed
one dram, infuse these in 4 ounces of
Seville oranges juice for 1 hour in a close
covered pot over warm ashes, then press
out the liquor thoroughly, in it dissolve
6 drams of syrup of violettes and give
moderate spoonfuls for 3 mornings. (M)

Wormwood draughts: 30 grains of salt of
wormwood, 2 spoonfuls of juice of
Lemmon [sic], 2 spoonfuls of water,
1 lump of sugar. 10 grains of salt of
Prunella bruised makes them more
cooling. (M)

Wounds

Apply a slice of horseradish to the cut,
put pepper on it and bind it up. (O)

Apply a cobweb. (O)

Apply mouldy cow dung. (O)

Clean and grease the instrument which
made the wound. (P)

Notes

Chapter 1: Introduction

1. Alsace Street, Walworth, South London
2. F. B. Smith, *The People's Health 1830–1910*, Croom Helm 1979, p.52
3. Interview with Mrs Coker, Lambeth, February 1980
4. Interview with Mrs Wallace, Suffolk, May 1977. The interview continued: 'If you want to know, I don't think it matters much. I'll have to leave it behind for somebody. It's only sulphur of flowers, but it just depends on how big a pot you've got. Mix it with paraffin, and then put a few drops of Dettol, that destroys the smell of the paraffin. But make it as thick as you can so as it will stay on and bandage it round, and do it three or four times a day. Keep it away from food, and that's all there is to it.'
5. D. Landy, 'Role Adaptation: Traditional Curers Under the Impact of Western Medicine' in D. Landy (ed.), *Culture, Disease and Healing*, Macmillan New York 1977, p.468
6. A. Rich, *Of Woman Born*, Virago 1977, p.17

Chapter 2: From Goddess to Sorceress

1. E. Gellner, *Thought and Change*, Weidenfeld and Nicolson 1964, p.1
2. I. Seibert, *Woman in the Ancient Near East*, Edition Leipzig 1974, p.11
3. D. McKenzie, *The Infancy of Medicine*, Macmillan & Co. 1927
4. M. Stone, *The Paradise Papers*, Virago/Quartet 1976, p.19
5. *Ibid.*
6. *Ibid.*
7. A collection of Egyptian medical writings believed to date from approximately 1550 BC and named after the German archaeologist, Georg Ebers, who discovered them in 1872–3
8. W. Von Soden, *Die Hebamme in Babylon und Assyrien*, Archiv für Orientforschung 18, 1957–58, pp.119–21, quoted in Seibert (*op.cit.*), p.28
9. R. Briffault, *The Mothers*, Allen and Unwin 1927; quoted in Stone (*op.cit.*), p.165
10. For a fuller discussion of this thesis see, for example, Merlin Stone, *op.cit.*
11. Stone (*op.cit.*), p.68
12. We do not know why embalming became the particular prerogative of men. Herodotus reports that the job was both smelly and filthy and, as a result, embalmers were shunned socially, especially by women. As a result, many high-ranking families would retain their female corpses for as long as possible before handing them over to the embalmers.
13. An inscription found at Sais records: 'I have come from the school of medicine at Heliopolis and have studied at the women's school at Sais where the divine mothers taught me how to cure diseases.'

K. Campbell Hurd-Mead, *A History of Women in Medicine from the Earliest Times to the Beginning of the 19th Century*, Haddam Press 1938, p.16

14. There is some speculation that opium may have been used, but this would only have dulled, not eliminated, the pain.

15. M. Gimbutas, *The Gods and Goddesses of Old Europe 7,000–3,500*BC, Thames and Hudson 1974, p.142

16. Hurd-Mead (*op. cit.*), p.29

17. Quoted in Hurd-Mead (*op. cit.*), p.33

18. Quoted in Stone (*op. cit.*), p.69

19. Hurd-Mead (*op. cit.*), p.43

20. Hurd-Mead (*op. cit.*), p.45

21. H. Trimp, 'Witchcraft' in the *Dictionary of the History of Ideas* Vol. IV, Charles Scribner and Sons, New York 1973, p.521

Chapter 3: From Sorceress to Witch

1. It is impossible to estimate the total number prosecuted and killed for witchcraft, though individual cases can provide some indication of the scale. In the Swiss canton of Vaud between 1591 and 1680 3,371 persons were tried and executed. In southwest Germany from 1561 to 1670, 3,229 were executed. In Wiesensteig 63 women were burned in 1562; in Obermachtel 7 per cent of the population were burned between 1586 and 1588. Between 1560 and 1680 some 314 people were prosecuted at the Essex assize and Quarter Session courts.

2. R. M. S. McConaghen, 'History of Rural Medical Practice' in Poynter (ed.), *The Evolution of Medical Practice in England*, Pitmans Medical Publishing Company 1961, p.120

3. There may also be a connection between the association with, and fierce condemnation of, women and healing by the Church of Rome and that Church's earlier conflict with the gnostics of the first and second centuries AD. Elaine Pagels demonstrates, for instance, that the gnostics questioned the belief that suffering and death were God's ordination for the sins of the world, and also elevated the feminine aspects of the Divinity, celebrating God as both father and mother. She argues that the gnostics lost out in the power struggle within the Church and that their interpretations of dogma became branded as 'heresy', while 'orthodox' Christianity – supported by the military and political might of the Roman Empire after the conversion of the Emperor Constantine – began to stress certain notions which essentially supported their position with the Church. 'We can see, for example, how the orthodox doctrine of Christ's bodily resurrection is connected with the power of the clergy originating from Peter, "first witness of the resurrection"; how the orthodox doctrine of "one God" served to support the rule of "one bishop" over the Christian community and indicates how gnostic opposition to that doctrine involves a challenge to the bishop's authority.' E. Pagels, 'Who was the real Jesus?' *Observer*, 23 December 1979

4. E. Maple, *Magic, Medicine and Quackery*, Robert Hale 1968, p.42

5. Quoted in J. Payne, *English Medicine in the Anglo-Saxon Times*, Oxford 1904, p.112

6.   Quoted in *Anglo-Saxon Leechcraft*, Lecture Memoranda BMA 1912, Burroughs Wellcome 1912

7.   Quoted in T. Szasz, *The Manufacture of Madness*, Routledge & Kegan Paul 1971, p.114

8.   Quoted in N. Cohn, *Europe's Inner Demons*, Paladin 1976, p.158

9.   BMA Lecture Memoranda, *op. cit.*

10.   BMA Lecture Memoranda, *op. cit.*

11.   BMA Lecture Memoranda, *op. cit.*

12.   Harnack *Medicinisches aus der Aeltesten Kirchen Geschichte*, Leipzig 1892, quoted in J. Walsh *Old Time Makers of Medicine*, New York 1911

13.   Melton *Astrologaster* p.20; quoted in T. J. Pettigrew *On Superstition*, London 1844, p.36

14.   W. Bonser, *The Medical Background of Anglo-Saxon England*, Wellcome History of Medicine Library, London 1963, p.121

15.   E. LeRoy Ladurie, *The Territory of the Historian*, Harvester Press Ltd 1979, p.99

16.   B. Ehrenreich and D. English, *Witches, Midwives and Nurses*, Writers and Readers Publishing Co-operative 1976, p.32

17.   '*mulieres et vetule et conversi et rustici, non nulli apothecarii et herbarii quam plures, insuper scholares in medicinae Facultate nondum docti – ignari scientie medicine, ignoratesque complexiones hominum.*' (Translated by Alan Thomas and Sue Smith.) Hurd-Mead (*op. cit.*), p.269

18.   Trimp (*op. cit.*), p.522

19.   W. Perkins, *A Discourse of the Damned Art of Witchcraft*, 1608, p.3

20.   M. J. Hughes, *Women Healers in Medieval Life and Literature*, New York 1943, p.85n

21.   Quoted in E. Maple, (*op. cit.*), p.66

22.   J. Cotta, *A Short Discoverie of the Unobserved Dangers of Severall sorts of Ignorant and Unconsiderate Practisers of Physicken in England*, 1612

23.   *Ibid.*

24.   Quoted in Szasz (*op. cit.*), p.111

25.   *Ibid.*

26.   Cotta *op. cit.*

27.   Michelet, quoted in Szasz (*op. cit.*), p.111

28.   A. Creighton, *A History of Epidemics*, Cambridge University Press 1891

29.   K. Thomas, *Religion and the Decline of Magic*, Penguin 1973, p.245

30.   D. Defoe, *Journal of the Plague Year 1665*

31.   Thomas (*op. cit.*), p.245

32.   A. Clark, *The Working Life of Women in the 17th Century*, George Routledge and Sons 1919

33.   H. Wolley, *The Compleat Servant Maid*, 1704

34.   T. Rogers, *The Character of a Good Woman*, pp.42–3, quoted in Clark (*op. cit.*), p.256

35.   N. Parry and J. Parry, *The Rise of the Medical Profession*, Croom Helm 1976, p.164

36.   *Ibid.* p.165; also Clark (*op. cit.*), p.256

37.   R. Josselin, *Diary* pp.163–4, quoted in A. Clark (*op. cit.*), p.257

38.   C. Creighton, *A History of Epidemics*, *op. cit.*

39.   *Ibid.*

40. Clark (*op.cit.*), p.258

41. W. Brockbank 'Country Practice in Days Gone By', *Medical History* 1960, Vol. 4

42. A. Martindale *Life Of*, 1632, p.21

43. The *Guardian* of 18 September 1980 contains a report by David Andrews on the introduction of a new course in family therapy which echoes the methods of a 'shaman', an East African folk healer. The report cites an article by Drs Rappaport and Dent in the *Journal of Medical Psychology* (1979, 52, 1, 49–54) on folk psychotherapy in Tanzania, which recognises the 'critical importance of the folk healer's personality'. The report continues: 'The medicine man usually functions as an extension of the predominant religious viewpoint and is seen as a sort of caretaker of traditional cultural values. Treatment is delivered in public, in front of the extended family, so that once it is all over the patient and his family share the belief that a cure has taken place. Rappaport and Dent say that this shared faith in the patient undoubtedly plays a vital part in helping him become part of the community again, as well as boosting their belief in the powers of the shaman.'

44. Quoted in Szasz (*op.cit.*), p.112

45. T. R. Forbes, *The Midwife and the Witch*, Newhaven, Yale University Press 1966, p.146

46. Quoted in T. Forbes, (*op.cit.*), p.126

47. *Ibid.* p.125

48. *Ibid.*

49. The physicians were also ignorant. Sir Kenelm Digby (1603–65), a court physician, was convinced that driving the blood out of the body of the child before tying the cord would prevent smallpox and other eruptive diseases for the lifetime of the individual. Digby believed that a pregnant woman, by failing to menstruate, retained impurities which would be passed on to the embryo.

50. S. X. Radbill, 'Pediatrics' in A. G. Debus (ed.), *Medicine in Seventeenth Century England*, University of California Press 1974

51. Quoted in C. H. LaWall, *4000 Years of Pharmacy*, Philadelphia and London 1927. This description varies little in basics from the counsel (tantamount to fraud) of a thirteenth-century physician: 'Do not be in a hurry to give an opinion for his (the patient's) friends will be grateful for your judgement if they have to wait for it. Tell the patient you will, by God's help, cure him but inform his friends that the case is a serious one. Suppose you know nothing, say there is an obstruction of the liver. Perhaps the patient will reply "nay, master, it is my head or my legs which trouble me" – repeat that it comes from the liver and repeatedly use the word obstruction, for patients do not understand it, which is important.' E. S. Turner, *Call the Doctor*, quoted in Maple (*op.cit.*), p.48

52. Quoted in F. N. L. Poynter *op.cit.*

53. Quoted in Poynter *op.cit.*

54. Quoted in A. MacFarlane, *Witchcraft in Tudor and Stuart England*, Routledge and Kegan Paul 1970, p.307

55. Ehrenreich and English (*op.cit.*), p.35

56.   MacFarlane (*op. cit.*), p.184
57.   Quoted in Maple (*op. cit.*), p.87
58.   Quoted in Thomas (*op. cit.*), p.640
59.   Ehrenreich and English (*op. cit.*), p.35
60.   Clark *op. cit.*
61.   Ladurie (*op. cit.*), p.103
62.   Ehrenreich and English *op. cit.*

Chapter 4: From Expert to Charlatan
1.   D. Landy *op. cit.*
2.   *The Paston Letters*, No. 490
3.   Quoted in Hurd-Mead (*op. cit.),* p.475
4.   As early as the fourteenth century the Abbess Hildegaard, from the Rhine country, wrote a number of medical works in which she included expensive remedies for the rich and cheaper ones for the poor. For the rich, concoctions would be made from the bodies of griffons, peacocks, storks, tigers and leopards. For the poor, mice and rats were thought adequate. And Margaret Paston, from a wealthy Norfolk family, requested in 1464 that her husband John send her from London a 'potte with treacle' – an ingredient presumably unavailable in Norfolk except to the wealthy with personal emissaries.
5.   Quoted in Hurd-Mead (*op. cit.*), p.477
6.   Creighton *op. cit.*
7.   Quoted in Clark (*op. cit.*), p.250
8.   Quoted in Clark (*op. cit.*), p.251
9.   E. Friedson, *Professional Dominance: The Social Structure of Medical Care*, Chicago/New York 1970
10.   Clark (*op. cit.*), p.288
11.   J. Peterson, *The Medical Profession in mid-Victorian London*, University of California Press 1976, p.14
12.   Quoted in Parry and Parry (*op. cit.*), p.166
13.   Quoted in Parry and Parry (*op. cit.*), p.166
14.   Creighton *op. cit.*
15.   Fifty guineas was not an uncommon price to pay in the early nineteenth century for a visit from the physician. The average working wage was about 5/-. Although apothecaries did not charge such exorbitant fees, they were nevertheless only open to the middle classes or, at the very most, the more affluent artisan.
16.   Creighton *op. cit.*
17.   A. McLaren, *Birth Control in 19th Century England*, Croom Helm 1978, p.80
18.   The sale of patent medicines increased greatly in the 1870s, when for the first time some of the working class began to have some surplus wages to spend on purchases other than the bare essentials. Some estimates place the increase in sales at this time at around 400 per cent. It seems obvious that a priority purchase would be medicine.
19.   Quoted in S. Chapman, *Jesse Boot of Boots The Chemist*, London 1974, p.17

Chapter 5: Alternatives for the Sick

1. In 1800 there were approximately 3,000 hospital patients in England and Wales, which had a population of 8,000,000. Even in 1851, when hospital patients were included in census returns, the patient population stood at only 7,619 when the population was approaching 18,000,000.

2. Chapman (*op. cit.*), p.21

3. *How the Minority Report Deals with the Children*, National Committee to Promote the Break-up of the Poor Law 1902, p.4

4. A. Digby, *Pauper Palaces*, Routledge and Kegan Paul 1978, p.168

5. M. W. Flinn 'Medical Services Under the Poor Law' in D. Fraser (ed.), *The New Poor Law in the 19th Century*, Macmillan Press 1976, p.58

6. S. and B. Webb, *English Poor Law History*, Part II, F. Cass & Son 1963, p.320

7. *How the Minority Report Deals with the Children* (*op. cit.*), p.4

8. Proposals were made to this Commission to establish a Government Insurance scheme. These were rejected on the grounds that it might encourage existing and potential members of Friendly Societies 'to look to the State for support in time of need, and thus to break down the barrier of honourable pride which now deters many from claiming assistance from the Poor Rates.'

9. S. and B. Webb, *The Break-up of the Poor Law*, 1909, p.258, quoted in H. Levy 'The Economic History of Sickness and Medical Benefit since the Puritan Revolution', *Economic History Review* 1944. The Friendly Societies and Medical Clubs, like the Poor Law, tried to secure their doctors at the cheapest possible rates. Although the BMA (British Medical Association), founded in the mid-nineteenth century to improve working conditions and standards for its members, fought long and hard to improve employment conditions for its members within all these organisations it met with little success. For by the mid-nineteenth century the middle-class market for doctors had become saturated and doctors were forced to turn to working-class practice in order to make a living. However minimally the Poor Law or Friendly Societies paid, it was at least a guaranteed income. The Friendly Societies, Medical Clubs and the Poor Law were not slow to exploit this position.

10. Quoted in J. Pickstone 'Medical Botany', *Memoirs of the Manchester Literary and Philosophical Society*, 119 (1976–7), p.85

11. Malnutrition, especially among poor women, did not die out in the nineteenth century. Dolly Davey writes of her experience just after the Second World War: 'I'd been in hospital with malnutrition. With six children to bring up, and Fred to look after, I always saw that they had enough to eat, and I would go without. Fred didn't know the half of it. I wouldn't admit I was going hungry. I always thought: "the children have got to have meals".' D. Davey, *A Sense of Adventure*, SE1 People's History Project 1980, p.31

12. P. Thane, 'Women and the Poor Law in Victorian and Edwardian England', *History Workshop*, Vol. 6, Autumn 1976, p.34

13. R. W. Harris, *National Health Insurance in Great Britain 1911–46*, London 1946

14. Flinn (*op. cit.*), p.56

15. *How the Minority Report Deals with the Sick, the Infirm and the Infants,*

National Committee to Promote the Break-up of the Poor Law, p.5

16.   *Ibid.*

17.   Interview with Mrs C. (wishes to remain anonymous), Suffolk, May 1977

18.   Quoted in Smith (*op. cit.*), p.46

19.   Mrs C. (Suffolk), *op. cit.*

20.   Interview with Mrs Coker, Lambeth, February 1980

21.   Mrs C. (Suffolk), *op. cit.*

22.   A. Mitchell, *Now We Have an Act*, unpublished Thesis 1974

23.   See, for instance, the article by R. Sauer, 'Infanticide and Abortion in Nineteenth-Century Britain', *Population Studies* 1978, 32; and by P. Knight, 'Women and Abortion in Victorian and Edwardian England', *History Workshop Journal* 4, Autumn 1977

24.   M. Woodside, 'The Woman Abortionist' in *Abortion in Britain* (Proceedings of a Conference held by the FPA at the University of London, 22 April 1966) Pitman's Medical Book 1966

25.   F. Tennyson Jesse, *A Pin to See the Peepshow*, Virago 1979, p.378

26.   Woodside *op. cit.*

27.   *Maternity: Letters from Working Women*, Virago 1978

28.   Mrs C. (Suffolk) *op. cit.*

29.   *Quarterly Medical Journal* 10, 1901–2, pp.148–52

30.   S. and B. Webb, (*op. cit.*), p.324

31.   Interview with Mrs Murray, Lambeth, March 1979

32.   *Ibid.*

33.   E. Porter, *Cambridgeshire Customs and Folklore*

34.   W. H. Barrett and R. P. Garrod, *East Anglian Folklore and Other Tales*, Routledge and Kegan Paul 1976, p.13

35.   Quoted in Parry and Parry (*op. cit.*), p.149

36.   *Ibid.* p.145

37.   *Ibid.* p.156

38.   Interview with Mrs Heiser, Lambeth, April 1980

39.   Mrs Murray (Lambeth), *op. cit.*

40.   A. J. Willcocks, *The Creation of the National Health Service*, Routledge & Kegan Paul 1967

41.   Interview with Mr Stronger, Lambeth, March 1980

42.   Interview with Mrs Johnson, Lambeth, February 1980

43.   Interview with Mrs B. (wishes to remain anonymous), Lambeth, February 1980 (interview conducted by Jenny Mauthe)

44.   *Bristol As We Remember It*, Bristol Broadsides 1978, p.19

45.   Mrs Murray (Lambeth), *op. cit.*

46.   Mrs Johnson (Lambeth), *op. cit.*

47.   Mrs Murray (Lambeth), *op. cit.*

48.   *Ibid.*

49.   Mrs Heiser (Lambeth), *op. cit.*

50.   Mrs Johnson (Lambeth), *op. cit.*

Chapter 6: Conclusions

1.   M. Barrett and H. Roberts, 'Doctors and Their Patients', in C. and

B. Smart (eds.) *Women, Sexuality and Social Control*, Routledge and Kegan Paul 1978, p.41

2.   D. Scully, *Men Who Control Women's Health*, Boston 1980; quoted in S. Kitzinger 'The American Way of Birth', *The Times Literary Supplement*, 1 August 1980

3.   Boston Women's Health Book Collective, *Our Bodies Ourselves*, British Edition by A. Phillips and J. Rakusen, Allen Lane 1976, p.547

4.   Barrett and Roberts (*op. cit.*), p.46

5.   J. Donnison, 'The Role of the Midwife', *Association of Radical Midwives Newsletter*, June 1979, No. 4, p.9

6.   J. R. Butler, J. M. Bevan, R. C. Taylor, *Family Doctors and Public Policy*, Routledge and Kegan Paul 1973; quoted in J. Robson 'Planning and Integration in Primary Care', *Medicine in Society* Vol. 5, No. 2, p.13

7.   R.. M. Titmuss, *Problems of Social Policy*, Longman 1950, quoted in Robson *op. cit.*

8.   Robson *op. cit.*

9.   J. Donnison *op. cit.*

10.   'Birth of A New Hope', *Peace News*, 21 April 1978, p.13

11.   Kitzinger *op. cit.*

12.   N. MacKeith, *The New Women's Health Handbook*, Virago 1978, p.5

Chapter 7: Remedies; introduction

1.   Trotula, *Diseases of Women*, ed. Elizabeth Mason-Hohl, Ward-Ritchie Press 1940

2.   M. Chamberlain, *Fenwomen*, Virago/Quartet 1975, p.75

3.   V. Berridge, 'Opium and Oral History', *Oral History*, Vol. 7, No. 2, p.51

4.   Bonser (*op. cit.*), p.121

5.   *Anglo-Saxon Poetry* (Everyman edition), p.87

6.   Quoted in W. Henderson, *Folklore of the Northern Counties of England and the Borders*, Wakefield 1866, p.137

7.   Quoted in G. Tindall, *Handbook on Witches*, Arthur Barker, London 1965, p.118

8.   E. Vaughan, *These for Remembrance*, Benham and Co., Colchester 1934, p.53

9.   W. G. Black, *Domestic Folk Medicine*, Folk Lore Society, 1883

10.   *Ibid.*

11.   Interview with members of the *East Suffolk Federation of Women's Institutes*, 1976–7

12.   *Ibid.*

13.   Black *op. cit.*

14.   Quoted in Maple (*op. cit.*), p.145

15.   G. White, *The Natural History of Selbourne*, 1789

16.   *East Anglian Magazine*, February 1948

17.   In both the Soviet Union and China traditional medicine still plays an important part in medical treatment. The Soviet Union, for instance, is particularly proud of its 'national medicine' – a mix of orthodox medicine and traditional healing methods. In the *Soviet*

Pharmacopoeia of 1978, 10 per cent of the monographs were on plants – a much larger proportion of the whole than in Western equivalents. Dr S. Fulder, 'The Hammer and the Pestle', *New Scientist* 10 July 1980, p.121

18.   LaWall (*op.cit.*), p.334

19.   Berridge (*op.cit.*), p.50

20.   Ergot has been used to prevent post-partum haemorrhage from at least the sixteenth century, administered as a liquid extract of ergot. In 1906 a British pharmaceutical company isolated what they believed was the active alkaloid and labelled it Ergotoxine. In 1918 a Swiss company came up with another alkaloid, which they called Ergotamine. The latter was a big commercial success on the Continent. British midwives, however, refused to give up the use of their liquid extract of ergot and their position was vindicated in 1932 by Dr Chassar Moir, who showed that both ergotoxine and ergotamine were inactive if not given orally and in any case neither was the substance which gave ergot its effect. In 1935 this substance was isolated and called ergotometrine.

21.   D. Silcock, 'The Healing Power of the Tongue', *Sunday Times* 14 September 1980

22.   H. Marcovitch, 'Mother's Milk: Beware of Imitations', *New Scientist* 6 November 1980

23.   Berridge *op.cit.*

24.   *Paston Letters*, No. 898

25.   W. Salmon, *The Family Dictionary or Household Companion*, 1696

26.   *Ibid.* These ingredients, similar in spirit if not in letter, were part of the stereotype of the witch and her pharmacy:
      Scale of dragon, tooth of wolf,
      Witches mummy, maw and gulf
      Of the ravin'd salt-sea shark,
      Root of hemlock digg'd i' the dark,
      Liver of blaspheming Jew,
      Gall of goat and slips of yew
      Sliver'd in the moon's eclipse,
      Nose of Turk and Tartar's lips . . .

27.   *The Queen's Closet Opened*, 1696

28.   Trotula *op.cit.*

29.   *Ibid.*

30.   *Ibid.*

31.   *Ibid.*

32.   J. Sharp, *The Midwives Book*, 1671

33.   T. Forbes (*op.cit.*), p.67

34.   T. Forbes (*op.cit.*), p.68

35.   N. Culpeper, *A Directory for Midwives*, 1651

36.   Trotula advised pregnant women to drink 'every morning a good draught of sage ale, Garden Tansy Ale, Mallow' – herbs not only rich in iron but which also have an action on the urinary tract and digestion (retention of water and flatulence being two of the banes of pregnant women).

37.   J. Sharp, *Compleat Midwife*, 1724

38.   Culpeper *op.cit.*

39.   O. Cockayne, *Leechdoms, Wort-cunning and Star-craft of Early England*,
       London 1864
40.   Kelly, *Indo-European Folk-lore*, p.145, quoted in Black *op. cit.*

Chapter 8: The Tales
Oral Sources
East Suffolk Federation of Women's Institutes, friends, relatives and
acquaintances

Manuscript sources   (Suffolk Record Office)

Reference Number	Subject of remedy
461/457	eyes; lavender water; medicine; bite of mad dog, tincture of rhubarb; typhus, ague; billious pills; burn; julep of camphire; diabetes
622/383	eyes; infusion of roses; teeth; gnat bites; bruises; cholera; cough, dropsy
HA11/C47/31	for a frozen patient; teeth; corns
HA11/A18/4	rheumatism; bite from mad dog; cancer; corns
HA11/C47/26	for the distemper
HD363	for a cough
AA11/C47/31	for influenza
50/19/4.7/8	family medicine; flush; hair; humour in the mouth; imbrocation; lance; rheumatism; disruption of spirits; sprain; tonic; teeth; bite of viper; ague; aperient draught; biliousness; blisters; bowel; colds; cough; debility, digestive pills
50/19/4.7/13	fever powder; partial insanity; ague; biliousness; 'Henry's complaint'.

Published sources
Domestic Remedies (title page missing, late nineteenth century), G. W. Black,
Domestic Folk Medicine, E. Porter, *Cambridgeshire Customs and Folklore*,
E. Porter, *The Folklore of East Anglia*, W. Henderson, *The Folklore of the
Northern Counties of England and the Borders*, *East Anglian Magazine*, Vols 1–34
(various)

Bibliography

BOOKS

Anonymous, *The Case of the Hertfordshire Witchcraft Consider'd*, 1712

Aristotle, *Book of Problems, Wherein is contain'd divers Questions and Answers Touching the State of Man's Body*, (26th edition) 1749

Aristotle, *The Experienced Midwife*, 1793

Aveling, J. H., *English Midwives*, London 1872

Barrett, W. H. and Garrod R. P., *East Anglian Folklore and Other Tales*, Routledge and Kegan Paul 1976

Black, W. G., *Domestic Folk Medicine*, London 1883

Blackwell, Elizabeth, *The Curious Herbal*, 1737

Blair, Peter Hunter, *An Introduction to Anglo-Saxon England*, Cambridge University Press 1970

Blunt, Wilfrid and Raphael, Sandra, *The Illustrated Herbal*, Weidenfeld and Nicolson 1979

British Medical Association, Lecture Memoranda Liverpool 1912, *Anglo-Saxon Leechcraft*, Burroughs Wellcome and Co., London 1912

Bonser, Wilfrid, *The Medical Background of Anglo-Saxon England*, Wellcome History of Medicine Library 1963

Boston Women's Health Book Collective, *Our Bodies Ourselves*, English edition (ed. Angela Phillips and Jill Rakusen) Allen Lane 1978

Branca, P., *Silent Sisterhood: Middle Class Women in the Victorian Home*, Croom Helm 1977

Brim, Charles, *Medicine in the Bible*, Froben Press, New York 1936

Bristol As We Remember It, Bristol Broadsides 1978

Brockington, C. Fraser, *Public Health in the Nineteenth Century*, E. & S. Livingstone, Edinburgh 1965

Buchan Peter, *Witchcraft*, 1823

Buchan, William, *Domestic Medicine or the Family Physician*, Edinburgh 1769

Camp, John, *Magic, Myth and Medicine*, Priory Press 1973

Cartwright, F. F., *A Social History of Medicine*, Longman 1977

Cartwright, Frederick, *Disease and History*, Hart-Davis MacGibbon 1973

Chambers, J. D., *Population, Economy and Society in Pre-Industrial England*, Oxford University Press 1972

Chapman, Stanley, *Jesse Boot of Boots the Chemists*, Hodder and Stoughton 1974

Child, Mrs, *The Frugal Housewife*, London 1860

Clark, Alice, *The Working Life of Women in the 17th Century*, George Routledge & Sons 1919

Clark, Sir George, *A History of the Royal College of Physicians of London*, Clarendon Press 1964

Clarke, Sir A., *The Mother's Medical Assistant*, London 1820

Cockayne, Oswold, *Leechdom, Wortcunning and Starcraft of Early England*, London 1864

Cohn, Norman, *Europe's Inner Demons*, Paladin 1976

Cole, G. D. H., *A Short History of the British Working Class Movement*, Gollancz 1927

Cotta, John, *The Trials of Witchcraft*, 1616

Cotta, John, *A Short Discoverie of the Unobserved Dangers of Severall Sorts of ignorant and Unconsiderable Practisers of Physicken in England*, 1612

Coulton, G. (Ed.), *The Pastons and Their England*, Cambridge University Press 1922

Creighton, Charles, *A Hiistory of Epidemics in Britain*, Cambridge University Press 1891

Crossley-Holland, Kevin, *The Battle of Malden and Other Old English Poems*, Macmillan 1965

Culpeper, Nicholas, *A Directory for Midwives*, 1651

Dawson, G., *Healing: Pagan and Christian*, SPCK, London 1935

Dawson, Warren R., *Magician and Leech*, Methuen 1929

Davey, Dolly, *A Sense of Adventure*, S.E.1. People's History Project 1980

Debus, A. G., *Medicine in Seventeenth Century England*, University of California Press, Berkeley 1974

Defoe, Daniel, *A Journal of the Plague Year 1665*, Oxford University Press facsimile 1969

Digby, Ann, *Pauper Palaces*, Routledge and Kegan Paul 1978

Donnison, Jean, *Midwives and Medical Men*, Heinemann 1977

Dunglison, Richard J., *History of Medicine*, Philadelphia 1872

Eckstein, Harry, *The English Health Service*, Oxford University Press 1959

Edelstein, L., *Greek Medicine*, John Hopkins 1967

Ehrenreich, Barbara and English, Deirdre, *For Their Own Good*, Pluto 1979

Ehrenreich, Barbara and English, Deirdre, *Witches, Midwives and Nurses*, Writers and Readers Publishing Co-operative 1976

Elliott, James Sands, *Outlines of Greek and Roman Medicine*, John Bale Sons and Danielsson 1914

Ericksen-Brown, Charlotte, *The Use of Plants*, Breezy Creeks Press, Ontario 1979

Flück, Hans, (in collaboration with Dr R. Jasperson-Schub), translated J. M. Rowson, *Medicinal Plants and Their Uses*, W. Foulsham & Co. 1976

Forbes, Thomas, *The Midwife and the Witch*, Yale University Press 1966

FPA, *Abortion in Britain*, Pitman's Medical Book 1966

Fraser, Derek, *The New Poor Law in the Nineteenth Century*, Macmillan 1976

Friedson, E., *Professional Dominance: The Social Structure of Medical Care*, Chicago/ New York 1970

Fullom, S. W., *The History of Women*, London 1855

Gellner, E., *Thought and Change*, Weidenfeld and Nicolson 1964

Gimbutas, Marija, *The Gods and Goddessess of Old Europe 7000–3500BC: Myths, Legends and Cult Images*, Thames and Hudson 1974

Gosden, P. H., *Self-help: Voluntary Associations in Nineteenth Century Britain*, Batsford 1973

Grattan, J. and Singer, C., *Anglo-Saxon Magic and Medicine*, Oxford University Press 1952

Graves, Robert, *The White Goddess*, Faber 1961

Haggard, Howard W., *Devils, Drugs and Doctors*, Heinemann 1929

A Handbook of Domestic Recipes, Cassell, Petter and Galpin 1862

Harris, Ben Charles, *The Compleat Herbal*, Barre Massachusetts 1972

Harris, R. W., *National Health Insurance in Great Britain 1911–1946*, London 1946

Henderson, W., *Folklore of the Northern Counties of England and the Borders*, Wakefield 1866

Henschen, Folke (tr. Joan Tate), *The History of Diseases*, Longmans 1966

Hodgkinson, Ruth G., *The Origins of the National Health Service 1834–1871*, Wellcome Inst. Hist. Med., London 1967

Horrobin, David F., *Medical Hubris*, Churchill-Livingstone 1978

Hughes, Muriel Joy, *Women Healers in Medieval Life and Literature*, King's Crown Press, New York 1943

Hurd-Mead, Kate Campbell, *A History of Women in Medicine*, Haddam Press 1938

Illich, Ivan, *Limits to Medicine*, Penguin 1976

Jayne, Walter, *The Healing Gods of Ancient Civilisations*, Yale University Press 1925

Jeaffreson, John Cordy, *A Book About Doctors*, London 1861

Jewkes, John and Sylvia, *The Genesis of the British National Health Service*, Oxford 1961

Jex-Blake, Sophia, *Medical Women*, Oliphant, Edinburgh 1886

King, L. (Ed.), *Mainstreams of Medicine*, University of Texas 1971

Klaaren, Eugene H., *The Religious Origins of Modern Science*, Erdman's Publishing Company, Michigan 1977

Kremer, E. and Urdang, G., *A History of Pharmacy*, (4th edition, revised by Glenn Sonnedecker) J. B. Lippincott, Philadelphia 1976

Ladurie, E. LeRoy, *The Territory of the Historian*, Harvester Press 1979

Landy, David (Ed.), *Culture, Disease and Healing*, Collier Macmillan 1977

LaWall, C. H., *Four Thousand Years of Pharmacy*, Philadelphia and London 1927

Leff, S. and V., *From Witchcraft to World Health*, Lawrence and Wishart 1956

Lewis, Walter, *Medical Botany*, John Wiley, New York 1977

Llewelyn Davies, Margaret (Ed.), *Maternity: Letters from Working Women*, Virago 1978

Longmate, Norman, *Alive and Well*, Penguin 1970

Lubenow, William C., *The Politics of Government Growth*, David and Charles 1971

Maple, Eric, *Magic, Medicine and Quackery*, Robert Hale 1968

Marshall, Dorothy, *The English Poor in the Eighteenth Century*, Routledge 1926

Martindale, Adam, *Life of*, 1632

Mitchell, Averil, *Now We Have An Act*, Unpublished Thesis 1974

MacFarlane, Alan, *Witchcraft in Tudor and Stuart England*, Routledge and Kegan Paul 1970

MacKeith, Nancy, *The New Women's Health Handbook*, Virago 1978

Mackness, James, *Moral Aspects of Medical Life*, London 1846

McKay W. J. Stewart, *A History of Ancient Gynaecology*, Bailliere, Tindall-Cox 1901

McKenzie, Dan, *The Infancy of Medicine*, Macmillan and Co. 1927

McLaren, Angus, *Birth Control in Nineteenth Century England*, Croom Helm 1978

Oxley, Geoffrey W., *Poor Relief in England and Wales 1661–1834*, David and Charles 1974

Parry, Noel and Parry, Jose, *The Rise of the Medical Profession*, Croom Helm 1976

Payne, Joseph, *English Medicine in the Anglo-Saxon Times*, Oxford 1904

Perkins, W., *A Discourse of the Damned Art of Witchcraft*, 1608

Peterson, H. Jeanne, *The Medical Profession in Mid-Victorian London*, University of California Press 1978

Pettigrew, Thomas J., *Superstitions Connected with Medicine and Surgery*, 1844

Pinchbeck Ivy, *Women Workers in the Industrial Revolution 1750–1850*, Virago 1981

Pomet, Monsieur, *A Complete History of Drugs*, London (4th ed.) 1748

Porter, Enid, *The Folklore of East Anglia*, Batsford 1974

*Porter, Enid, *Cambridgeshire Customs and Folklore*, Routledge & Kegan Paul 1969

Power, Sir D'Arcy, *British Medical Societies*, Medical Press, London 1939

Poynter, F. N. L. (Ed.), *The Evolution of Medical Practice in Britain*, Pitman Medical Publishing Company 1961

Precope, John, *Medicine, Magic and Mythology*, Heinemann 1954

Queen's Closet Opened, 1696

Reece, R., *A Practical Dictionary of Domestic Medicine*, 1808

Rich, Adrienne, *Of Woman Born*, Virago 1977

Riley, Madeleine, *Brought to Bed*, Dent 1968

Rivers, W. H. R., *Medicine, Magic and Religion*, London 1924

Roach, John, *Social Reform in England*, Batsford 1978

Rose, Hilary and Steven, *The Political Economy of Science*, Macmillan 1976

Ross, James Stirling, *The National Health Service in Great Britain*, Oxford University Press 1952

Rubin, Stanley, *Medieval English Medicine*, David and Charles 1974

Salmon, W., *The Family Dictionary or Household Companion*, 1696

Salzman, L. F., *English Life in the Middle Ages*, Oxford University Press 1928

Scot, Reginald, *The Discovery of Witchcraft*, 1584

Seibert, Ilse, *Women in The Ancient Near East*, Edition Leipzig 1974

Sharp, Jane, *The Compleat Midwife's Companion: or the art of midwifery improved*, 1724

Sharp, Jane, *The Midwives' Book*, 1671

Sigerist, Henry, *A History of Medicine*, Oxford University Press 1951

Simms, Madeleine and Hindell, Keith, *Abortion Law Reformed*, Owen 1971

Simon, E. D. and Inman, J., *The Rebuilding of Manchester*, Longmans 1935

Simon, John, *Public Health Reports*, London 1887

Smart, C. and B. (Eds.), *Women, Sexuality and Social Control*, Routledge and Kegan Paul 1978

Smith, F. B., *The People's Health 1830–1910*, Croom Helm 1979

Stephens, G., *Extracts from an Old English Medical Manuscript*, 1844

Stone, Merlin, *The Paradise Papers*, Virago 1976

Swanton, Michael, *Anglo-Saxon Prose*, Dent 1975

Szasz, Thomas, *The Manufacture of Madness*, Routledge and Kegan Paul 1971

Szasz, Thomas, *The Theology of Medicine*, Louisiana State University Press 1977

Tindall, Gillian, *A Handbook on Witches*, Arthur Barker 1965

Thomas, Keith, *Religion and the Decline of Magic*, Penguin 1973

Thompson, C. J. S., *Magic and Healing*, Rider and Co. 1947

Thomson, William A. R., *Herbs That Heal*, Adam and Charles Black 1976

Trail, H. D., and Mann, J. S., *Social England*, Cassell 1901–4

Trotula, *Diseases of Women*, Elizabeth Mason-Hohl (Ed.), Ward-Ritchie Press 1940

Tylor, Edward, *Primitive Culture*, London 1903

Underwood, E. A., (Ed.), *Science, Medicine and History*, Oxford 1953

Vaughan, Eliza, *These for Remembrance*, Benham and Co., Colchester 1934

Vaughan, Paul, *A Short History of the BMA*, Heinemann 1959

Vitalyos, Dominique, *Phytotherapie dans la Medicine Traditionelle Domestique a Hatouba-Papaye (Guadaloupe)*, unpublished thesis Paris 1979

Wall, Richard, *Slum Conditions in London and Dublin*, Gregg International Publishing Ltd. 1974

Walsh, James, *Old Time Makers of Medicine*, Fordham University Press, New York 1911

Webb, Sidney and Beatrice, *English Poor Law History*, Vols I and II Frank Cass 1963

Webb, Sidney and Beatrice, *English Poor Law Policy*, London 1910

Weiner, P. (Ed.), *Dictionary of the History of Ideas*, Scribner & Sons, New York 1973

Wesley, John, *Primitive Physic*, 1781

White, Gilbert, *The Natural History of Selbourne*, 1789

Williams, J. H. Harley, *A Century of Public Health in Britain 1832–1929*, London 1932

Willcocks, A. J., *The Creation of the National Health Service*, Routledge & Kegan Paul 1967

Willoughby P., *Observations on Midwifery*, (H. Blenkinsop Ed.) 1863

Wohl, Anthony, *The Eternal Slum*, Edward Arnold 1977

Wolley, Hannah, *The Accomplisht Ladys Delight*, 1675

Wolley, Hannah, *The Complete Servant-Maid*, 1704

Woodward, John and Richards, David (Eds.), *Health Care and Popular Medicine in 19th century England*, Croom Helm 1977

Woolley, Ann, *Pharmacopolinum muliebris sexus*, 1674

Zilboorg, Gregory, *The Medical Man and the Witch during the Renaissance*, John Hopkins Press 1935

ARTICLES AND REPORTS

Abortion Law Reform Association, *Conference Report* 1936

Anderson, Alan and Gordon, Raymond 'Witchcraft and the Status of Women – the Case of England', *British Journal of Sociology* Vol. 29 No. 2 June 1976

Berridge, Virginia 'Opium and Oral History', *Oral History* Vol. 7 No. 2

Biggar, J. 'When Midwives Were Witches ... White Ones Of Course', *Nursing Mirror* 134, 26 May

Blake, J. 'The Compleat Housewife', *Bulletin of the History of Medicine* 1975, 49

British Medical Association, *Secret Remedies*, London 1909

British Medical Association, *More Secret Remedies*, London 1912

Brockbank, William 'Country Practice in Days Gone By', *Medical History* 1960, 4

Carnegie Report on the Physical Welfare of Mothers and Children (Hope and Campbell) 1917

Crellin, J. K. 'British Pharmacy and Nineteenth Century Domestic Medicine', *Veröff. int. ges. Gesch. Pharm.* 1969 N.F.32 (*Die Vorträge der Hamptversammlung der Internationaten Gesellschaft für Geschichte der Pharmazie*)

Claxton, Ros 'Some Homeopathic and Herbal Preparations for Pregnancy and Childbirth', *Newsletter No. 2*, The Birth Centre, London

Cohn, Alfred E. 'Changes in Public Attitudes Toward Medicine: Historical Aspects', *Bulletin of the History of Medicine* Vol. XI, 1942

Dodd, J. Theodore 'The Majority Report of the Poor Law Commission – Why We Should Reject It', *The National Committee to Promote the Break-up of the Poor Law*, 1910

Donnison, Jean, 'The Role of the Midwife', *Association of Radical Midwives Newsletter* No. 4, June 1979

East Anglian Magazine Vols. 1–34 (various)

Francome, Colin 'How Many Illegal Abortions?' *British Journal of Criminology* 1976, 16

Fulder, S. 'The Hammer and the Pestle' *New Scientist*, 10 July 1980

Guthrie, Leonard 'The Lady Sedley's Receipt Book 1686, and Other Seventeenth Century Receipt Books', *Proceedings of the Royal Society of Medicine* 1913, 6

Hartung, Edward 'Medical Education in the Twelfth Century' *Medical Life* 41 (1934)

Hoffman, Susanna Weinbach 'A Collection of Home Remedies 1742– 1803', *Academic Bookman* 1972, 25(1)

Kitzinger, S. 'The American Way of Birth', review in *Times Literary Supplement*, 1 August 1980

Knight, Patricia 'Women and Abortion in Victorian and Edwardian England', *History Workshop Journal* 4, Autumn 1977

Lane Committee 1974, *Report of the Committee on the Workings of the Abortion Act*, HMSO 1974

Levy, H. 'The Economic History of Sickness and Medical Benefit', *Economic History Review* 1944, 14

Manson, C. G. 'Craft Unions, Welfare Benefits and the Case for Trade Union Law Reform 1867–75', *Economic History Review* 1975, 28

Marcovitch, H. 'Mother's Milk: Beware of Imitations', *New Scientist*, 6 November 1980

McLaren, Angus 'Women's Work and Regulation of Family Size', *History Workshop Journal* Issue 4, Autumn 1977

How The Minority Report Deals with the Sick, the Infirm and the Infants, The National Committee to Promote the Break-up of the Poor Law, 1909

New Suffolk Garland, Ipswich 1866

Notes and Queries, 1955

Pagels, Elaine 'Who Was the Real Jesus?' *Observer*, 23 December 1979

Pettigrew, T. J. 'Observations on Extracts in Prose and Verse from an Old English Medieval Manuscript, preserved in the Royal Library at Stockholm', *Archaeologic* XXX, 1844

Pickstone, John V. 'Medical Botany', *Memoirs of the Manchester Literary and Philosophical Society* 119 (1976–7)

Roberts, R. S. 'The Personnel and Practice of Medicine in Tudor and Stuart England', *Medical History*, October 1962 and July 1964

Robson, J. 'Planning and Integration in Primary Care', *Medicine in Society* Vol. 5 No. 2

Rosen, G. 'People, Disease and Emotion', *Bulletin of the History of Medicine*, Vol. XII, 1967

Silcock, D. 'The Healing Power of the Tongue', *Sunday Times*, 14 September 1980

Singer, C. 'Early English Magic and Medicine', *Proceedings of the British Academy* IX, 1919–20

Sue, Jilly and Jenny 'Birth of a New Hope', *Peace News*, 21 April 1978

Sauer, R. 'Infanticide and Abortion in Nineteenth Century Britain', *Population Studies* 1978, 32

Teall, John 'Witchcraft and Calvinism', *Journal of the History of Ideas* 1962 23(1)

Thane, Pat 'Craft Unions, Welfare Benefits and the Case for Trade Union Law Reform 1867–75', *Economic History Review* Vol. 29, 1976

Thane, Pat 'Women and the Poor Law in Victorian and Edwardian England', *History Workshop Journal*, Issue 6, Autumn 1976

Webb, Mrs Sidney *The Minority Report and its Relation to Public Health and the Medical Profession*, The National Committee to Promote the Break-up of the Poor Law 1910

Index

Virago

If you would like to know more about Virago books, write to us at
Ely House, 37 Dover Street, London W1X 4HS for a full catalogue.

Please send a stamped addressed envelope